Moral Repair

Reconstructing Moral Relations after Wrongdoing

Moral Repair examines the ethics and moral psychology of responses to wrongdoing. Explaining the emotional bonds and normative expectations that keep human beings responsive to moral standards and responsible to each other, Margaret Urban Walker uses realistic examples of both personal betrayal and political violence to analyze how moral bonds are damaged by serious wrongs and what must be done to repair the damage. Focusing on victims of wrong, their right to validation, and their sense of justice, Walker presents a unified and detailed philosophical account of hope, trust, resentment, forgiveness, and making amends – the emotions and practices that sustain moral relations. *Moral Repair* joins a multidisciplinary literature concerned with transitional and restorative justice, reparations, and restoring individual dignity and mutual trust in the wake of serious wrongs.

Margaret Urban Walker is Professor of Philosophy and Lincoln Professor of Ethics at Arizona State University. She is the author of *Moral Understandings: A Feminist Study in Ethics* and *Moral Contexts*; editor of *Mother Time: Women, Aging and Ethics*; and co-editor of *Moral Psychology: Feminist Ethics and Social Theory* with Peggy DesAutels. She has published numerous articles in journals such as *Ethics, Journal of Human Rights, Metaphilosophy*, and *Hypatia*.

T0312069

Moral Repair

Reconstructing Moral Relations after Wrongdoing

MARGARET URBAN WALKER

Arizona State University

CAMBRIDGE UNIVERSITY PRESS
Cambridge, New York, Melbourne, Madrid, Cape Town, Singapore,
São Paulo, Delhi, Dubai, Tokyo, Mexico City

Cambridge University Press
The Edinburgh Building, Cambridge CB2 8RU, UK

Published in the United States of America by Cambridge University Press, New York

www.cambridge.org
Information on this title: www.cambridge.org/9780521009256

First published 2006

A catalogue record for this publication is available from the British Library

ISBN 978-0-521-81088-3 Hardback
ISBN 978-0-521-00925-6 Paperback

To Hilde and Robin

Contents

Acknowledgments   *page* ix

1 What Is Moral Repair?   1
2 Hope's Value   40
3 Damages to Trust   72
4 Resentment and Assurance   110
5 Forgiving   151
6 Making Amends   191

Bibliography   231
Index   245

Acknowledgments

I am deeply grateful to several institutions and individuals whose support has made the completion of this book possible. Fordham University, my academic home until 2002, provided a Faculty Fellowship in Spring 2001, as well as teaching reductions in previous semesters, which permitted me to get the ideas for this book well off the ground. The College of Public Programs at Arizona State University generously supported a full year's fellowship leave just a year after I arrived in 2002, so that I might bring this book to completion. I thank Anne Schneider, then Dean of the College of Public Programs; Marie Provine, Director of the School of Justice & Social Inquiry; and Arizona State University for their unhesitating and gracious support for this opportunity. The opportunity was a Laurance S. Rockefeller Fellowship in 2003–2004 at Princeton University's Center for Human Values, where I enjoyed a splendid working environment for most of the final writing of this book. I thank Stephen Macedo, Center Director, and Center faculty Kwame Anthony Appiah, Josh Ober, Peter Singer, and Chris Eisgruber for their generous interaction with Fellows. I thank my cohort of Fellows in 2003–2004 for many valuable discussions.

I rely on notes in the chapters to record my debts to various individuals, institutions, and audiences who provided opportunities and responses that continually reshaped parts of this book through many presentations and discussions in many places. I thank especially some close colleagues who contributed in important ways to this project. Great thanks to Michael Stocker, whose own work on emotions has taught me much and who gave good advice and concrete support early on for this book. Peter A. French, now Lincoln Chair of Ethics at Arizona State University, engineered two successive years of visiting appointments at the Ethics Center of the University of South Florida, 1996–1998, which not only allowed me to complete two previous books, but also to embark on the first stages of this one, as I began to think about those emotions and attitudes in which our sense of responsibility is seated. Robin N. Fiore provided the first opportunity for an exploration of the theme of moral repair by inviting me to give the David Ringelheim Lecture at Florida Atlantic University in 1999. Robin has extraordinary abilities to match up people, projects, and occasions with happy results. I am grateful that she urged me to consider pursuing the idea of moral repair; she has been a constant supporter of the project in word and deed. Hilde Lindemann has more energy than one person is entitled to, and I have had to borrow some of hers on too many occasions to detail. I am grateful to Hilde for forms of support and assistance – philosophical, editorial, and emotional – too numerous to detail, including many readings, discussions, critiques, and edits of every bit of this book. This book is dedicated to Robin and Hilde with great fondness.

Victoria McGeer offered observations that proved decisive in rework-ing the chapters on trust, hope, and forgiveness; her own work on these topics repeatedly refreshed and reshaped my perspectives. Alicia Partnoy, poet, activist, and former political prisoner in Argentina, had a galvaniz-ing effect on my thinking when she responded to one of my earlier uses of Ariel Dorfman's play *Death and the Maiden.* Neta Crawford provided the invaluable opportunity to participate in Brown University's Steering Committee on Slavery and Justice and its wide-ranging final conference, Restitution and Reconciliation in International Perspective, in March 2005. Rebecca Tsosie, my ASU colleague in the College of Law, has been a great dinner companion and friend, whose own work on cultural repair and repatriation of Native American remains and artifacts has helped me to appreciate the distinctiveness of particular cases of moral disre-pair involving groups with long histories. They might not have known it, but both Neta and Rebecca contributed to steering this book toward its present conclusion. Needless to say, none of these fine interlocutors is responsible for where I ended up.

Three opportunities to present ideas from this work to colleagues and to graduate students in some faraway places were exceptionally valuable as well as enjoyable for me. I thank Marian Verkerk, Henk Manschot, Guy Widdershoven, Selma Sevenhuijsen, and Joan Tronto for the vibrant Summer School on the Ethics and Politics of Care, Netherlands School for Research in Practical Philosophy, held in Soesterberg, the Netherlands, in August 2000. My thinking about trust was deepened at this meeting;

to my lasting regret, jet lag caused me to miss the charades at which Selma acted out the concept of "normative expectations." An invitation to Brisbane, Australia, to keynote a week's activities for the conference New Ways of Applying Ethics, in the Research Concentration in Applied Ethics at Queensland University of Technology in June 2001, helped me link my former work to this present one. I thank Trevor Jordon for being a great host and the program's faculty and graduate students for being excellent interlocutors. Finally, it was a great honor to be the first woman appointed to the Cardinal Mercier Chair at the Institute of Philosophy at the Catholic University of Leuven, Belgium, in 2002. I was able to present work on moral repair and on reactive attitudes to faculty and graduate students with helpful feedback. Warm thanks, especially, to Herman De Dijn. Of course it is fun to travel, but it is also a joy to discover and to knock off some parochial edges of one's thinking and to be part of wider and more diverse philosophical and political dialogues. I am grateful to have had these and other opportunities to do so.

Several graduate assistants in recent years have provided exactly the leg, finger, and brain work needed to move this project along or, equally important, to get other projects expeditiously out of its path. Thanks to Shelley Erickson, Jill Thomas, Judson Garrett, and Gregory Broberg at ASU and to Silas Langley, Michael Kelly, David Zinn, and Rachel Waterstradt earlier at Fordham. Special thanks to Jill for going over the final text with a sharp eye, Shelley for excellent research assistance, Judson for being a superb teaching assistant and my wingman, and Greg for always helping out while deepening my understanding of restorative justice. Thanks also to Michael Coyle for steering me to good resources on restorative justice. David Miller prepared the bibliography and helped me to straighten out many last-minute kinks; I am responsible for those that remain. All of these folks have been moving parts in a network of intellectual support and good fellowship during the writing of this book. I literally could not have done it without them.

Thanks to Beatrice Rehl, my editor at Cambridge University Press, for her assistance in obtaining the moving cover image, and to Sally Nicholls for excellent copyediting and swift production.

I have felt constant sadness and unease that much of the material researched for this book involves the terrifying, cruel, and shattering experiences of many people and that I have made their suffering the subject matter of an academic work. I have tried to be accurate about what human beings are capable of doing, good and evil. I hope that I have shown respect for the profound suffering of those among us who are subjected to withering disrespect and to brutalities that remain for many others safely beyond imagination. I have learned many more facts about violence and suffering than I knew when I began, but I am sure that my understanding of the human cost and meaning of those facts, especially of the consequences of violence, is profoundly inadequate. I do not imagine this book can do anything for anyone who has suffered the kind of violence to which I refer so often in these pages. I hope that the book contributes something to others' understanding of why it is important not to turn away.

Passages of Chapter 1 are reprinted from "'The Cycle of Violence,'" *Journal of Human Rights* 5 (2006): 81–105, © Taylor and Francis Group, LLC. Chapter 4 is a much extended version of "Resentment & Assurance," which first appeared in *Setting the Moral Compass: Essays by Women Philosophers*, edited by Cheshire Calhoun, copyright © 2003 by Oxford University Press, Inc. Used by permission of Oxford University Press, Inc.

1

What Is Moral Repair?

A woman is at home in an isolated house by the sea. It is night, and she sits on the terrace. When a car turns in toward the house, the woman gets a gun. When she hears her husband's voice, she puts the gun away – until later. This is the opening of Ariel Dorfman's play about Paulina Salas, an imagined survivor of political violence by the former military government of her Latin American country. Under that regime she was kidnapped, secretly detained, repeatedly raped, and otherwise tortured.[1] Paulina's husband Gerardo Escobar is a distinguished lawyer; Paulina surmises correctly that her husband has agreed to head a truth commission that will investigate those – and only those – human rights violations that ended in death; those that are, as the play describes them, "beyond repair." Because Paulina survived her torture, her story will not be heard and her case will not be investigated.

Gerardo, who, returning home in a rainstorm, had a flat tire on the highway, invites the stranger who drove him home to stay the night. Paulina believes this "good Samaritan" is the physician who raped her and presided over her torture when she was kidnapped and held in detention by the state. Paulina believes she recognizes his voice and phrases, and, when she gets closer, his scent. While Gerardo sleeps, Paulina takes Dr. Roberto Miranda captive; she knocks him unconscious, binds him to a chair, mocks and humiliates him with sexual taunts, and proceeds to interrogate him and terrorize him with threats of death if he does not confess. Gerardo is horrified and terrified when he awakes to find Paulina holding Miranda at gunpoint. He cajoles, pleads, and remonstrates with

---

[1] Ariel Dorfman, *Death and the Maiden.*

1

her that her behavior is "crazy," but she is not moved. In the middle of the play, Paulina tells Gerardo what she wants. She begins with the thought of doing to Miranda, in exact detail, everything that was done to her; she says that she wants to have him raped. But she concludes that what she really wants is for him to confess, in his own handwriting with his own signature, to everything he has done, so that she can keep the copy for her own protection and satisfaction. When Gerardo reminds her she might be making a mistaken identification, and so might be holding and tormenting an innocent man, Paulina replies, "If he's innocent? Then he's really screwed."[2]

Gerardo tries to conspire with Miranda to produce a plausible enough confession to win his freedom; he feeds Miranda details of Paulina's torture that he has wrested from her for this purpose. But Paulina is one step ahead. She has fed Gerardo small inaccuracies in order to see if Miranda will correct them; he does, and thus reveals himself as in fact her torturer. The penultimate scene ends in ambiguity, with an increasingly agitated Paulina threatening to kill an unrepentant and evasive Miranda. In the concluding scene Paulina and Gerardo are attending a concert of Shubert's *Death and the Maiden* when Miranda appears to enter the theater. The Commission has done its work. Paulina is finally able to listen to Shubert's piece, her favorite, which Dr. Miranda had played while he raped her. It is unclear in this scene whether Miranda is real or is an apparition of Paulina's. She turns to look at him, then turns back to face the stage.

Paulina Salas is a fiction, but her experience of violation and its political context is not. Dorfman, a Chilean citizen in exile during Pinochet's rule, knows the facts of Pinochet's brutal regime and the voices of its victims. Investigations of Pinochet's rule by Chile's National Commission on Truth and Reconciliation and its successor Reparation and Reconciliation Corporation found 3,197 cases of disappearance leading to extrajudicial execution or deaths under torture.[3] Like the commission in Dorfman's play, Chile's National Commission on Truth and Reconciliation was charged to investigate and document only the cases of victims who were killed or are presumed dead. So, like the imagined Paulina Salas, the real surviving victims of torture in Pinochet's Chile had no

---

[2] Dorfman, *Death and the Maiden*, Act 2, Scene 1, p. 42.
[3] Amnesty International, "Transition at the Crossroads: Human Rights Violations under Pinochet Rules Remain the Crux." The summary figure is reported at AI Index: AMR 22/01/96.

opportunity at that time to testify about their violation or to have their cases investigated, and the numbers of those surviving torture were uncertain. In 2004, the Chilean government commissioned a new investigation, and the report issued in November 2004 reflected, at last, the testimony of 35,000 torture survivors.[4]

Since opening in Chile in 1991, *Death and the Maiden* has been performed in at least thirty countries in many productions; it has been made into a major motion picture starring Sigourney Weaver and Ben Kingsley.[5] The play is morally disturbing and dramatically gripping. But what does the play depict as the reaction and reality of the victim? Dorfman's Paulina is unstable, wounded, crazed, and vengeful, and it is her aggressive, threatening, and violent acts that drive the story. She has been confined, tormented, and violated; she in turn confines, torments, and violates her torturer, threatening him with death and shrugging off the possibility that he is an innocent man wrongly under suspicion. Paulina not only needs and desires to inflict in return what she suffered at the hands of Dr. Miranda, but she seizes the first opportunity to act out her vengeful desires with startling ferocity. The scenario of *Death and the Maiden* embodies, up to a point, a stock plot and a popular genre: righteous fury and retaliation turned on wrongdoers with grim inevitability. "From the ancient Greeks to the evening news, every age has been transfixed by the spectacle of people driven to exact blood for blood," says Jeremiah Creedon.[6] Does this familiar and mesmerizing plot and favored motif of journalism capture some truth about what victims of serious wrong and injustice need and want?

Dorfman has said of the victims, "I am not their voice: I make a space for those voices, a bridge."[7] Some people who have suffered detention and torture like Paulina's, however, do not see the reality of "the victim"

---

[4] Larry Rohter, "A Torture Report Compels Chile to Reassess Its Past," describes the impact of the 1,200-page report of the National Commission on Political Imprisonment and Torture. A common but conservative estimate had been 40,000 torture survivors. See Priscilla Hayner, *Unspeakable Truths: Confronting State Terror and Atrocity*, 36.

[5] See Dorfman's website http://www.adorfman.duke.edu/, accessed 21 May 2005, for information on the play and movie. The movie version resolves the final ambiguity that lingers in Dorfman's play; in the movie Miranda finally admits his guilt and Paulina does not follow through on her threats.

[6] Jeremiah Creedon, "To Hell and Back: To Break the Cycle of Revenge Countries Must Look Beyond the Law," 56.

[7] Ariel Dorfman, "Ariel Dorfman on Memory and Truth," Interview by Carlos Reyes, Maggie Paterson, http://www.amnesty.org.uk/journal'july97/carlos.html, accessed 27 April 2004.

or hear her voice in Dorfman's play. Poet and human rights activist Alicia Partnoy, author of *The Little School*, stories based on her own months of secret detention and torture in Argentina in the 1970s, objects to the "thriller's devices" in Dorfman's play by which the victim of political torture becomes "a victimizer and a mad woman...We hear a victim that is out of her mind and committing an act of violence totally out of context...Where is the acknowledgment to the stories and lives of all the women who did not need to resort to a gun and did not appear as – however justifiable – crazy as Paulina[?]"[8] Partnoy also notes the presence of disturbingly titillating details: Paulina, who has been raped and sexually tortured, is portrayed in both the play and the film versions as gagging Miranda by removing her underpants and stuffing them in his mouth. Ana Roca, in an essay on the movie *Death and the Maiden*, observes as well that "the film manipulates viewers' allegiances, making us doubt the victim herself to make the evening's entertainment more suspenseful and exciting."[9] No doubt *Death and the Maiden* is performed widely because its dramatic excitement draws attention to political realities from which people would otherwise rather turn away. Yet the depiction of the victim of disappearance and torture in the play and in the film follows too well a stylized generic formula: the victim wants and justice requires "payback," and that means visiting on the offender equivalent violence or suffering, or vengeance compounded with interest.

This tried and "true" – not to mention exciting – formula threatens to overwhelm the other important details that are worked into Dorfman's drama. Paulina's racing for a gun at the sound of a car reveals terror, not rage. Paulina has just learned that her case will not be investigated and her story will not be told as part of the official truth the new commission seeks. Paulina is suspended between the power Gerardo believes inheres in the legal system's standards of proof and due process, a system that remains powerless to deliver justice to her, and the power to demand some satisfaction, which Paulina has learned belongs to the person with the gun. Once Miranda is captive, Paulina first makes him *listen to her story*,

---

[8] Alicia Partnoy, correspondence, quoted with permission. See Alicia Partnoy, *The Little School: Tales of Disappearance and Survival*. There is also an intriguing interlude in Antje Krog's *Country of My Skull: Guilt, Sorrow, and the Limits of Forgiveness in the New South Africa*, 312–13, in which she recounts a conversation with Dorfman, not her own, in which he defends his work as "a sort of mixture – some of it is what he's heard, and some he makes up" (313).

[9] Ana Roca, "Madness or Divine Sense? Revisiting Ariel Dorfman's *Death and the Maiden*," 7–9.

before she insists on exacting a confession from him. Paulina recites a litany of violent reprisals that she has, to her own horror, imagined turning back on him. In the end, however, it is Miranda's accountability in a full and signed confession – a durable and publicly accessible testimony – that admits everything he has done, and so confirms everything she and others have wrongly suffered and endured, that Paulina seeks. In the final moments of the penultimate scene, Paulina asks only for Miranda's repentance as the price to spare his life; and she asks why it is always "people like me" – victims of violence – who are forced to make concessions in seeking a resolution to an episode or era of violence.[10]

Paulina's needs for validation, voice, and vindication go unanswered. The character of Paulina is not only a victim of horrible violence; she is also a victim who is abandoned and isolated. Dorfman's play troubles us with the tension between a fantasy of vengeance that is dramatically exciting and the reality of victims who deserve and need some kind of justice in a world that typically offers them little or none. If Paulina is driven to a crazed vengeful rage, is this solely because of the terrible violence done to her by Miranda and others? Or is it also because, given the brutal, terrorizing, and humiliating violence she has endured, no other way has been available to reclaim her equilibrium, her safety, her dignity, and the recognition of her loss, pain, and blamelessness? Would Paulina be driven to act out that rage violently if there were other ways to claim what she needs? What difference would it make if her membership in a community – as a neighbor, a citizen, a fellow human being – entitled her to make these claims, and if it assured her that she would be respected and supported in pursuing them?

There is no simple answer here, for there is no one thing victims of serious wrongdoing feel and want. Yet there is a pattern of evidence that suggests that many victims of wrongful harm face similar terror, grief, affront, and distress, and that victims are deeply sensitive to the ways provided or denied them in coming to terms with the wrongful harm

---

[10] Teresa Godwin Phelps's recent book, *Shattered Voices: Language, Violence, and the Work of Truth Commissions*, uses Dorfman's play to illustrate her view that "the need to take revenge is a deeply rooted human need that cannot be moralized away; it is an inevitable and indestructible part of the human psyche" (6). Yet in the next paragraph Phelps acknowledges that what Paulina wants once she has her former torturer solely within her power is *not* "comparable violence" but "words." I thank Alicia Partnoy for first drawing my attention to the dangers in Dorfman's depiction, and Thomas Brudholm for urging me to recognize the tension between the revenge motif and the other features of the presentation of Paulina.

others have done them. The question arises: what does it mean, in moral and human terms, to respond adequately in the wake of wrongdoing and serious harm, both individual and large scale, and both personal and political? What does it mean to respond to wrongdoing and wrongful harm in a way that serves justice in an ancient and enduring sense, putting individuals in right relationship with each other and communities as a whole into a sustainable order of reciprocal expectations by which their members measure what is due to each other?

This book is an examination of an unavoidable human task: moral repair. As human beings, we need, over and over, to decide how to respond to wrongdoing and wrongful harm in our midst, whether we are the victims, offending parties, or others. Moral philosophers following Immanuel Kant have often described ethics as answering the question: "What ought I to do?" This seems to imply a set of choices on a fresh page. One of our recurrent ethical tasks, however, is better suggested by the question "What ought I – or, better, *we* – to do *now?*" after someone has blotted or torn the page by doing something wrong. I am seeking here to understand how responses to wrong and harm, in personal and political cases, can be ways to repair and sustain the grip of morality as a force in our shared lives. The chapters that follow try to clarify the moral psychology of stable and disrupted moral relations, finding what the relatively stable ones consist in, and what has been lost in the damaged or shattered ones. Moral repair is the process of moving from the situation of loss and damage to a situation where some degree of stability in moral relations is regained. This process of restoration or recreation is not always possible; in cases of serious wrong, if repair is possible in some degree, it will usually be at some cost – for the victim, the cost of absorbing some irreparable loss, pain, and anger; for the wrongdoer, the cost of some shame, vulnerability, and compensating action; for communities, the costs of providing acknowledgment and vindication for victims, placing responsibility and its demands on wrongdoers, and showing that standards are affirmed and enforced.

I want in this book to keep a focus on the victim, the one who has experienced wrongful harms and losses for which human actors bear responsibilities, the one who has been brutalized, terrorized, insulted, demeaned, or diminished by violence, mistreatment, disrespect, contempt, or negligent disregard. Although the roles of victims, wrongdoers and other responsible parties, bystanders, and communities are all key to repairing moral relations, I orient my discussion to the victim's plight, need, and desert, for if moral repair means anything it means the attempt to address offense, harm, and anguish caused to those who suffer wrong. It is about "setting things right," in the first case, for the victim. In the cases of serious, violent, traumatic, and shattering harm that most concern me here, it is a simple and poignant fact that no wrong is ever undone. At best, it is the sequel to the wrong that either "does right" by the victim or does not do so. In the end, no matter what others do or fail to do, no one who suffers grave wrong is relieved of the considerable burdens and pain that the sufferer alone must struggle to absorb or transcend. It is true that there are situations in which the same people who are victims of wrong in one respect are responsible for wrongs to others in another. While this is an important feature of some situations, I will still speak of "the victim," for two reasons. In many cases, both personal and political, there *is* a blameless victim. In those cases where wrongs are done mutually or all around, however, the same person may be a victim and a perpetrator (or a complicit or negligent bystander), but that person is a victim of some *particular* wrong and a perpetrator of *another* distinct one. I understand that reciprocal violence and disrespect in real cases creates practical difficulties for reparative efforts. Clarity is not served, however, and justice cannot be attempted when these matters are not distinguished. People need to get what they deserve as victims, *and* to be called upon to do what they are obliged to do to make amends as wrongdoers.[11]

I will also emphasize the responsibilities of communities to demand and support repair. Communal responsibility is nothing exotic; it figures in familiar and everyday practices in which a public supports institutions that are charged to maintain, reiterate, and enforce social order. Communities also can be harmed by serious wrongdoing, because it may shatter individual members' sense of security and call into question the authority of standards and the effectiveness of protective institutions.

Of course, wrongdoers will also be central to the discussion. Certainly, those most directly responsible for wrong are also those with paramount and unique responsibilities for attempting to make amends for it. Yet there might be less concentration here than some might expect on the offending party or parties. In fact, repeated hard experience shows that often it is in the gravest cases, including cases of mass violence and terror,

---

[11] A good discussion of the victim/perpetrator/bystander complexity in context is found in Tristan Anne Borer, "A Taxonomy of Victims and Perpetrators: Human Rights and Reconciliation in South Africa." See also Jon Elster's taxonomy of wrongdoers in *Closing the Books: Transitional Justice in Historical Perspective.*

that wrongdoers are least inclined to accept responsibility. I begin my discussion of amends in Chapter 6 with this sad fact. Even in fairly ordinary matters, there is a human propensity to evade and diminish responsibility. Those responsible for wrong and harm must remain at all times clearly in the frame, but moral repair is too essential to our lives to be left entirely to wrongdoers: why should victims be left to the double jeopardy of injury and then the insult of wrongdoers' denial and refusal to repair?

Philosophical discussions of responding to wrong, have tended to center on the wrongdoer, and on society's punitive responses to those who break laws or violate moral norms.[12] There are long-running debates on shame, guilt, blame, and, above all, punishment in the history and contemporary literature of philosophy. By comparison, bodies of philosophical writing on apology, reparation, or forgiveness are fairly small, although recently growing. Traditional exceptions to this pattern are discussions of "righteous anger," "resentment," or "indignation" experienced by those who are wronged or by others on their behalf. There is a long philosophical history to the idea that anger at wrongdoing (called either resentment or indignation or both indifferently) usefully prompts us to defend ourselves when we are treated ill and suffer injury, disregard, disrespect, or insult.[13] Often this anger, in turn, is used to explain or to defend retribution, retaliation, or revenge – socially organized or

---

[12] Historical exceptions are Joseph Butler's and Adam Smith's work on moral sentiments, and contemporary ones include Jeffrie G. Murphy and Jean Hampton, *Forgiveness and Mercy*, and Jeffrie G. Murphy, *Getting Even: Forgiveness and Its Limits*. Nietzsche's famous discussion of "ressentiment" might be thought an exception, but I believe it is not; it is an artful recasting of victims as envious "losers" from the (imagined) point of view of those winners who might otherwise be taxed with responsibilities. See Chapter 4 for my own discussion of resentment, which incidentally places Nietzsche's in this particular light.

[13] The idea that a person responds, not only naturally but properly, with anger, resentment, or indignation to another's violence or disregard toward that person, and perhaps toward others, has a long history in philosophy. One of the circumstances that makes anger appropriate, on Aristotle's account of the virtue of "good temper," is that in which oneself or one's friends are insulted, and in which without anger one who suffers insult is "unlikely to defend himself." Aristotle, *Nichomachean Ethics*, 97, 1125b. The more modern views of Joseph Butler and Adam Smith see resentment or indignation (anger that rises toward a wrongdoer upon the perception of a wrong) as natural human responses that are proper to the extent that they prompt proportionate rebuke or punishment, and are objectionable only when excessive and vengeful. Joseph Butler, "Upon Resentment," in *Butler's Fifteen Sermons*, 79; Adam Smith, *The Theory of Moral Sentiments*, 86. The most widely cited recent accounts of resentment are those of Jeffrie Murphy and Jean Hampton in their *Forgiveness and Mercy*.

freelance punishment.[14] I share the view that anger is a defensive response to wrongdoing and is something most victims feel intensely at some points. However, anger at wrong is not all that victims feel, and the distinctive kind of anger in question – resentment – requires a more complex account. In Chapter 4 I present an account of what resentment tries to defend and what resentment is likely to dispose people to do and to seek. Retaliation, punishment, and retribution are only some of the responses that victims seek and are not always or only the ones that lead a victim to experience vindication.

I would not deny that punishment, when proportionate and humane, is one indispensable response to wrongdoing. But I do not intend here to add to reams of discussions on the nature and justice of punishment. Philosophers, politicians, jurists, penologists, and the rest of us continue to debate the issue of what justifies punishment as a social practice, and almost everyone intuitively knows the main (not necessarily exclusive) rationales include retribution, deterrence, re-education or rehabilitation, and the unequivocal expression of society's negative judgment. Yet whatever is an occasion for punishment is just as much an occasion for alternative or additional responses to come into play, sometimes seeking the same ends, and sometimes seeking different ones.[15] It's important to remember that when people behave wrongly and hurt others, we don't always think, or only think, of punishing them. Spouses and lovers are unfaithful, children selfish, associates unfair, friends deceitful; there are slights, insults, lies, acts of indifference, betrayal, aggression, or violence among us, and in some instances these dent or shatter lives. While we do sometimes seek to punish people who wrongfully harm us or others (or wish that we could), there are a lot of alternatives to punishment that in fact are always there, and we often need and use them. Some of these responses exclude each other while others can be combined or deployed in sequence.

---

[14] There are many variations on this theme. Some contemporary defenses include Susan Jacoby, *Wild Justice*; Robert Solomon, *A Passion for Justice*; and Peter French, *The Virtues of Vengeance*.

[15] See Randy E. Barnett, "Restitution: A New Paradigm of Criminal Justice," and Geoffrey Sayre-McCord, "Criminal Justice and Legal Reparations as an Alternative to Punishment," for arguments that other practices serve, or serve better, some of the aims of punishment. A burgeoning literature on restorative justice questions some of the aims of punishment as well as the results claimed for it. A good sample of this literature is found in Gerry Johnstone, ed., *A Restorative Justice Reader: Texts, Sources, Context.*

We can "let it go," by accepting the offense or forgetting it. We can blame or reproach the offender, resort to public denunciation or censure, or simply turn away, pushing those we no longer trust to the margins of our lives. We can demand acknowledgment of responsibility and wrongdoing, a show of guilt, shame, or remorse, and reparative acts such as apology, repentance, and amends. Sometimes we pardon or excuse, deciding that the offense does not require redress, or that it is better to forgo redressing it, or that although redress is in order, there are reasons to be merciful and demand less than is owed. Those who are injured may forgive, and may in turn seek to restore connections with those who hurt them or to let those connections go. In some cases we feel a need to insist on a truth's being established "for the record," whether that record is the formal one of history books or the shared understanding of a friendship, a marriage, an institution, or a nation. Some historic wrongs call out for memorials or commemorations that preserve a rebuke to wrongdoers, the dignity of victims, and a warning to others. We might, finally, aim at the prevention of like wrongs in the future, whether by severing contact with untrustworthy parties, selectively withholding trust, extracting promises, passing legislation, or creating new institutions. All of these alternatives have personal and public versions and variations. Any of these responses might in some situations be reparative while in other cases might not be. Can we explain why?

I intend my discussion of moral repair to bear on the whole field of ways to address and redress wrongdoing, including punishment and other responses that can replace punishment or accompany it. While I mention punishment in these pages only in passing, I do not mean to rule it out or to imply it is unimportant, either as a social expedient or as a morally reparative process. I do, however, intend my discussion to provide a resource for questioning whether and when punishment *is* morally reparative, just as I intend it to provide a background for asking the same question about telling the truth about wrongs or memorializing them, or publicly denouncing wrongdoers or forgiving them, or compensating victims or extending apologies to them. My project here is to expose the *conditions of moral relationship* that are a reference point for assessing whether an intended repair of moral relationship achieves its aim. This is a crucial part of understanding when responses to wrongdoing are morally reparative, and some reasons why those responses can fail. First, I want to explain where my own project fits into a current preoccupation with repairing wrongs that is emerging on several fronts.

Responding to Wrongs: A Cultural Moment and a Moral Agenda

Reckoning with wrongs has in recent years become the aim of political projects around the world. International tribunals and domestic trials for severe abuses of human rights – genocide, war crimes, and crimes against humanity – have sprung to life half a century after Nuremburg.[16] Truth commissions seek to find out what still remains unknown, or to render conclusive and public what is known by perpetrators and victims or surmised by anguished survivors, in cases of massacre, extrajudicial execution, torture, mass rape, sexual slavery and atrocity, illegal detentions and other human rights violations during repression or conflict.[17] Reparations movements for wrongful harms and losses have proliferated in recent decades, seeking official apologies, restitution, material compensation for losses, public education and commemoration, and legal and institutional protections against the repetition of abuses and injustice.[18] Some reparations programs have addressed war crimes and crimes against humanity, including genocide, and death, disappearance, torture, sexual violence or severe mistreatment during episodes of political violence and persecution. The successful movement to secure recognition, apology, and symbolic monetary compensation for Japanese-American citizens interned during the Second World War provides one kind of model of what such programs might look like, as do the reparations of the German Federal Republic to Jewish victims of the Holocaust, and

---

[16] On the history and politics of tribunals, see Gary Jonathan Bass, *Stay the Hand of Vengeance: The Politics of Wartime Tribunals*. In defense of retribution for mass violence, see Aryeh Neier, *War Crimes: Brutality, Genocide, Terror, and the Struggle for Justice*. See Martha Minow, *Between Vengeance and Forgiveness: Facing History After Genocide and Mass Violence*, on the power and limits of trials in comparison to truth commissions and reparations. See also Carlos Santiago Nino, *Radical Evil on Trial*.

[17] In addition to Minow, *Between Vengeance and Forgiveness*, see Hayner, *Unspeakable Truths*; Robert I. Rotberg and Dennis Thompson, eds., *Truth v. Justice: The Morality of Truth Commissions*; and Phelps, *Shattered Voices*. The United States Institute of Peace offers documentation on truth commissions in a "Truth Commissions Digital Collection" at http://www.usip.org/library/truth.html#tc.

[18] The international standard for reparations, the Van Boven principles, can be found in the United Nations Document "The Administration of Justice and the Human Rights of Detainees: Revised Set of Basic Principles and Guidelines on the Right to Reparation for Victims of Gross Violations of Human Rights and Humanitarian Law Prepared by Mr. Theor van Boven Pursuant to Sub-Commission Decision 1995/117." The four main categories recognized internationally are restitution, compensation, rehabilitation (medical, psychological, social and legal services), and satisfaction (including apology, truth-telling, and commemoration) and guarantees of non-repetition.

payments made by some Latin American governments to survivors of torture and to families of the disappeared.[19] Reparations are also proposed, so far with less success, as ways to deal with unrepaired injustices with roots decades or centuries long, such as histories of slavery and segregation, colonization and exploitation, the forced removal of indigenous peoples and theft of their lands, remains, and cultural objects, the forced removal of children from their parents and indigenous communities, and the knowing suppression and destruction of cultures by colonizers.[20]

Interwoven with political movements and social consciousness come the theories and research programs explaining, justifying, comparing, and contesting specific practices of moral and social repair. The questions range over legal remedies, political and institutional processes, moral order, and social cohesion, tolerance, and reconciliation. The practices at issue – trials, truth commissions, administrative reorganization, institutional reform, amnesties, constitution and nation building, reparation, and commemoration – try to do some kinds of justice or offer some kinds of repair, or both, in the wake of horrifying violence. Much of this discussion now goes under the rubric of "transitional justice." The terrain comprises protracted interstate and intrastate wars that kill, and indeed increasingly target for violence, ever higher percentages of civilians, especially women and children, genocides, and targeted systemic oppression policed by terror, torture, and the disappearance of opponents and critics.[21]

---

[19] See Minow, *Between Vengeance and Forgiveness*, ch. 5, and Roy L. Brooks, ed., *When Sorry Isn't Enough: The Controversy Over Apologies and Reparations for Human Injustice*, on the Japanese-American internment case. Hayner, *Unspeakable Truths*, summarizes Latin American programs, as does Sharon F. Lean, "Is Truth Enough? Reparations and Reconciliation in Latin America." Elazar Barkan surveys the German programs in *The Guilt of Nations: Restitution and Negotiating Historical Injustices.*

[20] An overview of reparations programs and movements is provided in Barkan's *The Guilt of Nations,* and a compendium of original documents and arguments by Brooks, *When Sorry Isn't Enough.* Naomi Roht-Arriaza, "Reparations in the Aftermath of Repression and Mass Violence," explores the "discrepancy between word and deed" in achieving reparations. John Torpey, ed., *Politics and the Past: On Repairing Historical Injustices,* and Carol A. L. Prager and Trudy Govier, eds., *Dilemmas of Reconciliation: Cases and Concepts,* explore both practical and conceptual issues involved in specific attempts at reparation and conciliatory repair. See also Pablo de Greiff, ed., *The Handbook of Reparations,* for case studies and theoretical issues. Janna Thompson's *Taking Responsibility for the Past: Reparation and Historical Injustice* is an extended philosophical argument for reparations for historical wrongs rooted in a conception of justice.

[21] Wenona Mary Giles and Jennifer Hyndman, eds., *Sites of Violence: Gender and Conflict Zones,* 5, cites sources that place figures on civilian deaths in the post-World War II era between 60–80 percent and 90 percent. Laurel E. Fletcher and Harvey M. Weinstein, "Violence

Transitional justice is not a new phenomenon. This is unsurprising inasmuch as war, tyranny, and political oppression have always left bitter legacies, volatile political situations, guilty parties seeking cover, and outraged victims seeking vindication and resolution. The concept of transitional justice, however, and the literature articulating its methods and challenges, has grown rapidly in recent years.[22] Transitional justice incorporates both retributive and compensatory or reparative projects, and the legal and philosophical arms of compensatory or reparative justice have widened to embrace causes that include claims to restitution of land, human remains, and cultural resources by indigenous people; the enslavement and ensuing diminished legal status of African-Americans; and the systematic rape and sexual abuse of women as a tactic of war and repression, although still without much success.[23] Some books assumed to be closed are lately being reopened, as in the emergence in the United States of what some call "atonement trials" for brutal acts of violence during the civil rights era, or the overruling of 1980s amnesty laws in Argentina, or renewed prosecution in Uruguay for offenses occurring under military governments in the 1970s.[24] Pressure toward retributive justice is not the only way to reawaken an awareness of outstanding and unredressed injuries: a privately organized Truth and Reconciliation Commission, created in 2003, conducted hearings in

---

and Social Repair: Rethinking the Contribution of Justice to Reconciliation," 576, cites the Carnegie Commission on Preventing Deadly Conflict, "Preventing Deadly Conflict: Final Report," 25–30, as finding that civilian deaths increased from 14 percent to 90 percent of all war-related deaths from 1914 to 1997.

[22] Elster, *Closing The Books*, takes transitional justice back to ancient Greece. Ruti Teitel, *Transitional Justice*, provides an excellent systematic overview of legal issues. See also Neil Kritz, ed., *Transitional Justice: How Emerging Democracies Reckon With Former Regimes: Laws, Rulings, and Reports*; Carla Hesse and Robert Post, *Human Rights in Political Transitions: Gettysburg to Bosnia*; and Charles Villa-Vicencio and Erik Doxtader, eds., *The Provocations of Amnesty: Memory, Justice, and Impunity*. The International Center for Transitional Justice was founded in 2001 to develop expertise and consult worldwide on issues that confront societies in transition, at www.ictj.org.

[23] See Roy L. Brooks, *Atonement and Forgiveness: A New Model for Black Reparations*; Colleen Duggan and Adita Abusharaf, "Reparation of Sexual Violence and Democratic Transition: In Search of Gender Justice." Barkan, *The Guilt of Nations*, discusses restitution of land and remains to Native American nations.

[24] Shaila Dewan, "Revisiting '64 Civil Rights Deaths, This Time in a Murder Trial," provides a timeline of cases. On Argentina, see Hector Tobar, "Argentina Justices Overturn Amnesty for Soldiers Linked to Rights Abuses." Nino, *Radical Evil on Trial*, provides earlier background. The Uruguayan government has charged Juan Maria Bordberry, President in the 1970s, with illegal killings that, having occurred outside Uruguay, skirt the 1986 amnesty law: Larry Rohter, "Uruguay Tackles Old Rights Cases, Charging Ex-President."

Greensboro, North Carolina, to revisit and document the murders of five antiracist community activists in 1979 for which no one was ever convicted despite the existence of videotapes of the murders.[25] In 2005 the United States Senate issued an apology for its failure to enact federal law to make lynching a crime in the early twentieth century.[26] Exhumations of human remains at massacre sites stretching back to the Second World War and of more recent date in Central America and the Balkans continue to provide both forensic and humanitarian opportunities, while memorial sites that commemorate mass deaths and genocides evoke deep feeling and controversies.[27] These events remind us that desires to "close books" are not disinterested and often not society-wide, and that for some who have suffered wrongs that have been insufficiently acknowledged and redressed, books are still open, and blood stains the page.

Restorative justice has also entered the contemporary field as a distinctive view of justice and wrongdoing. South Africa's Truth and Reconciliation Commission, launched in 1995 by a new democratic government, famously used restorative justice as the foundational vision for its transitional process.[28] After much international and internal consultation, South Africa remodeled the investigatory mechanism of the truth commission into a participatory public event. Victims and perpetrators of gross human rights violations came forward, many in public testimonies, to seek redress of injury or amnesty for terrible crimes, while at the same time creating a more complete and authoritative record and a public discourse about the reality of apartheid and the armed struggle against it in South Africa's past. In some instances, victims and survivors were able to confront directly those who had tortured them or murdered their family members. East Timor's national Commission for Reception, Truth, and

[25] The Commission's site is http://www.greensborotrc.org/. See also Ellis Cose, *Bone to Pick: Of Forgiveness, Reconciliation, Reparation, and Revenge,* 119–25, on the Greensboro Commission.

[26] Sheryl Gay Stolberg, "Senate Issues Apology Over Failure on Lynching Law."

[27] Eric Stover and Rachel Shigekane, "Exhumation of Mass Graves: Balancing Legal and Humanitarian Needs." Edward T. Linenthal, *The Unfinished Bombing: Oklahoma City in American Memory,* explores one such case in detail. On the broader issue, see also Sanford Levison, *Written in Stone: Public Monuments in Changing Societies,* and Jenny Edkins, *Trauma and the Memory of Politics.*

[28] On South Africa's Commission, in addition to Hayner, *Unspeakable Truths,* Rotberg and Thompson, *Truth v. Justice,* and Prager and Govier, *Dilemmas of Reconciliation,* see Charles Villa-Vicencio and Wilhelm Verwoerd, eds., *Looking Back, Reaching Forward: Reflections on the Truth and Reconciliation Commission of South Africa,* and Antje Krog, *Country of My Skull: Guilt, Sorrow, and the Limits of Forgiveness in the New South Africa.*

Reconciliation, following the country's independence struggle, has gone farther, with local public participation and a system of direct mediation for low-level offenders who come forward.[29] Restorative justice, however, originated long before these truth commissions as an alternative or an adjunct to criminal prosecution in a domestic context. Restorative justice embodies a view of crime or violence as a violation of people and relationships that entails an obligation to set things right, repairing victims and communities, and ideally humanizing and reintegrating offenders. The emphasis for restorative justice is on repairing relations through acknowledging the needs of victims and requiring accountability of those responsible for harm, through truth-telling, apology, and restitution or compensation.[30] In ordinary criminal contexts, the framework of focusing on harm, repair, and relationship leads to forms of mediation and conferencing, sometimes involving not only victims and offenders but communities of varying descriptions. On the national and international levels, the same framework can furnish a distinctive moral rationale for truth commissions and programs of reparation, education, and commemoration responding to political violence. While these measures are not exclusive of retribution, they can offer different, and in some instances superior, outcomes for victims and offenders.

A growing empirical literature on the effects of restorative justice practices dealing with ordinary crime, including violent crime, shows promising results. Almost all victims desire some forms of resolution and satisfaction, what Howard Zehr calls "an experience of justice."[31] Some may value a traditional court process that leads to punishment, but many victims, as quite a few studies show, may both be and feel well-served ("done justice") by a process that is less punitive but that offers participation,

---

[29] Roht-Arriaza discusses the much less known East Timor process (as well as some details of the Rwandan gacaca system) in "Reparations in the Aftermath of Repression and Mass Violence."

[30] Howard Zehr's influential *Changing Lenses: A New Focus for Crime and Justice* is a simple introduction. Gordon Bazemore and Mara F. Schiff, eds., *Restorative Community Justice: Repairing Harm and Transforming Communities*, and Johnstone, *A Restorative Justice Reader*, provide good coverage of empirical, conceptual, and critical issues in restorative justice practice. Dennis Sullivan and Larry Tifft, *Restorative Justice: Healing the Foundations of Our Everyday Lives*, situates restorative practice in a larger "needs-based" picture of social justice. John Braithwaite, *Restorative Justice and Responsive Regulation*, powerfully combines empirical results and theoretical analyses to support "responsive" approaches as a first resort in criminal justice, business and environmental regulation, and peacemaking. Many essays in Rotberg and Thompson, *Truth v. Justice*, discuss restorative justice in the South African case.

[31] Zehr, *Changing Lenses*, 28.

control, and a direct response from their offender.[32] In the wake of political violence, participants in national transitional movements for "truth and reconciliation" express some wonder at the willingness of many victims and survivors to be moderate in their responses and demands. José Zalaquett, a member of Chile's influential National Commission on Truth and Reconciliation, reported after interviewing thousands of the relatives of people who had been killed or disappeared under the Pinochet regime, "Certainly, many of them asked for justice. Hardly anyone, however, showed a desire for vengeance. Most of them stressed that in the end, what really mattered to them was to know the truth, that the memory of their loved ones would not be denigrated or forgotten, and that such terrible things would never happen again."[33] Retributive responses are not the only way, and in isolation may not be a completely adequate way, for victims to achieve personal, but also public and socially shared, validation and vindication. When victims do seek prosecution and (they hope) retribution as the gold standard of accountability, they are willing to accept that impersonal, measured, and socially sanctioned act of retribution as vindication; they do not typically seek "wild justice," mirroring the violent perpetrator's behavior in trying to "pay back" what they have suffered themselves. For many victims of violence, this is more than an emotional fact; it is a moral position. In a stark statement of this position, Susan Brison, a survivor of sexual violence and attempted murder, says, "I have seen the face of a killer set on exterminating a fellow human being. It is not a face I want to see when I look in the mirror."[34]

Those involved with assisting victims of crime and violence, and psychologists assisting victims of trauma and intimate betrayal, know that the range of emotions victims commonly experience includes "anger,

---

[32] Braithwaite, *Restorative Justice and Responsive Regulation*, ch. 3, provides a detailed and analytical overview of the empirical literature, concluding that restorative justice practices seem to provide greater satisfaction for victims, offenders, and communities than do typical court processes. See also Daniel W. Van Ness and Mara F. Schiff, "Satisfaction Guaranteed? The Meaning of Satisfaction in Restorative Justice." Findings of greater satisfaction with restorative justice practices might reflect failures of our bureaucratic administration of criminal justice rather than simply the superiority of restorative justice in principle. Yet there are functions that criminal prosecutions simply cannot, and do not try to, perform. See Minow, *Between Vengeance and Forgiveness*, 26.

[33] *Report of the Chilean National Commission on Truth and Reconciliation*, "Introduction to the English Edition," xxxiii.

[34] Susan Brison, "Letter to the Editor," accessed 3/1/2004. Thanks to Susan Brison for directing me to her eloquent letter. Margaret Urban Walker, "The Cycle of Violence," examines in detail the dangers of seeing retaliatory violence as the spontaneous and "natural," if not inevitable urge, of victims.

fear, terror, frustration, confusion, guilt, self-blame, shame, humiliation, grief, and sorrow."[35] Howard Zehr offers us a window into this world of "the intense and contradictory feelings of victims" in his remarkable photo essay of interviews, *Transcending*. Zehr asked victims of violent crime and families of murder victims to discuss their experiences.[36] The sample is not random, as Zehr's interview candidates were referred by victim services agencies and restorative justice programs. But the feelings they describe vividly illustrate the general picture given by psychologists of victimization and trauma.[37] The thirty-nine victim statements include repeated references to "anger," "anger and frustration," "enormous anger," "horrible anger," "rage," and "hatred." Reported alongside the anger in many of the interviews are shame, grief, distrust, humiliation, depression, self-blame, shock, fear, and, in unforgettable phrases, "shattering, howling pain," and "visceral, animal anguish."[38] Victims repeatedly say "in the beginning . . . " when they describe what they feel. More than a narrative convention, this signals how important to victims is the succession and course of emotions that they traverse in reacting to their experience, riding out the complex synergy and interaction of feelings: being ashamed of one's fear, or frightened of one's anger, or even, in a pattern too common to be dismissed, finding that grief or sadness over their own loss gives way to compassion for the offender.[39] Many

[35] Mary Achilles and Howard Zehr, "Restorative Justice for Crime Victims," 88, summarizes findings of Marlene Young of the National Organization for Victim Assistance.

[36] Howard Zehr, *Transcending: Reflections of Crime Victims*.

[37] See Ronnie Janoff-Bulman, *Shattered Assumptions: Towards a New Psychology of Trauma*; Judith Herman, *Trauma and Recovery: The Aftermath of Violence – From Domestic Abuse to Political Terror*, 33, on the exposure to "the extremities of helplessness and terror"; and Susan Brison, *Aftermath: Violence and the Remaking of a Self*, on the massively altered senses of self and self-control of victims of violence.

[38] Zehr, *Transcending*, on anger, rage, resentment, and hatred, 15, 48, 82, 86, 96, 97, 102, 112, 115, 134, 136, 138, 162, 168, 170, 177; on grief, hurt, pain, anguish, and depression, 10, 15, 26, 48, 56, 60, 115, 118, 162, 177; on shame, humiliation, self-blame, and mistrust, 34, 36, 136, 168, 170, 180; on shock and fear, 56, 130, 136, 168, 170, 180. "Shattering howling pain" is described by Debra Franke, 26; "a visceral, animal anguish" by Kim Muzyka, 48.

[39] John Conroy's study of torture and torturers recounts several startling cases of later friendship between torturer and tortured or good will by the tortured person toward the torturer. In a particularly poignant one, a victim of torture during the Greek civil war in the 1940s is approached twenty-five years later by the man who tortured him; the man seeks employment for his son. The two drink and dance together, but do not discuss the torture. The victim reports, "We were both ashamed." See Convoy, *Unspeakable Acts, Ordinary People: The Dynamics of Torture*, 172–77, quotation 176. While this story is exceptional, there are more reports of astounding magnanimity, and even compassion, by torture victims toward those who perpetrated obscene and violent acts upon them.

respondents describe intensely vengeful feelings, and only some of them repudiate those feelings. Some report a psychological passage or a moral conviction that has caused them to overcome or leave behind vengeful feelings. The variety and complexity of emotional responses of victims predicts that while victims will have needs that are varied and complex, they will value many of the same things. They will value and seek reassurance, safety, recognition of suffering, and appropriate placement of blame. Victims of grave wrongs are likely to feel they deserve this from both offenders and others, whether or not they desire to see offenders punished.

Research on criminal victimization, traumatic injury, and the aftermaths of political violence have explored the extensive network of fractures to a person's basic assumptions and attitudes that occur when they encounter violent, threatening, and profoundly disrespectful behavior at others' hands. The literatures of restorative justice, reparation for violence and injustice, and traumatic victimization begin to tell us what the wronged party seeks and what elements figure in their experience of justice and their own grasp of repair. In the case of Dorfman's fictional Paulina Salas, voice, validation and vindication are denied her, and she is isolated and abandoned. Victims must be able to tell, or have someone else tell in ways basically faithful to their own experience, the truth about what they have endured. Serious violation occasions a "rupture" in the human world and the understandings of the victim, and people seek to incorporate their experience of violation, betrayal, and terror into an intelligible part of the story of their lives, something they may not be able to achieve fully when they have experienced traumatic violence.[40] They need to transform violation or betrayal that may be nightmarish or phantasmic into matter that is accessible within a world of experience and

Lawrence Weschler describes Luis Perez Aguirre, a young Jesuit priest repeatedly imprisoned and tortured in Uruguay, in 1981, who actively approached the man who tortured him with forgiveness. See Weschler, *A Miracle, A Universe: Settling Accounts with Torturers,* 154–55. In another astonishing story, years of rage and bitterness are resolved into compassion by a meeting between torturer and victim, in Eric Lomax, *The Railway Man: A POW's Searing Account of War, Brutality and Forgiveness,* and reprised in Aaron Lazare's *On Apology,* 242–48. These instances are meant only to suggest the complexity of victim's responses, which can be completely lost in a simplistic account focusing only on rage and anger, and on vengeful anger, at that.

[40] In addition to Herman, *Trauma and Recovery,* Janoff-Bulman, *Shattered Assumptions,* and Brison, *Aftermath,* see also Yael Danieli, "Introduction," on the rupture and the victim's painful sense of silence and estrangement. Beverly Flanigan, *Forgiving the Unforgivable: Overcoming the Bitter Legacy of Intimate Wounds,* explores similar, if less catastrophic, phenomena in betrayals and severe harms by intimates.

description shared with others.[41] Victims may be uncertain about their own blamelessness and what they deserve. They need to know that others grasp the fact of the violation, its clear wrongfulness, the culpability of the perpetrator, and the reality of the harm and suffering caused them, in order to be validated. They need the affirmation of their entitlement to repair, and to be supported in seeking it or to have others seek it on their behalf. Whether that repair includes a confession, an apology, an acceptance of punishment, or some kind of amends, this is something to which they are entitled.

Another's faulty, disrespectful or violent action inflicts costs on the victim. The costs are often material, almost always emotional and moral, and sometimes they are difficult or impossible to bear. It is justice for the victim to have these costs reduced or relieved, ideally by the responsible party; to the extent and in the ways that this is achieved, victims are vindicated. What victims seek and deserve, then, has to do not only with what the victim or society can do to the offender, such as demanding accountability, voluntary or otherwise, but also with what the victim needs the offender or the community to do for her or him. Victims also need and deserve support in seeking to do things for themselves that are integral to restoring what they have lost: to regain self-respect, to avoid self-blaming, to re-establish moral equilibrium, to trust again, to hope, to live without terror, to feel safe from those who have harmed them, to forgive if they choose.

Voice, validation, and vindication are not neatly separable; being willing to hear victims is already validating, and sometimes the ability to tell or to have wrong acknowledged by others is vindicating. What matters is to secure these responses from others in some degree, especially from those others one perceives as one's "community," and to whom one looks for both reaffirmation of standards and affirmation that one's value and membership are recognized. When these responses are not forthcoming,

[41] A haunting passage, more resonant than any psychological analysis, comes from Clementine, a victim of the Rwandan genocide: "Me, I see that the survivors and the killers do not remember the same way at all. If the killers agree to speak up, they are able to tell the truth in every detail about what they did. They have kept a more normal memory of what happened on their hill. Their memory doesn't bump up against anything they've lived, it doesn't feel overwhelmed by horrible events. It is never mired in confusion . . . The survivors do not get along so well with their memories, which zigzag constantly with the truth, because of fear or the humiliation of what happened to them . . . Survivors must get together in little groups to add up and compare their memories, taking careful steps, making no mistakes." In Jean Hatzfeld, *The Machete Season: The Killers in Rwanda Speak*, 161–62.

the victim's situation is worse than unaddressed, it is aggravated. If the community or authority to whom the victim looks for validation and vindication ignores the victim, challenges the victim's credibility, treats the victim's complaint as of little import, shelters or sides with the perpetrator of wrong, or, worse, overtly or by implication blames the victim, the victim will feel abandoned and isolated. That abandonment is a "second injury" that can be humiliating.[42]

That second wound can also precipitate anger, grief, fear, terror, or despair, the same commonplace feelings that victims are liable to experience due to the original injury or wrong. That is because *to fail to confirm the victim's sense of wrong is itself another wrong.* It violates the morally essential trust that there are recognized, shared rules by which we live and which we can count on to protect and guide us. *Normative abandonment* is especially painful, enraging, and humiliating, and can feel disastrous for victims. This explains a common phenomenon in the testimonies of victims: they often experience as much or more rage, resentment, indignation, or humiliation in response to the failure of other people and institutions to come to their aid, acknowledge their injury, reaffirm standards, place blame appropriately on wrongdoers, and offer some forms of solace, safety, and relief, as they experience toward the original wrongdoer.[43] It is bad enough to have one's expectations of minimal respect and decent treatment violated, to feel one has lost control of one's life, or to be injured and rendered vulnerable to a storm of painful feelings. It can be unendurable to be ignored, to be denied credibility, or to run up against the fact that others, including those institutionally empowered to deal with crime and violence, do not seem to care about one's experience of violation and its consequences.[44] This is as true on the individual level of personal betrayals, cruelty, and violence as on the level of victimization

---

[42] Janoff-Bulman, *Shattered Assumptions,* 147, cites Martin Symonds on the "second injury." See also Danieli, "Introduction," 7, on the "second wound" and the "conspiracy of silence."

[43] A blistering and unnervingly intense presentation of the sense of abandonment is Jean Améry's expression of "Resentments" in his *At the Mind's Limits: Contemplations By a Survivor on Auschwitz and Its Realities.* I return to Améry's anguished discussion of resentment in Chapter 4.

[44] Thomas Brudholm explores three layers of violation involved in pressuring victims of political violence to take up a forgiving attitude to unpunished perpetrators, as he and others argue happened in the atmosphere of South Africa's Truth and Reconciliation Commission: there was the original violation, an amnesty policy that precluded legal redress for victims, and then a celebration of forgiveness that discouraged or implicitly criticized the victims' continuing resentment. See Brudholm, "'An Ugly Intrusion': Resentment in the Truth and Reconciliation Commission of South Africa."

by political terror: the stability of a moral world and our senses of trust and responsibility within it depend critically on how others respond to wrongs inflicted on us and among us.

There is a new and fruitful development in studies of responses to mass violence and oppression. Close empirical studies of the real problems that stand in the way of restoring relationships or imparting a sense of hopefulness to battered populations are starting to appear. Investigators are pressing beyond hopeful theoretical declarations about repair of individuals and societies to examine the actual effects of practices that address violence and explore the perceptions of victims, perpetrators, and bystanders of their meaning and impact. Two impressive studies are James Gibson's detailed examination of the impact of South Africa's Truth and Reconciliation Commission on several types of reconciliation and the report by Erik Stover and Harvey Weinstein of investigations of attitudes toward justice and reconciliation in the Balkans after the grisly warfare of 1991–95 and in Rwanda after the 1994 genocide.[45] Among many interesting findings of detail, a similar theme emerges in both studies: human beings' understandings of justice are more multi-form than most philosophical or legal conceptions account for. Gibson found that while South Africans perceived amnesty for violent wrongs as basically unfair, "alternative forms of justice," specifically voice, apology, and compensation, weighed significantly in tempering the injustice of amnesty.[46] Stover and Weinstein report that "For some, justice was testifying at a trial against the soldiers and paramilitaries who had murdered their families and destroyed their homes. For others, justice had to be exacted by revenge. Some said justice could only take place once their neighbors looked them directly in the eye and apologized for betraying them. Still others said it was finally learning the truth about their missing relatives

---

[45] James L. Gibson, *Overcoming Apartheid: Can Truth Reconcile a Divided Nation?*, and Eric Stover and Harvey M. Weinstein, eds., *My Neighbor, My Enemy: Justice and Community in the Aftermath of Mass Atrocity*. Roman David and Susanne Choi Yuk-ping, "Victims on Transitional Justice: Lessons from the Reparation of Human Rights Abuses in the Czech Republic," found satisfactory compensation and restoration of occupational standing to be particularly satisfactory in achieving sociopolitical redress and inner healing, but the study had a low rate of response. Naomi Roht-Arriaza, "Reparations in the Aftermath of Repression and Mass Violence," reports the finding of a Chilean human rights organization that interviewed families of persons killed and disappeared in Chile, Argentina, El Salvador, and Guatemala: "for victims, moral and legal measures of reparation are fundamental, while monetary compensation is controversial and problematic" (127).

[46] Gibson, *Overcoming Apartheid*, ch. 7, "Judging the Fairness of Amnesty," 284; and see also ch. 9, "Lessons for South Africa's Future and the World."

and receiving their bodies for proper burial."[47] "Setting things right" and hence "doing justice" is a broadly encompassing category from the point of view of those harmed, and this begs for explanation.

These studies and others suggest the need for factual inquiry and objective evidence to test broad generalizations that truth heals, that only criminal trials create accountability, that only retribution satisfies victims, or that reconciliation requires forgiveness.[48] Detailed empirical inquiries suggest that concrete situations create specific opportunities and obstacles to redress and repair, depending upon what is possible and what victims and perpetrators can experience as useful and just. Yet as much as empirical inquiry is needed, so is a deeper understanding of the main normative ideas – and ideals – at issue in responding to wrongs. We need to keep a clear sense of what it is that reparative measures are attempting to repair. Certain themes repeat throughout the literature on transitional justice, reparation, and restorative justice. There are constant references to "social repair," "social reconstruction," "restoration of relationships," "restoring the dignity of the victim," "restoring trust," "reweaving the moral fabric," "moral reconstruction," or "moral reparation."[49] These phrases function most often as touchstones that are not closely analyzed and are not situated in a broader perspective on moral relationship.

My project is to try to provide that broader perspective. I start with an account of what a moral relationship involves in order to identify precisely the kinds of damage that serious wrongs do. At the same time,

---

[47] Stover and Weinstein, *My Neighbor, My Enemy*, 4.

[48] Fletcher and Weinstein, "Violence and Social Repair," offers a sustained criticism of the lack of empirical investigation of ambitious claims made for the primacy of criminal trials, including international tribunals.

[49] Variations on these phrases are too numerous to cite. For a few examples, Jose Zalaquett speaks of "moral reconstruction" in Naomi Roht-Arriaza, "The Need for Moral Reconstruction in the Wake of Past Human Rights Violations: Interview with Jose Zalaquett," and Naomi Roht-Arriaza speaks of "moral" (vs. material) reparations in her "Reparations in the Aftermath of Repression and Mass Violence." Minow, *Between Vengeance and Forgiveness*, speaks of "reconstruction of a relationship" (26), and "repairing social connections and peace" (92). Eva Hoffman speaks of Holocaust atrocities in Poland in terms of "ravages of the moral sense" and the need for "restoration of that moral world and moral order" in *After Such Knowledge: Memory, History, and the Legacy of the Holocaust* (267). Psychologist Beverly Flanigan speaks of the foundation of trust between people that sets expectations in a relationship as a "moral history" disrupted by intimate betrayal that may or may not be reparable, in her *Forgiving the Unforgivable*, 20–21. South Africa's TRC described its job in part as "restoring the human and civil dignity of the victims." See Rotberg and Thompson, *Truth v. Justice*, for frequent use of this expression. These formulations sometimes blend with others couched in the therapeutic language of "healing," or a sociological language of "social repair."

the prominence of themes of trust, hope, resentment, despair, and the importance to victims and others of responses or lack of response to wrongs in discussions of restorative justice, reparations, and trauma, tend to support the account I will offer. This account of fundamental issues in moral repair aims to make clearer when repair is, as it may not always be, a possibility, and where, at a deep level, attempts at repair may run up against limits.

Moral Repair

Moral repair is the task of restoring or stabilizing – and in some cases creating – the basic elements that sustain human beings in a recognizably moral relationship. By "moral relationship" I refer to a kind of relationship or mode of relating rather than to an order governed by a particular scale of values, set of imperatives, or system of role-bound obligations. Such "moralities" are the shared terms that societies set for responsible conduct and properly lived lives. Any such morality (including those streamlined normative ethical systems that philosophers elaborate, were they to be enacted in life) must be embedded in the responses, feelings, and attitudes, as well as the beliefs, of human beings in order to become and remain a functioning moral order in actual time and space. By "moral relationship" in the generic sense I mean a certain disposition of people toward each other and the standards they trust, or at least hope, are shared.

On this view, morality as a phenomenon of human life in real time and space consists in trust-based relations anchored on our expectations of one another that require us to take responsibility for what we do or fail to do, and that allow us to call others to account for what they do or fail to do. This is a way of living by rules or norms that set mutual expectations and ground social practices of giving and demanding accounts; in this way of living we rely on each other to be responsive to expectations and to understand that accounting is owed when we do not behave in the ways upon which others rely. This way of going on together stands in contrast to other ways people have of getting others to behave as they expect or wish, such as violence, force, coercion, and some kinds of manipulation. These are ways of securing human behavior through compulsion rather than through reliance on self-guidance through shared recognition of norms and values, the mutual expectations they create, and responsiveness to what they demand. In social life, threat and compulsion thread through and run alongside our mutual reliance on each other's senses of responsibility, teaching and reminding us of the expectations in play, and providing examples and incentives for that self-guidance on which human societies mostly rely.

The attitudes that support moral relationship in this generic sense are also the keys to moral repair. To sustain moral relationship we require *confidence* in shared standards (that some standards as we know them are shared, that they are recognized as such, and that there is reason to think they lead to worthwhile lives), and *trust* among individuals, and in a common human environment, that we ourselves and others will be responsive to these standards (and to the reproach we deserve when we transgress them). At bottom, living in moral relationship requires a residual and renewable *hopefulness* that we and others are worthy of the trust we place in each other, and that our world allows us to pursue the goods to which our shared understandings are meant to lead us.[50] Moral relationship also requires distinctive forms of response – resentment and indignation – that register violations of shared understandings, demand accountability, and prompt corrections of unacceptable behavior. Hope, trust, and resentment are linked through a particular kind of expectation – a *normative expectation* – that rests on those standards we believe authoritative.

A sensibility attuned to norms is a basic part of human social functioning.[51] We navigate the human world around us by forming and acting on normative expectations of others and of ourselves. Our normative expectations embody what we expect *of* people, whether or not we expect that they are likely to behave compliantly (although in many instances we do expect that people will behave as they are supposed to behave).[52] A normative expectation anticipates compliance more or less (and sometimes scarcely at all), but always embodies a *demand* for that form of behavior we think we've a right to. A simple explanation of that "right" is the presumed authority of a norm of some kind. The basis for our sense of entitlement is our trust, always more or less hopeful, in the authority of the norm and in others' responsiveness to it. The expression of our

---

[50] In Margaret Urban Walker, *Moral Understandings: A Feminist Study in Ethics*, I develop a critical epistemology of this trust-based view of actual moral relations.

[51] It is not exclusively human, however, and this should not be surprising. See Frans de Waal *Good Natured: The Origins of Right and Wrong in Humans and Other Animals*, 89–97, on the "sense of social regularity" in primates.

[52] An early paper that draws this distinction clearly is Anthony Woozley, "Injustice." Woozley concludes, suggestively, that injustice fundamentally is "the affront done to a man as a human being by not treating him as he can expect to be treated," and that this arouses indignation even where one is treated as one expects one in fact *will* be treated.

sense of entitlement is our readiness to be aroused angrily at one whose noncompliant behavior threatens the authority of a norm by defying it. Resentment and indignation are this distinctive *accusing* and *rebuking* anger. When we or others are injured or treated ill it is not the fact of harm or suffering in itself but the sense of the *wrongfulness* of that harm or suffering that is embodied in this kind of anger. So, too, are the boundaries of our sense of entitlement represented in our readiness to feel and express gratitude when others go beyond normative bounds in treating us with undue generosity, kindness, or care. The feelings that are cued by the fulfillment or disappointment of normative expectations – ones philosophers call "reactive attitudes," following Peter Strawson's classic discussion – literally embody our senses of responsibility.[53] Reactive feelings and the reactions and responses that express them are the ways we concretely hold others (and ourselves) to account. The responses can be immediate and expressive (an angry scowl), articulate ("How dare you!"), or elaborately institutionalized in custom or law. In these responses and by them we participate in the reiteration and enforcement of shared norms and the normative expectations they entail.

Reactive feelings in their natural and learned forms of expression have been described as a form of "moral address": they call on us to recognize the propriety or impropriety of what goes on between us and in our midst.[54] Strawson called the way we live with others in constant readiness to express these reactions, and so to address each other as responsible beings, a "participant attitude."[55] In that stance, when disqualifying or excusing circumstances are absent, we hold others responsible for their intentional actions and see ourselves in a form of relationship to others that entails mutual accountability and the right to demand it. Resentment and indignation in particular express a finding of *fault* of others and a *demand* on them for an appropriate response. Appropriate responses from offenders include at the very least acknowledgment of fault and responsibility (when justification and excuse do not apply), and, beyond that, some attempt at repair, including apology or amends. Resentful and

---

[53] P. F. Strawson, "Freedom and Resentment." I focus here mainly on reactive attitudes to others; Strawson emphasizes self-reactive attitudes such as guilt or remorse, and these are also fundamental features of our senses of responsibility.

[54] See Jonathan Bennett, "Accountability"; Gary Watson, "Responsibility and the Limits of Evil"; and Barbara Houston, "In Praise of Blame," on reactive attitudes as forms of address. The phrase seems to be Watson's.

[55] Strawson, "Freedom and Resentment," 79–80.

indignant responses also seek an audience in others who one assumes will share the judgment of faulty action and will join in or support the demand for an accounting. This turns out to be crucially important for moral repair.

Resentment and indignation arise as responses to behavior that contravenes normative expectations. Among our normative expectations are expectations that others, with whom we think we are playing by rules, not only play by them, but also rise to the reiteration and enforcement of those rules when someone goes out of bounds. *Normative confirmation* and enforcement is something we usually feel we have a right to expect of each other in addition to the behavior that specific rules require. When we express and direct our resentment or indignation at a norm violator, we demand some rectifying response from the one who is perceived as out of bounds. When we express our resentment to others, we invite confirmation from others that we have competently judged a normative violation and that others share our interest in affirming the norms we hold, in showing disapproval of conduct out of bounds, and perhaps in seeking redress of violations. Most fundamentally, we seek confirmation that these norms are meant to include and protect *us*; that we are recognized by others and that our dignity is valued by others. All the more so when the violation is a serious one, a cause of harm, indignity, or insult that is apt to be seen as moral matter.

There is, however, a large complication. The reality is that moral relations are seated in and expressed through social relations. More often than not, in human societies the extant moral order will to a great extent track or implement a social order that privileges some over others.[56] Not all "participants" are equal in most human social and moral orders. In this commonplace situation, moral repair may address wrongs within the extant order, or the moral repair sought may be repair of the social and moral order itself and the normative expectations that house it. Moral repair may be directed to shoring up ongoing understandings, however morally questionable from a critical point of view, or it may target those understandings for change. In these cases, the possibilities and the stakes are different. Repair cannot mean return to the status quo, but must aim

---

[56] On the intricate meshing of social and moral orders, and the roles of de facto moral understandings in sustaining what are often questionable or disturbing orders that arbitrarily demean or subordinate some of their members, see my *Moral Understandings*. See also Annette Baier, *Commons of the Mind*, on our practice of holding people accountable as "part and parcel of intentional agency itself" (37–38), not specific to moral evaluation but part of the "social subsoil of morality" (39).

at bringing morally diminished or shattered relations closer to morally adequate form. Where there are deeply embedded social patterns of disregard, subjugation, or violation among members of certain groups, the normative expectations of the powerful may be more or less understood as a rigged game by those dominated or oppressed. At the extremes of violence, it is not only trust that can be extinguished but also the residual hope that nourished that trust. In the more everyday situation of hierarchical relationships that rest ultimately on coercive power, relations of trust are likely to be asymmetrical, and to appear differently to those who rule and those who must obey. Keeping hope and self-respecting normative expectations alive under conditions of social disregard is a special burden on those targeted for diminishing or abusive treatment. It compounds the problems of redress and affects what it means to forgive as well as what can count as amends in the wake of mass violence and historical injustice. I try to keep this complication in view throughout the book.

In sum, then, reactive feelings testify to normative expectations that define the scope and nature of our senses of responsibility. Resentment and indignation rise to defend normative boundaries when they are seen as threatened by action that is out of normative bounds. In the more serious cases, the bounds are moral ones, but they need not be. Resentment and indignation are all-purpose emotions for human beings, inhabiting as they do an elaborate structure of norms that organize almost all areas of life. Normative expectations require a background of trust and hope. Hope is an energizing attitude that mobilizes our attention and efforts toward a desired but uncertain state that need only be barely possible. Trust, in several varieties, is an attitude of reliance on others that holds those others responsible for the performance on which we rely. Trust is always more or less hopeful; when trust is crushed, there is only hope that others may yet, or yet again, be worthy of trust. When hope is crushed, a moral world cannot be sustained. The nature of and relations among hope, trust, and resentment are taken up in Chapters 2, 3, and 4.

Serious and particularly violent wrongdoing, as well as systemic oppression, creates a situation of disruption, distortion, damage, and even despair of moral relations. In Chapters 5 and 6 I explore two morally emblematic forms of "exit" from this situation, forgiveness and making amends. Victims have the power to forgive, releasing themselves from a position of anguish, anger, and protest, and releasing a wrongdoer from continuing reproach and demand. What is involved in forgiving is surprisingly elusive and complex, given how familiar and indispensable this act is to human relationships; I try to honor this complexity in my account in

Chapter 5. Wrongdoers from their side may offer amends, and communities may demand, support, or join in amends, in order to acknowledge responsibility, reaffirm shared standards, answer resentment, fear, and despair, and reinvite trust and hopefulness. Taking responsibility, apologizing, and making amends is an everyday business and our repertory of reparative gestures is learned early and used frequently in the general run of life, where we often have reason to anticipate success in smoothing breaches and regaining normal relations with others. Our ordinary conceptions of responsibility and amends-making may come under strain, however, in cases that involve severe betrayal or violence, or that transcend the scale and time-frame of our usual reparative gestures and exchanges. I conclude in Chapter 6 with a discussion of violence, historical injustice, and the resources of restorative justice theory and practice to engage individuals and communities in responsible reckoning with their individual and collective pasts.

I can now say in brief: *moral repair is restoring or creating trust and hope in a shared sense of value and responsibility*. More precisely, moral repair encompasses six tasks.

1. Moral repair is served by placing responsibility on wrongdoers and others who share responsibility for wrongs.
2. Moral repair is served by acknowledging and addressing wrong, harm, affront, or threat to victims and communities.
3. Moral repair is served by authoritatively instating or reinstating moral terms and standards within communities where wrong may have caused fear, confusion, cynicism, or despair about the authority of those standards.
4. Moral repair is served by replenishing or creating trust among individuals in the recognition of shared moral standards and in their responsiveness to those standards and support of the practices that express and enforce them.
5. Moral repair is served by igniting or nourishing hope that moral understandings and those who are responsible for supporting them are worthy of trust.
6. Moral repair is served by connecting or reconnecting in adequate moral relationship those who have done wrong and those who have been harmed as a result, where and to the extent that this is possible, practically and morally. Where this is not possible, moral repair aims to stabilize or strengthen moral relationship among others and within communities.

Communal Responsibilities for Repair

Wrongdoers and victims – whether individuals or groups – are a natural focus for moral repair. It is less obvious but essential to see that moral repair is always at the same time a communal responsibility.[57] The task of reproducing standards of responsibility and senses of responsibility is the basic shared task of every community, including those very amorphous communities that are called, sometimes with rhetorical purpose but usually with practical necessity, "society." This is why communities must reiterate the standards that have been contravened in wrongdoing or in allowing undeserved harms; they need to reanimate the grip of standards in the minds and, more deeply, in the feelings of those who are expected to honor them. This is nothing less, but also nothing more, than the condition for the existence and reproduction of moral and other normative standards and relations in groups on any scale. Groups must succeed through many redundant and mutually reinforcing actions and practices, by their members singly and in concert, in sustaining practices of responsibility and keeping them running on the rails of some shared standards. If they fail, they cannot conserve a moral culture, and in fact cannot sustain a culture embodying other norms, such as norms of dress, etiquette, or decorum.[58]

Any serious wrongdoing (or persistent wrongdoing, even where less serious) raises the question of whether certain standards are really taken seriously, and often whether the interests and dignity of individuals harmed by wrongdoing are taken seriously. It is the responsibility of communities to answer those questions, for the business end of the authority of moral standards is some community's willingness to enforce them in a variety of ways. One part of effective practices of repair will be actions undertaken by communities that reiterate moral understandings, clarify their scope, and stabilize our confidence in their authority. Wrongdoing always raises the question "What do we stand for?" in two senses: "What are the shared norms on which we rightfully base our mutual expectations of each other's behavior?" and "What will we do to express the authority of those standards for us when someone has violated them, and

---

[57] Trudy Govier, *Forgiveness and Revenge*, ch. 5, discusses groups as agents and subjects of harm, and so capable of offering reparative gestures and receiving them.

[58] The concept of "practices of responsibility," socially authoritative patterns of assigning, accepting, and deflecting responsibility for matters open to human care and effort, is developed, and the claim that the moral practices are never modular with respect to social roles and practices is defended in Walker, *Moral Understandings*.

so put that authority in question?" Communities have an abiding need
to keep in circulation their authoritative understandings, and to try to
make sure that these understandings continue to be seen as authoritative.
Communities have a responsibility also to telegraph the need for changes
in community standards that are found to be disrespectful or indecent to
some. A "community" can be a household, or a neighborhood, or a society, or a nation, and perhaps the "world community" or the "community
of nations" of which we in the twenty-first century now often hopefully
speak. The "community" in question is the collective of moral judges to
whom people look as a reference point for the validity of claims of injury
and claims to repair.

Communally shared responsibilities are those that inhere in a collectivity that is defined principally as a community of judgment defined
by its members' shared recognition of some basic standards that predictably set normative expectations among them. Some communities of
judgment are perfectly clearly bounded; the members of a club or organization who hew to certain standards of conduct among themselves is an
example of a clearly defined community of normative judgment. Other
such communities have fuzzier boundaries; consider professions where
there are widely shared standards of conduct, but where membership is
not always clearly defined (credentials or activity?), and where it is less a
question of precise rules of conduct than of folkways and accepted modes
of interaction. Then there are those communities whose reality lies somewhere between the ways they are imagined to embody certain histories
and values, and the historical consciousness and values that are actually
embodied in their major institutions, stabilized by law and custom. Often
the match between the "imagined community" and the reality is only very
rough. Societies are such communities.[59]

Communities have three ongoing tasks with respect to their practices
of responsibility. First, communities are responsible for the reiteration of
the *standards* that have been contravened and reassertion of their authority, at least if the wrongdoing has put the standards or their authority
in question. Second, communities are responsible for the legitimiza-
tion and enforcement of the individual *wrongdoer's* proper acceptance
of responsibility and consequent obligations to submit to or perform
reparative action, at least if the wrongdoer is identified, available, and

---

[59] Benedict Anderson's phrase refers to communities such as modern nations that preclude
face to face contact but to which vast numbers of people see themselves as belonging
together. See his *Imagined Communities: Reflections on the Origin and Spread of Nationalism*.

subject in some degree to the community's control. Third, communities are responsible for seeing that injustice to the victim does not go unaddressed, or, more precisely, that the *victim* does not go unaddressed, but receives acknowledgment that the treatment by the wrongdoer was unacceptable to the community, and assurance that this is a matter of record and due importance to the community. The last communal responsibility is as commonplace as the first two, but its importance is magnified where those who are responsible for wrongful harm are unidentifiable, unavailable, or unwilling to acknowledge their responsibility and their obligations of repair.

The latter two responsibilities – making wrongdoers accountable and validating victims – are instrumental in achieving the first, but they also have independent import. They are instrumental because among the ways that any group shows what it believes its standards to be and whether it takes them seriously as effective standards is to respond clearly to their violation, and that means responding both to those who violate and to those, should there be any, who are wronged. There are other ways that standards are defined, for example, by being taught and promulgated in formal and informal ways, and publicly invoked as justification for actions, including the actions of enforcing standards. But an important way of asserting and defining standards is to respond with rebuke to the violator and with assurance or redress to the injured. Addressing offenders and those wronged asserts standards and also signifies membership in the community for which the standards are presumed to hold. It is in these applications that the actual meaning of standards in a community is defined.

At the same time that addressing violators and victims is part of the process of reasserting a norm, doing so has other important and independent functions. Reproving wrongdoers – which can range from labeling to reproaching to punishing, excluding, or demanding amends – confirms that membership is conditional upon certain responsibilities. Assuring or satisfying victims – which again can range from labeling and pronouncing wrongs to support for redress or direct redress for victims – confirms that membership entails forms of recognition and protection. Notoriously, the application of what appear to be quite general norms in human communities are in fact selective with respect to whom and what they protect. Norms may be reasserted selectively with respect to some and not others, just as acknowledgment of needs to repair and obligations of repair may be offered to some and denied to others. So communal assertion or reassertion of norms carries two constitutive and signifying features.[60] The first is that there is a norm, a boundary between what is acceptable and what is not; the second is that some are guaranteed membership under the norm in either or both of two modes: they are subject to demand in case of violating the norm, and they are within the community's protective mantle under the norm. To fail to reprove wrongdoers or to fail to hold responsible those to whom responsibility reasonably falls is to cast doubt on the authority of norms, to authoritatively if implicitly mark exceptions to them, or to indicate that wrongdoers are beyond the reach of the community or its norms. To fail to reassure or to satisfy victims is to cast doubt on the authority of norms, to authoritatively if implicitly mark those victims as outside the norm's protective cover, or to indicate that those victims are not members to whom the community's general responsibility reaches, or are not members at all.

Systems of law that, among other functions, codify some moral and social understandings into rules enforceable at public cost and, in democratic societies with some transparency, by collectively owned and accountable institutions, formally represent communal responsibilities. Although law serves many purposes, its popular image is precisely that of a protective and expressive order: "the law" says what society will and will not tolerate, and the legal system provides mechanisms of accountability and sanction. The legal apparatus, however, is only a partial and partially effective expression of such moral consensus as exists in communities. This consensus is always rough and is usually being contested in significant part at any given time, but it nonetheless holds over wide territories of behavior that do serious harm to people. This nexus of moral understandings is a common resource that provides terms of shareable (even if not always shared) judgment. We renew this resource individually and as a collective by our repeated articulation and enforcement of these standards. Much of this is done by informal social "policing," which includes punishing or protective actions as well as emotional expression – resentment, indignation, reproach, blame, reprisal, penalty, exclusion, or punishment. Much is also done through social, religious, legal, and political institutions.[61]

---

[60] Adeno Addis, "Economic Sanctions and the Problem of Evil," says that sanctions against wrongdoers invoke norms in "constitutive and signifying roles." Addis explains the sense in which there is an "international community" that is imagined and enacted through shared history, institutions, and the values it expresses in invoking norms.

[61] I have avoided the terminology of "collective responsibility." Theories that ascribe collective responsibility to groups such as corporations, institutions, or nations in virtue of a well-defined decision-making structure do not capture diffusely located communal

Communities do not always fulfill these responsibilities, or make adequate attempts to do so. In cases of deeply conflicting standards and at times of social change, there is a real question about how to define the relevant community. One way, though, that communities bring themselves into existence, sustain themselves, and define and refine their identities is by the progressive articulation and the enforcement of their norms and of their membership. When individuals take up the role of judges, invoking norms and affirming membership, they make use of something that is common property, the moral authority of a community. In judging, they exercise a prerogative and undertake to fulfill a responsibility that is not uniquely theirs. This is why it matters a great deal that individuals enjoy confidence in the rightful authority of standards, trust in themselves and others as responsive and responsible to standards, and have a hopeful attitude that the community's standards and its members are worthy of that confidence and trust. Individuals can only take up their parts in the rough and ready business of stabilizing and reproducing – and in some instances modifying – practices of responsibility that embody moral and other values if they enjoy this confidence, trust, and hope in some degree. What this comes to is that communal responsibilities are nothing exotic, and appeal to them is not a novelty on the fringes of ethical experience.

Moral repair falls upon us as individual parties who have done wrong, or caused or failed to prevent wrongful harm, *and* as members of a community intended to be defensibly just. Even in fulfilling our purely individual responsibilities when we are responsible for wrong, we will be guided by communally understood and supported gestures and practices of repair. We will use what our societies have established, a collectively sustained resource, as meaningful ways to demonstrate accountability and to address the harm or insult suffered by victims. In the fulfillment of responsibilities of communities such as "our neighborhood" or "the United States," our means of fulfilling communal responsibilities will typically be organizational or institutional, and individually we will play our roles

responsibilities as I have described them, although they do explain the collective responsibility that characterizes the institutions that often carry out communal responsibilities. Perhaps the notion of "shared responsibility" is better suited to explaining the nature of communal responsibilities. On collective responsibility in virtue of a certain kind of organization and execution of decisions, see Peter A. French, *Collective and Corporate Responsibility*, and Toni Erskine, "Assigning Responsibilities to Institutional Moral Agents: The Case of States and 'Quasi-States.'" On shared responsibility, in which individuals each bear some portion of responsibility for actions or outcomes that none determined alone, see Larry May, *Sharing Responsibility*. Another approach to shared responsibility is found in Christopher Kutz, *Complicity: Ethics and Law for a Collective Age*.

in accepting, supporting, and perhaps participating in the organizational or institutional programs of repair. Where we have no individual link to wrongs, there is no purely individual responsibility (or individual portion of shared responsibility) in which we can be derelict. Yet in cases where we have no individual link to wrong we do not cease to have a role in communal responsibilities as community members, and we can still fail to support (or in some cases to support the creation of) those practices and institutions that are designed to fulfill communal responsibilities of repair. Only wrongdoers and other responsible parties can be in a position to offer some forms of amends – apologies for the act of wrongdoing, for example. But only communities, at different levels, are in a position to give certain kinds of validation, such as the assurance that the community is on the side of the victim, not of the wrongdoer. There are nonetheless many kinds of validation and vindication to which both wrongdoers and communities may contribute.

Limits of Moral Repair

I understand the claim that a wrong should be set right as a moral claim. Like any moral claim, a claim to have wrongs "righted" may compete for fulfillment or may conflict with other moral claims, and so it does not follow that every such claim can be or should be fulfilled. If it cannot be fulfilled, this itself is apt to constitute a wrong, thus giving rise to another claim of essentially the same sort, a special kind of "remainder": a claim that someone should make right a prior failure to make something right.[62] When justified claims to repair might have been fulfilled but are not, whether because of conflicting moral claims or because of ignorance, indifference, or unwillingness, there is a continuing failure of repair, culpable to a greater or lesser degree. This sort of continuing failure can be additive, or can compound an original wrong, like a debt that grows larger with interest. There really is such a thing as adding moral insult to injury, whether wilfully or not, and thus adding additional injuries, and there is also the fact that certain wrongs over time become larger ones when they involve continuing neglect or disrespect, or when wrongful harms themselves worsen for lack of response to them. Unremedied historic injustices toward groups or peoples have these

---

[62] The idea of "remainders" that survive as sources of regret or of further obligation is rooted in discussions of moral dilemma and moral luck. Christopher Gowans, *Innocence Lost: An Examination of Inescapable Moral Wrongdoing*, provides detailed discussion.

features of added and compounded injuries, as do continuing neglectful or bad treatment among individuals.

Continuing failure to attempt reparative action reveals and adds to severe distortions in the conditions of moral relationship. The understandings and attitudes that enable people to meet in relations of responsibility can be diminished or extinguished. In cases where some human beings are scarcely seen as within consideration at all, there is not only an absence of the understandings and attitudes that should be there but there are counter-attitudes and distorted understandings. There are understandings, for example, among those who acknowledge each other as worthy of consideration that some others – the woman, the native, the slave, the lower orders, the foreigner, the enemy – are not within the same circle of consideration or not worthy of consideration at all. Understandings like these, utterly commonplace in human societies, are invariably buttressed by mythologies, ideologies, religious dogmas, pseudo-scientific discourses, and "noble lies." Most societies continue to live with some such understandings or continue to struggle with their legacies. Recent episodes of genocide, ethnic cleansing, and mass rape and killing in such places as Rwanda, the former Yugoslavia, or Sudan remind us how alarmingly easily these attitudes can be ignited in their most malignant forms.

Talk of "repair" is not out of place even in cases of extreme disregard and worse. For it is never only a question of creating the conditions of moral relationship where they have been lacking; it is always a case of reforming or replacing some attitudes and understandings that are distorted and injurious, even malignant. It is true, however, that a deep distortion in moral relationship, or the denial of moral relationship, has a depth that no isolated reparative measures can reach. Applying remedies for this kind of distortion will inevitably be a long-term process on many fronts, most likely including orchestrated political, legal, and social change, changes in education and custom, carefully considered displays and rituals of recognition and respect, and substantial reparative measures of several kinds. This is especially true of historic situations in which some groups or peoples have been persistently denigrated, subordinated, conquered, colonized, terrorized, exploited, or excluded by other groups or peoples.[63]

---

[63] Stover and Weinstein, in *My Neighbor, My Enemy*, suggest "reclamation" as a more fitting term in cases of where relations are severely damaged – see "Introduction: conflict, justice, and reclamation," 15.

The difficulty, complexity, and variety of measures needed to respond at all effectively to historic injustice, mass violence, or terror, and the extended commitment, perhaps over generations, to reparative measures is not a persuasive argument for "letting bygones be bygones." This argument is often made, and seems usually to be made by those who stand guilty of having mistreated others on a large scale, as when state officials responsible for systemic violence argue for amnesties so that "old wounds" are not "reopened," and that it is "impossible" to set right such grave and extended wrongs. This argument is also tempting to the beneficiaries who reap the bounty of historic patterns of discrimination that, though no longer enforced, still pay handsomely to their advantage. Arguments from practical difficulty and social discord are not conclusive arguments against undertaking sustained and systemic repairs where moral relations have been denied, distorted, or repeatedly damaged. On the contrary, if repair is owed, then repair must be attempted. If it has not been attempted, then wounds are still open and injuries and insults continue.

Nonetheless, there are concrete problems of "too much" and "not enough" that will predictably confront individuals and societies when repair is at issue. Communities and individuals have finite resources and time. Societies in transition, for example, must often balance programs of reparation with urgent demands for rebuilding infrastructure, coping with displaced and injured populations and orphaned children, and creating the legal and political institutions that will serve normal life. Often societies emerging from conflict are desperately poor ones that face huge demands to re-establish an economy and create housing, education, and medical services; these demands compete for resources with programs of judicial redress and reparation. In addition, new resentments can be aroused by monetary compensation or differential access to benefits and services provided to victims as compensation.[64] Since wrongdoers and beneficiaries of wrongdoing typically are resistant to the admission of wrong and wrongful gain that reparation predicates, it may be hard to stand up against pressures to settle fast and cheap, or not at all. If what is at issue where people must go on living together is the restoration of social bonds of trust and bases for hope, reparation must neither slight victims nor be a source of dangerous envy and hostility. There are trade-offs and zero-sum moments in undertaking and implementing any program of repair, and these are not present only in large-scale and political cases.

---

[64] These problems are clearly discussed in Roht-Arriaza, "Reparations in the Aftermath of Repression and Mass Violence."

Individuals too, after offense or harm to others, must reckon how much they are prepared to offer and how hard they are prepared to try to make amends and mend fences; when injured, they must decide what is meaningful and adequate as an offering of repair. The costs may be found to be too high on either end to attempt to continue the relationship.

Yet we have a repertory of common moral gestures that aim at repair, such as owning up, apologizing, making amends, showing repentance, and seeking or offering forgiveness. These are the familiar everyday maneuvers of individuals that are effective in restoring relationships after everyday wrongdoing. We may worry that resorting to these socially familiar and common formats in more complicated cases is feeble or insulting. An apology for several hundred years of chattel slavery, apartheid, and racist violence? A compensatory payment for wartime sexual slavery? An official truth-telling to address an epoch of state-controlled murder, disappearance, and widespread torture? Still, where repair is owed, morally repair must be sincerely attempted. Otherwise, those of us who have done wrong, or others of us who are witnesses, bystanders, or beneficiaries, but who refuse to address that wrong, will add to, compound, or deepen the damage done and augment the insults it carries. If no wrongs can be fully righted as no bell can be unrung, there is still plenty of room for reparative gestures that work on the moral plane to relieve suffering, disillusionment, isolation, and despair. Too little is better than nothing, and small gestures can carry larger meanings or can be a starting point for a broader reconsideration of relationships between individuals and within societies. The refusal of even the small gesture, on the other hand, can feed bitterness, rage, and despair.

Finally, the language of repair is a natural and straightforward one for the tasks that I examine here, but to speak of "repair" may be misleading in an important respect.[65] It might seem to imply that a "broken" moral relationship *can* be fixed, and that when fixed it will be fully or largely restored, if not "good as new." This can indeed happen where wrongdoing does not strike deeply or where the nature of the relationships it affects allows not only for reconciliation but also for an actual strengthening of bonds. A breach healed in a friendship can be an occasion for friends' deeper understanding of each other and of what connects them. A prodigal relation may be reaccepted with familial generosity that creates deeper and new durable bonds of connection. Old enemies may

---

[65] Many nuances of the idea and practices of repair are explored in Elizabeth V. Spelman, *Repair: The Impulse to Restore in a Fragile World.*

carry the memory of some place of conflict they wish never to revisit, and this wisdom achieved through shared history may become a basis for keeping peace. Many instances of wrongful injury, however, do not permit relations to be continued as they were, or to be continued at all. The perception of repair as possible, however, may hinge on whether the parties have a choice about going on together or not. If they cannot part ways, then they had better be imaginative in seeking possibilities of repair and energetic in pursuing them.

I do not intend my account to preclude either cases of moral repair that lead to a "better than new" state of affairs, on the one hand, or the case of irreparable damage, on the other. Nor do I see the effects of wrongdoing and or available repairs as ordered along a continuum, for that would suggest that there is a single dimension along which wrongdoing does damage and repair undoes it. I hope to keep in view the multiple aspects of moral relationship that can be threatened, damaged, or put out of reach by wrongful harms, and the multiple reparative responses that do not all touch the same points of damage, nor touch all of them with the same effect from case to case. My objective is an account that sheds light on why reparative activity can in many cases restore or create moral relations in varying degrees and also why some injuries are irreparable. The simple formula, to be elaborated in what follows, is that repair of relations involves creating or stabilizing normative expectations, trust, and hope of some types for those parties affected by wrongdoing. The parties include primarily wrongdoers, victims, and communities, where communities also frequently include bystanders and beneficiaries, as well as those injured who are not the immediate or primary victim but who have suffered wrongful losses due to others' choices and actions. There is perhaps no case where in principle trust and hope of the relevant kinds might not be restored, but what matters for moral repair is what human beings can actually feel and do, as well as what they choose to do. Communal support can make a great deal of difference to whether wrongdoers will accept responsibility and undertake amends, and whether victims will be inclined to consider forgiveness or even wary reconnection.[66]

There is an old saying that "Time heals all wounds." We know that this is not true: human beings tortured and terrorized are not simply healed by time even when they are able to reclaim their lives, and some hearts

---

[66] See Jodi Halperin and Harvey M. Weinstein, "Empathy and Rehumanization After Mass Violence," on the intensity of pressures *not* to reconcile across groups in a study of the Balkans.

broken by betrayal or cruelty never mend. There is truth, however, in the power of time to soften and distance harms and losses of many kinds for many people, and to allow them to rebuild lives, trusting relationships, and hopeful expectations. The possible healing powers of time do not excuse us from individual and communal responsibilities for repair. They offer us the hope that our always limited powers of setting things right may be strengthened by the remarkable ability of human beings to go on. Yet the experience of bitter abandonment in misery is something that can last a lifetime too, and time can cause wounds to fester. What must always be done is to acknowledge wrong and to make clear efforts at repair. All too often, this is all that can be done. If this is all that can be done, it is better than the insult of doing nothing. When there is more to do, acknowledgment and willingness to seek repair opens the way.

2

Hope's Value

Marion Halligan tells a story of Wendy, a pretty young woman, who works, saves, marries, honeymoons on a package trip to Fiji, has three children, is abandoned by her husband who drinks and runs up gambling debts, and continues to work raising her children alone, buying the occasional lottery ticket. In other words, it's a story of a life that is pretty common-place in a certain kind of society at a particular time. It takes seven pages to tell. Halligan then asks the reader to count the hopes in the story, as one would count the animals hidden in the puzzle picture in the news-paper. The author has planted fifty-five hopes in this brief and realistic tale, and reckons that some readers may spy more. "It's a story full of hopes. Some easy to see, some hidden. Hopes for a good skin by using certain cosmetics, for the good life in a planned city, for a bridal bou-quet bringing a husband, modest hopes many of them, and domestic, but none the less hopeful for their simplicity."[1] Halligan says of Samuel Johnson's quip that remarriage is a triumph of hope over experience: "That's a description of life."[2]

Hope appears as the warp in the everyday weave of the imagined Wendy's life; it defines the shape of the garment over varying lengths – planning a beauty treatment for a summer, saving for a vacation holi-day, anticipating the adult life of a tiny child. Specific hopes come to an end when what they yearn toward is either realized or no longer seen as possible. Yet overlapping lines of hope at most points form a sturdy enough bridge to the future in this life. Not all lives are so thickly or

[1] Marion Halligan, "Hope," 221.
[2] Halligan, "Hope," 231.

uniformly threaded with hopes. In some lives at some times the threads fray to breaking, are cut by violence, or are snapped by deprivation.

War correspondent Chris Hedges tells the story of a Bosnian Serb couple, Rosa and Drago Sorak, who fled the Muslim enclave of Goražde after a siege and heavy bombing by Serbs. While still in Goražde, increasingly isolated from their Muslim neighbors, they lost both their sons. One son, Zoran, disappeared after being taken for interrogation by Muslim police. When Zoran's wife gave birth to a baby girl months after her husband's arrest, food shortages were severe and the mother was unable to nurse the child. On the fifth day, as the child languished, Fadil Fejzić, a Muslim neighbor, arrived at the door with half a liter of milk from his cow. He came each day for over a year, refusing money and facing the taunts of other Muslim neighbors, until mother and baby were able to leave for Serbia. Despite grief and hard feelings over their sufferings, Hedges says, the Soraks could not talk about Muslims without remembering what Fadil Fejzić did for the baby: "What this illiterate farmer did would color the life of another human being, who might never meet him, long after he was gone. In his act lay an ocean of hope."[3] Fejzić did not fare well under the siege, losing the cow and much else besides. Yet, when told of the Soraks, he asked "And the baby? . . . How is she?" Hope can aim for a future good even amid dim and dwindling possibilities. Hopeful acts on one person's part can be gifts of hope to others, who may find it possible because of them to continue living, to trust, and to believe something of value can yet be attained.[4]

As hope can be given and created, so can it be willfully destroyed. Lawrence Weschler quotes a Uruguayan therapist describing the torture routinely practiced on political prisoners in Uruguay under the military government from 1973 to 1985: "The original point of the torture was to take various individuals who had been politically or socially active, on behalf of their various causes, in a particular location at a particular moment and to gouge out their capacity for such activism: to leave them as if dead, unable any longer to aspire, let alone to act."[5] Weschler adds that "torture itself, during repressive regimes, has a dual role: the expunging of the capacity for subjective aspiration in specific individuals, and through their example (the whiff of terror their fate spreads), the

---

3 Chris Hedges, *War Is a Force That Gives Us Meaning*, 50–53.
4 A rich description of the ways we all, from infancy, require the "scaffolding" of others to learn and continue to hope is given by Victoria McGeer, "The Art of Good Hope."
5 Lawrence Weschler, quoting an unnamed Uruguayan therapist, in *A Miracle, A Universe: Settling Accounts with Torturers*, 240–41.

expunging of that capacity in the wider society."[6] Much violence, political and otherwise, aims at the extinction of hopes of certain kinds, or of every kind. A documentary account of perpetrators and victims of the 1994 Rwandan genocide attempting to come to terms with each other includes this report from a survivor, Annonciata Mukanyonga, whose children were murdered: "'Leave her,' she heard the killers say, 'she is sadness incarnate, she will die of sorrow.'"[7] Hope is both an individual and a social good; more than that, it is an individual and a social necessity. If you want to destroy people or a people, you can take away those things on which hope most depends, especially those things that show there is a future that they can value.

The destruction of hope, however, need not be dramatic or the product of specific intentional actions. Hope can leak away in lives of relentless hardship, loss, or injustice. Residents of desolate, dangerous, and impoverished American urban areas, disproportionately African-Americans or Latino/as, can feel like Juanita Moody, quoted in a *New York Times* interview: "it was stressful just to walk out of that place. You were always scared for the kids. . . . You wake up stressed, go to sleep stressed, you see all the garbage and the dealers. That is depressing. In a bad environment like that you say, 'What's the use of doing anything?'"[8] Yet Mrs. Moody, suffering from a serious chronic disease, managed to move with her husband to a middle-class area and to significantly improve her health as well. Fear, stress, sickness, loneliness, unemployment, racism, poverty, prison, violence, and the death of loved ones can kill hope or can drive it into odd corners where there might still be something to do and control. Even so, many people summon strength, make plans, reach out, and fight back, sometimes banking not on the smallest hopes but on the bigger ones that aim to change lives. The human capacity for hope can be astonishing, like weeds that can grow up through the smallest cracks in slabs of concrete. Hope, too, is a kind of growth toward the light.

Is there then hope wherever there is life, wherever a human being struggles simply to survive, however ill, injured, or afraid? Some of the most haunting testimonies in this regard come from the writings of Holocaust survivors, and they do not comfort us with clear answers. In "None of Us Will Return," the first piece in a trilogy now published as

---

[6] Weschler, *A Miracle, A Universe*, 241.
[7] Quoted from Anne Aghion's documentary "Gacaca: Living Together Again in Rwanda?" by Nancy Ramsey, "Filming Rwandans' Efforts to Heal Wounds."
[8] Helen Epstein, "Enough to Make You Sick?" 98.

Auschwitz and After, Charlotte Delbo, a French resistance worker and Auschwitz survivor, depicts the reality of camp survival with terrifying detail. In doing so she invents a suffocating poetics of hopelessness, a spare and repetitive prose of short sentences, many in the present tense, and of concrete imagery with blade-like sharpness framed by an eerie detachment. A dog is set on an inmate, lunging at her throat: "Something snaps. The head in the muddy snow is nothing but a stump. The eyes are dirty wounds."[9] And: "A female skeleton. She is naked. Her ribs and pelvic bones are clearly visible. She pulls a blanket up to her shoulders while continuing to dance. The dance of an automaton. A dancing female skeleton." Delbo evokes for a reader who can never truly grasp it a timeless, endless, and senseless present, a state of numb endurance punctuated by horrors, an existence without a past or a future, without desire or imagination. Suddenly she reintroduces time, imagination, and intention, reminding us with surreal clarity: "Presently I am writing this story in a café – it is turning into a story."[10]

Later in the text she pictures herself thinking of how she will "explain the inexplicable," how she will tell what thoughts kept her alive in that freezing hell with no past or present. She admits that "Actually, I did not say anything to myself. I thought of nothing.... I felt nothing. I was a skeleton of cold, with cold blowing through all the crevices in between a skeleton's ribs."[11] Where there is no future, no desire, no imagination, there is no hope in bare survival. Yet there are shards of hope scattered in Delbo's story, times in which imagination, foresight, and the ability to act toward a chosen end briefly reappear. Inmates chatter about imagined furnishings in an abandoned house, make plans for going home, and, improbably, stage a production of Molière in the women's quarters, where "while the smokestacks never stopped belching their smoke of human flesh, for two whole hours we believed in what we were doing."[12] The most piercing shard of hope is the sight, on a frigid march through stinging hail to a work detail, of a tulip in a window, "Pink beaker between pale leaves." Flowers, a traditional memento mori in European art, appear here as the fragile beauty of life itself. She describes the apparition as "a moment of hope."[13] Delbo exposes how much hope depends on our existence in a time lived backward and forward in memory and imagination, propelled

[9] Charlotte Delbo, *Auschwitz and After*, 29.
[10] Delbo, *Auschwitz and After*, 26.
[11] Delbo, *Auschwitz and After*, 64.
[12] Delbo, *Auschwitz and After*, 171.
[13] Delbo, *Auschwitz and After*, 61.

by abilities to think and plan, energized by purposes and possibilities that move us and give us direction. Delbo's story also gestures to the importance of human connection to hope: "Only surrounded by the others is one able to hold out."[14]

What is this powerful and pervasive emotional attitude we call hope? What aspects of hope most deserve our moral attention? I want to look at the nature, role, and value of hope in its elements of *futurity, desire, belief in possibility,* and, above all, its *efficacy,* hope's dynamic tendencies to move us in feeling, thinking, expression, and action toward what it seeks, sometimes in surprising and improbable ways. There is a view that hoping may not be very good for us or may even be a dangerous tendency. However, while hoping, like any emotional state or attitude, might be misplaced or out of proportion in particular circumstances, it is as basic to us as breathing, and basic in the same way: it is something we must do to live a human life. In particular, it is important to remember the intimate interaction of hope and trust in our moral relations. While our moral understandings are grounded on trust, this trust in turn is dependent on hope. A moral order requires a core of confidence in the shared understandings that make it up and trust in the responsiveness of its members to what the understandings require. If repairing moral relations requires securing or restoring that trust, and that trust needs hope to stabilize or recreate it, then morally reparative measures must often aim at restoring or igniting hope. This might mean giving people something to hope for, or supporting people's inclination or ability to be hopeful, or both. It also suggests that some wrongs are particularly disastrous in their assault on the conditions of hope, and might for that reason be seen as "irreparable" and even "unforgivable." One never can and never should write off the human ability to rekindle hope, but we should view the careless or intentional devastation of hope as one of the most morally abhorrent features of serious wrongdoing and as a grave wrong in and of itself.

What Is Hoping Like?

Hope is a "state of mind." Is it an emotion or feeling, a state of belief, or a combination of belief and desire?[15] Hope certainly involves a belief or perception, for there is always something that hope is "about," a future, or

---

[14] Delbo, *Auschwitz and After,* 104.
[15] J. P. Day, "Hope," frames this question clearly.

at any rate yet unknown, state of things. We hope that . . . , or hope for . . . , or hope to . . . , where these can be filled in with some state of affairs or other, including one in which we ourselves do or achieve something. Must this "object" of hope – the state of affairs hoped for – lie in the future? Perhaps not, since it is common for people to say things like "I hope she made it home safely" well after the fact of whether she made it home safely or not. One might also say of people and events many years, even centuries, past, "I hope they didn't die in vain." Despite these manners of speaking, I think hope is nonetheless oriented toward something future, toward something that is not yet certain from the point of view of one who hopes.

When we speak of hoping with respect to something already over and done, it seems "I hope that . . . " makes sense not because the event hoped about is not past, but because one remains uncertain about how it has come out. These ways of speaking borrow on the *futurity* of hope – hope goes to what hovers before us with a sense that all is not decided *for us*; what is not yet known is "as if" open to chance and action, for all one knows. Saying "I hope that . . . ," where the apparent object of hope is actually a fact already determined might be understood as short for "I hope I will discover that . . . " More than a turn of speech, I think this use of 'hope' reveals something important about hope: its nature is to engage our desire and agency, so that in hoping, the world is, in some respect that one cares about, construed as *open* to the outcome one favors. And this is not merely an "estimate of probability," but something else as well: there is a sense, and it can be an actual feeling, of "pulling for" the yet undetermined resolution one desires, as people clutch and pull the railing at the race track as the horses enter the home stretch. Of course, the expression "I hope that . . . ," is sometimes just a polite formula, in the manner of "How kind of you to come."

This much already reveals that hope involves an evaluative stance toward what is hoped for. What is hoped for is welcomed, sought, or desired; and should the object of one's hopes come to be realized and its reality come to be known, one will be pleased by that fact. So one does desire or want the thing hoped for. While one might be tempted to identify hope, then, with fervent longing, hope does not need to be fervent, and is more than longing or wishing. Some hopes are ardent or intense, but most hopes are slight and ordinary as they thread through the weave of our lives. Their objects are not grand. We hope the dry cleaner is still open, that the train is coming into the station rather than just pulling out as we arrive, that the wind outdoors is not lashing, that our supper will taste good, and that we can get to bed early. There need be nothing grand about hope's objects or strenuous in its expression or our experience of it. It is important to remember this in order to appreciate the degree of violence inflicted by situations that destroy many small and unassuming hopes, shredding the very fabric of what we sometimes, from a fortunate position, call "ordinary" or "everyday" life.

Nonetheless, ardent and arduous hopes are revealing. It is in these cases of ardent hopes, or hopes for improbable outcomes or for outcomes of very great importance, that the *efficacy* of hope is apt to be most clearly displayed. Where someone hopes for remission of a fatal disease or for recovery from a dangerous one, or where I hope to escape from a prison camp or a burning building, or hope to see the end of a savage war in my lifetime, there hope is likely to show its dynamic tendencies strikingly. It will steer thoughts and talk, and will stir other feelings; it will press us to actions that further the likelihood of our attainment of what we hope for and will strengthen those attitudes and patterns of attention that fortify our sense that the object of hope is attainable. These *dynamic tendencies* in hoping, as well as the belief in or perception of possibility underlying it, separate hoping from merely wishing, longing, or daydreaming that something desirable is so.

When we wish or long or fantasize, we can do so without any appraisal of the realism of what we would see happen. In wishing, the state of affairs we would like need only be logically possible, something we can conceive of or imagine. I can wish I could fly or that I was thirty-five again or that I might be in two places at once. When I hope, I must believe (or "half-believe," in the peculiar but apt expression of one philosopher) that what I hope for might be or come true.[16] Hoping requires some presumption of probability, however slight, and it may be vanishingly small. As important, when we wish or long or fantasize, it can be entirely a spectator sport, while hope somehow engages, encourages, or propels agency; it bends us toward "making it so." I've already mentioned hope's dynamic tendencies; and I'll say more about this dynamism of hope, for it is one of its most important as well as distinctive features and is crucial to understanding hope's value.

These, then, are some aspects of hoping: the *futurity* of what is hoped for in the agent's perspective; the *desirability* of what is hoped for; the real *possibility* (non-zero probability but less than certainty) of what is hoped for, at least in the estimate of the one who hopes; and the *efficacy* of hope

---

[16] See J. M. O. Wheatley, "Wishing and Hoping."

itself, its dynamic tendencies to attend to or be attuned to what is hoped for in a way that tilts or propels us toward making it so.

Is hope, then, an emotion? In a number of classical texts, it is assumed to be a "passion," "appetite," or "emotion." Contemporary philosopher J. P. Day argues that it is not, though he concedes that his view is at odds with "virtually all philosophers."[17] In Day's analysis, hoping entails wishing for or desiring that P, and thinking that P is to some degree probable. That is, hoping requires a desire and an estimate of probability, which estimate can range from very slight, on the one hand, to more probable than not, on the other, without taking it for certain. "I hope the weather is fair tomorrow" is true if and only if I want the weather to be so and believe that there is at least some slight possibility that it might be so. Further, in desiring P one is disposed to try to bring it about that P in those cases where the subject's own action is relevant to bringing it about that P, for that is generally true of desires; and in taking P as at least to some degree probable, however slight that degree, one who hopes must believe that he or she possesses some evidence relevant to P.

Something is missing in Day's desire plus possibility account. What's missing is precisely the commonplace but protean and often powerful *efficacy* of hope. This is captured, although not explained, in Aquinas's nice statements: "Hope adds to desire a certain drive, a buoyancy of spirit about winning the arduous good"[18]; and "Hope causes, or increases, love; sometimes by virtue of the emotion of pleasure, which it arouses; and sometimes by virtue of the emotion of desire, which it intensifies; for without some hope there is no strong desire."[19]

Merely to desire that something be the case, and to think it just barely possible that it could be, or even to think it very likely that it could be, can very well leave one pretty much where one was: unmoved to further attention, thought, or effort toward the wished-for situation. And then it seems pointless to say that one "hopes." Suppose I rise on a cloudy day, would like a cheering bit of sunshine, think that there's a tiny possibility it could break through, although the forecasts are against it. It could be true

---

[17] Day, "Hope," 89.

[18] Thomas Aquinas, *Summa Theologiae*, I–I, 25, 1.

[19] Aquinas, *Summa Theologiae*, I–I, 27, 4. In a striking parallel, contemporary psychologist Richard Davidson says hope involves "the comforting, energizing, elevating *feeling* that you experience when you project in your mind a positive future." Quoted in Jerome Groopman, *The Anatomy of Hope: How People Prevail in the Face of Illness*, 93 (emphasis in original). Groopman's own investigations of the role of hope and the absence of hope in healing, and of the biology of hope, appear largely consistent with the view I argue for here.

that I hope for sun, on this scenario, but if I do, there must be something more, for the desire and probability estimate are compatible with my just accepting the gloom and going about my day without hoping or even feeling dejected at the unlikelihood of some warming rays. Or, suppose I rise on a cloudy day, would like some sunshine, check the forecasts which predict the fog will burn off quickly, and now fully expect to see sunshine before the day is out. Now the space for hope might be closed in the opposite direction: despite the fact that my probability estimate of sunshine is less than a certainty, if I fully *assume* a sunny day ahead I might or might not find it natural to describe myself as "hoping" the sun will shine. I might simply expect it to. There is, I suppose, a use of "I hope so" that is a kind of energetic or affirmative way of underscoring what one fully expects; people do say things like "I certainly hope I can carry this job out to your satisfaction, and I know that I will!" The reverse point is that people get nervous if we say "I hope I'll be able to attend" instead of "I will attend"; "hoping" does, pragmatically if not logically, imply something less than certainty, and can even suggest some degree of doubt.

So, what is "added" to the necessary desire and the perception or belief in possibility that seems characteristic of hope? What reveals that the sun fancier is hopeful rather than diffident or resigned? What shows that the fully confident sun fancier is hopeful, rather than simply assured? I don't suggest that we try to detect a peculiar mental ingredient, but rather that we look at our concept of "hoping" as ascribing an emotional stance or "affective attitude," a recognizable syndrome that is characterized by certain desires and perceptions, but also by certain forms of attention, expression, feeling, and activity.[20] As Wittgenstein put it, there are "phenomena" of hope – what we go by in ascribing hoping to ourselves and to others; hope, like grief, "describes a pattern which recurs, with different variations in the weave of our life."[21] And: ". . . the characteristic mark of all 'feelings' is that there is expression of them, i.e. facial expression, gestures, of feeling."[22] On this view there is not a single "recipe" of specific ingredients in precise proportions that constitute hope, but there are patterns of ingredient perceptions, expressions, feelings, and dispositions to think, feel, and act that are part of the repertory of hopefulness.

If we look for features of the patterned syndrome that we characterize as hoping, we will see what is missing from an account like Day's, which

---

[20] I borrow on Karen Jones's way of characterizing trust as "a distinctive and affectively loaded way of seeing" in Karen Jones, "Trust as an Affective Attitude."
[21] Ludwig Wittgenstein, *Philosophical Investigations*, Part 2, Section I, 174e.
[22] Ludwig Wittgenstein, *Zettel*, paragraph 513, 90e.

describes hope as only a desire and a belief in probability. Two things are missing in capturing the character of hope. First, there are the forms of attention, expression, feeling, and activity that manifest hope. And, second, there is what these forms of attention, expression, feeling, and activity in turn reveal: that people have varied and characteristic ways they try to invite, affect, or produce an outcome for which they hope, *even when the outcome is not open directly, or at all, to their own effort.*

Peter Goldie's useful study of emotion sees emotional experiences as narratively structured episodes of thought, feelings, bodily changes, and expressive activity that embody an emotion.[23] The emotion itself is a complex and relatively enduring state weaving together emotional episodes and dispositions to the kinds of thoughts, feelings, bodily changes, and expressive behavior that contribute to these episodes. So one cannot have an emotion – say, jealousy – without having episodes of jealous thoughts or feelings, but one need not experience specific episodes of jealous feeling at all times to be jealous. Nor does one have to have reflectively available beliefs of a particular kind in order to have an emotion. As Goldie says, often "we first have an emotional response towards an object, a feeling which is often quite primitive," and then, in reflecting on the feeling, we seek to "make it intelligible" by looking for the beliefs that identify and explain the feelings. He suggests there is "too much talk of belief, and not enough talk of feeling, perception, and imagination" in some accounts of emotion.[24]

The account of hoping that fixes only on certain beliefs about probability and some desire that things be one way rather than another over-intellectualizes hope while failing to take a larger view of the complex repertory of thought, feeling, and expression in which hope reveals itself and exhibits its peculiar efficacy. To understand hoping, then, we need to consider feeling, perception, and imagination as well.

What Good Is Hoping?

Psychologists tell us that hope is "a vital coping resource."[25] While we need prudent and realistic assessments of situations in order to respond fruitfully but self-protectively to them, our need for measured and safe responses can be in tension with the need to sustain a sense of positive

[23] Peter Goldie, *The Emotions: A Philosophical Exploration.*
[24] Goldie, *The Emotions*, 45.
[25] Richard S. Lazarus, "Hope: An Emotion and a Vital Coping Resource Against Despair," 674.

possibility. We need to be realistic, but not so "realistic" that we fail to see the future as open, to experience desired changes or outcomes as possible, and to feel our own attitudes and actions as somehow relevant to making a difference. Too much prudent realism in the face of hard knocks can shrivel expectations and harden into cynicism. We need hope to mobilize those perceptions, feelings, and desires that prompt us to feel we might have an impact on getting the outcomes we desire. What happens in the mobilization of hope? Is it always beneficial?

Hoping goes beyond mere wishing – hope involves perceptions, feelings, and dispositions to feel, think, and act in some ways that move the one who hopes in the direction of having what is hoped for come about. What are some of the dynamic tendencies that are characteristic of hoping for something? When we are hoping for a certain state of affairs, our thoughts, imaginings, and feelings about the desired situation are stirred, and these can prompt actions, as well as spur further thoughts, imaginings, and feelings. In hoping, we become alert to the ways and means by which the hoped for circumstance could come about. We imagine scenarios in which what is hoped for comes to pass and plays out before us. We create ideas and plans and awaken anticipation, excitement, or pleasure about what its realization and consequences will be like. The most obvious effect of doing any of this is to create motivation and energy that drive us to contribute to the desired outcome: to move us to look for openings, imagine alternative routes, consider useful resources, preview motivating rewards, and thus to make what might be barely possible or simply uncertain appear somewhat more likely, and perhaps even within reach. Where our own actions form some part of the conditions for our hopes being realized – where we hope, for example, to graduate with honors, persuade someone to give us a job, or escape from prison – hope clearly can dispose us in a variety of ways to seek out, plan for, strive for, take heart about, concentrate on, put renewed energy into getting the outcome we want. Certainly this argues strongly for hope's value at least in those cases where our own endeavors might affect the outcomes for which we hope.

Luc Bovens points out that hope can also be a fruitful counterbalance to local risk aversion when it allows us to take the longer view that "averages over" short-term particular losses in favor of a larger share of good outcomes overall. I might fear failure on a particular project that I need to initiate in order to succeed in attaining my larger aims, but if I prepare for these particular opportunities, I'm likely over the longer haul, other things being vaguely equal, to get more by trying than I lose in any given round.[26] If I want to get a chance to win a tournament, I'll have to accept the disappointment of losing some games along the way. Bovens also identifies hope as a dynamic force in recharging or rearranging our larger picture of what we desire, including the nested goals and goods that make it up. Hope's impact on this larger picture can even reorganize our desires and expectations themselves. It can shift our beliefs about what is possible, our perceptions about what is important or desirable, and our levels of motivation to pursue particular situations. I can hope to get a better job so that I can afford a better car, but as I focus on developing my skills I might start to want to be good at what I do more than I want the car. Bovens says: "Through hoping we spend a certain amount of mental energy on the projected states of the world and we may come to realize that what we were originally hoping for is not worth hoping for after all."[27] Or we might come to see that what we hope for is more worth aiming at than we originally thought, as we pursue and enjoy the different phases of our achievement of the goal. At any rate, in hoping we are more inclined to exercise imagination that provokes feelings that shift interest and energy, so that we may not remain with the outlook from which we began. Our hopes may well expand, contract, or change target or focus. Hope's dynamic tendencies are not limited to what it might get us to do, but are just as powerful in the domain of thought, imagination, and feeling, and these in turn have consequences.

Finally, Bovens captures the contribution of hoping to refreshment, relief, fortitude, and resiliency that causes psychologists to see hope as a coping resource; hope can provide pleasure and solace that are a lifeline in hardship, and can draw us into more reflective understanding and imaginative testing of what we want and what that shows about who we are. Hoping holds open spaces in our awareness of ourselves and our worlds, spaces we can fill, experimentally but not idly, with possibilities that we value. Our inhabiting these spaces of positive possibility is both valuable instrumentally and valuable in itself. It is good to hope, and our hoping is good for our remaining open-minded, energetic, and even optimistic about the realization of goals and the satisfaction of needs. It is easy to see why despair, one contrary of hope, is often imaged as surrounding blackness or blank walls, and why desperation, another kind of contrary, invokes the images of something "closing in" or "running out." In feeling and attitude, hope spreads light and space

---

[26] Luc Bovens, "The Value of Hope," 671–72.
[27] Bovens, "The Value of Hope," 673.

around the hoped for objective; it expands the energy and tries to expand the space of possibility in which the situation that is hoped for comes true.

It is the lure of tapping into these pleasing, energizing, and motivating spaces of possibility, however, that might be the negative side of hoping. After persuasively arguing its considerable instrumental and intrinsic values, Bovens concedes that "hoping is an open invitation for wishful thinking and can interfere with my epistemic rationality." This danger threatens when hope's active "mental imaging" gives way to wishful thinking unconstrained by evidence. The space of possibility then becomes an imprisoning and opaque bubble that cuts one off from reality and from efficacy in dealing with it. Bovens faults an "illusion of agency" that he claims adheres to hope. This illusion is the product of mistakenly "generalizing" the effect of hope in situations dependent on our own performance to those that do not depend on us.[28] In effect Bovens is claiming that hope tempts us toward merely wishful or outright magical thinking.

I want to show that neither of these supposed dangers is actually a problem with hope. First, consider the view of one psychologist: "I have never quite understood what false hope is. All hope is 'false' in the sense that what is hoped for may not materialize.... If the hope serves to improve one's quality of life and does not cause one to avoid taking adaptive action when it is possible, nor be resentful when the hoped-for outcome does not materialize, then it is obviously desirable."[29] One can continue the argument in this vein: *any* emotion has dynamic properties that can charge or steer further perceptions, imaginings, and feelings in directions that are more or less realistic and useful. Any emotion can be more or less proportionate and apt to the circumstances to which it is a response. If this is so, then it is not obvious that hope is especially dangerous; like other emotions, but not necessarily more so than other emotions, hope may lack a reasonable basis or may be out of proportion (either too little or to much) to the basis it has. Emotions can get out of line. Bovens's point, however, seems to be one about a dangerous tendency inherent in hoping. It might be that the potential for emotions to get out of line takes different forms with different emotions. If that is true, it might be that

---

[28] Bovens, "The Value of Hope," 680.

[29] Lazarus, "Hope," 655, quoting Seymour Epstein, "Introduction," in A. H. Epstein, *Mind, Fantasy and Healing: One Woman's Journey from Conflict and Illness to Wholeness and Health* (New York: Delacourt Press, 1989), xxv.

Bovens is right to warn us about the special danger of hope becoming merely wishful thinking. That might be hope's particular pitfall.

If we are careful to distinguish hoping from wishful thinking, however, I think we can avoid attributing this inherent danger to hope. Hoping isn't merely wishing something is so and believing it possible; hope isn't merely wishful thinking. What counts as "really hoping" as distinct from "merely wishing"? Without proposing a bright line between these at one particular spot, we should expect characteristic differences between the syndrome of thought, feeling, expression, and behavior that is identifiable as wishing and the one that is identifiable as hoping. Here is where Bovens goes astray. Bovens's picture of hoping as desiring, plus believing possible, plus "mental imaging" identifies hope with too impoverished a repertory of expression and activity; hope is identified by Bovens with making satisfying mental pictures of desired things, obscuring "the line between reality and fancy."[30] This neglects the fuller range of attention, perception, feelings, and behavior that are constitutive of what we call "hope."

Someone who is hopeful of a letter's arrival does not sit in a chair picturing the letter without eagerly checking the mailbox or going out to meet the mail carrier. The candidate who hopes to get the job does not remain in a reverie of successful competition without attempting to prepare for the interview and showing up for it. The patient with a terminal illness who still has hope does not only imagine being well, but tends to question the physicians, to seek news of alternative treatments, or to exercise, take up a nutritional program, or to pray. In part, this is a conceptual point, a point about what we take hoping to be. We mark the difference between wishing and hoping precisely by noting whether individuals work to sustain and augment the feelings that will carry them through to some course of action, whether they look out for circumstances that bear on their hopes being fulfilled, whether they take care to seek and explore routes to achieving the end, whether they express their hopes to others who might provide what is desired or assist them in obtaining it; whether, in other words, they do anything *other* than engage in wishful thinking. These other things are among what Wittgenstein called the "phenomena" of hope – the features by which we have learned to identify someone's state as hope rather than something else, including the something else that we call "wishful thinking." Hope doesn't merely have an "illusion of agency," hope is displayed in a variety of actual exercises, expressions, and activities by hopeful agents.

---

[30] Bovens, "The Value of Hope," 678.

Consider also that while wishful thinking suggests turning inward and soothing oneself with good thoughts as an alternative to reality, hope is a complex affective landscape that often incorporates elements of tension and anxiety, and expressions and symptoms of these states are also indicative, in the presence of certain patterns of attention and effort, of hoping for something, even if we make no overt admissions of hope. Hope stirs and animates, and expresses itself in some tension and striving. At the same time we are able to discriminate hope from desperation, in which the will to get the object takes on a drive approaching panic; perhaps desperation, sometimes considered a "contrary" of hope, is an unstable mixture of hope and fear.[31] The momentum of hope is "buoyant," not rigid or driven, and there are characteristic earmarks of this energetic lightness in thought, feeling, and expression. Bovens seems to think that hope tends toward wishful thinking when the strength of our beliefs that something will come about is pushed beyond available evidence, rather than restrained or determined by evidence.[32] But this seems to confuse hope with *faith*. In having faith one believes beyond and even in defiance of evidence. But hope does not entail belief in the likelihood of the situation one desires; hope entails only that we believe it is actually, however remotely, possible. It doesn't seem integral to hope that one will dangerously inflate subjective probabilities. Instead, what is dangerous *to* hope (but not *in* hope) is the deflation of a sense of *possibility* and *efficacy*.

Maybe Bovens's complaint about hope's "illusions of agency" might be founded in a different way. If hoping isn't just wishing, and we know how to tell the difference (even if we cannot always make the distinction clearly or confidently in every particular case), then perhaps the problem with hoping lies in another, indeed almost the opposite, direction. Perhaps the danger in hope is magical thinking – exerting effort, but doing so vainly or irrationally because one's exertions do not, and in the nature of many cases cannot, be effective because the hoped for situation is not open to one's efforts. Think again here of the bettors who grip the rail at the racetrack as the horses go by, "pulling" for Lucky Lady in the home stretch. Pulling the rail and stretching forward will do nothing whatsoever to influence the outcome of the race. So there seems to be a mistake here, not about the probability of an outcome, but about what can possibly affect those probabilities. And this comes closer to the attitude and feeling at the heart of hope. It involves feelings, behavior, and perceptions

---

[31] See Day, "Hope," 98, on contraries.
[32] Bovens, "The Value of Hope," 678.

that things are still open, even if indeterminately so; and if they are open there is some room for me to make a difference. This is a better way of making Bovens's own point about an "aura of agency" that may spill over from cases where agency can matter to ones where it does not. Hope goes wrong, can waste effort, and could do damage, when the one hoping wrongly imagines that he or she can make the difference in the space of possibility that is believed to remain open, when in fact he or she cannot. Does hoping make us specially prone to this error? Again, I think it does not.

Notice first that there is a distinction here between the hopeful agent's point of view and that of an observer. If I pray for a cure when I am terminally ill, a nonbeliever may see me as engaging in irrational, magical thinking; there exists no being whom my prayers can reach and who might be swayed to assist me. But that is not the agent's perspective; I pray because I believe my prayers might be answered, or perhaps I simply believe that I do not know that they cannot be answered. If the praying agent is out of bounds, it is the agent's *belief* that is so, not the agent's hoping. I see there is time remaining for a cure or remission and I do something I think might help it to happen. The same goes for people who pursue what *others* think of as quack therapies or baseless rituals. I am properly moved by hope, it is efficacious for me in leading me to pursue a possible route to what I desire, but I might be mistaken or even irrational in my beliefs. That is not, so to speak, hope's problem. All complex emotional attitudes involve beliefs, and our beliefs can be wrong.

But now suppose that I am mistaken in believing that I can directly make a difference in the space of possibility I believe remains open. Even then I may not be mistaken that someone else could yet make a difference to the outcome. Since the possibility of a saving intervention by someone else, intended or purely fortuitous, is rarely something that can be *conclusively* ruled out, it seems that this is always fair game for hope, which requires only a bare possibility. The possibility can be vanishingly small. This leads to a curious yet significant result: the bare possibility of a saving intervention by someone, somehow, somewhere creates fresh opportunities for *my own* agency to be effective. For now I may set myself to imagine how an intervention might come about, and to discover any contribution that I can make to its arrival.

In a desperate situation one may set oneself the task of just staying sane or physically surviving in order to allow for the minute possibility of others saving one's life or restoring one's freedom. Luz de las Nieves Ayress, imprisoned, raped, and otherwise tortured like thousands of others in the 1970s in Pinochet's Chile, talked and sang to herself, to the door, to the window, to the dinner plate from which she ate like a dog due to a broken shoulder; she talked and sang loudly so that others could hear her. It was a way of being alive.[33] Trapped in a deserted mine shaft with diminishing air, one might control one's breathing in the hope of buying time. Or one might deliberately shift to hopes for things that someone might bring about even after one's death – for example, that one's children are cared for. This enlivening thought might provide the only solace available, a bulwark against madness or despair, and it might, intentionally or not, fortify one in ways that allow for rescue or survival. Detained and tortured, one might mentally construct in precise detail the house one will build when one is released, or one might recite to oneself every scrap of poetry or literature one can remember. Charlotte Delbo painstakingly remembered fifty-seven poems and recited them to herself during roll call at Auschwitz, and later memorized *Le Misanthrope* from a copy for which she traded her food.[34]

A more common situation is one of less dire straits in which the possibility of the intervention of others is less remote. One can still target and hone one's attention, looking out for opportunities to advertise one's hopes to others, and searching out any opening to badger, cajole, bargain, plead, inspire, or tempt others to do something that might affect the realization of one's desires, or to undertake a search for someone else who will do so. Bernard Dauenhauer makes the surprising claim that hope reveals not only an awareness that the future need not be like the present, but also a "conviction that the character of the future can somehow be influenced by the activity of free agents," even if not by one's own actions, and that "hope implies some expectation concerning the outcome of the agency of others."[35] This is not strictly true. One can very well hope that something one desires will be brought about when this seems possible *only* by grace of luck or impersonal forces. We can hope for rain without imagining that there is any agency – divine or human – that can intercede to produce it.

Yet, it may be true that for the most part our hopes naturally attach to ideas that *someone*, rather than something, could make a difference and might actually do so. Often despair or resignation sets in over the fact that

[33] Joyce Wadler, "Years After Torture, a Cry Against Pinochet."
[34] Delbo, *Auschwitz and After*, 188.
[35] Bernard Dauenhauer, "Hope and Its Ramifications for Politics," 457–58.

"nothing can any longer be *done*" even when there is something that could still *happen*. Some accounts of Holocaust survivors note how devastating for victims was the realization that so many onlookers, whether neighbors or strangers, remained *bystanders*, even if they avoided more active complicity.[36] It should not be surprising that the shock of discovering that no one *will* help is more devastating than the belief that no one *can* help. The former obliterates any sense of "extending" agency through the intentional or chance help of others, who in taking up the stance of bystanders actually intentionally foreclose the possibility of help. In doing so the lack of a basis for hope becomes a *deed*, something else done *to* (or in spite of) those who are in danger or need, rather than a plight that has unluckily befallen them. In such cases, hope is killed; it does not die the natural death of exhaustion in the face of waning possibilities.

Some people think it important, nonetheless, to curb or still hopes in situations where what is hoped for is extremely improbable. Sometimes people advise or insist that others not entertain "false" or "unrealistic" hopes. Hope itself can be false only in the sense that one is *mistaken* that there is *any* possibility, no matter how slight, that the object of one's desire will be attained. That is not so easy to establish, and hope is never "falsified" by the mere improbability of what it seeks. Hope is *misplaced* when one has false beliefs about the efficacy of oneself and other agents, and people do, I have suggested, very commonly "place" their hopes on others, even on unknown others whose interventions they cannot clearly imagine. Yet again, it is hard to be certain that *no intervention whatever is possible*, and this leaves room for hope, including hopes that can do no more than provide solace or stave off terror. Saving oneself from terror and despair is no small thing. So, it is unclear to me why entertaining hopes with little chance of fulfillment is, in and of itself, something to be avoided, although we might well be warned against certain dangerous or very imprudent actions based on such hopes. The fact remains that people not only have hopes for things they want or believe they need, but also have needs for hope itself, where that is all there is against inertness, terror, or despair. It is unclear why these needs should be chastised. Rather than condemning hope, we might do better to encourage imagination

---

[36] On the chosen passivity and elective ignorance widespread in non-Jewish populations during the Holocaust, see Victoria J. Barnett, *Bystanders: Conscience and Complicity During the Holocaust*, especially ch. 7, "The Dynamics of Indifference." See also Jean Améry's excoriating remarks on "laborers, file clerks, technicians, typists" who formed the mass of people who not only refused to help, but refused to know, in *At the Mind's Limits: Contemplations by a Survivor on Auschwitz and Its Realities*, 74.

and flexibility that would allow those who hope on meager grounds to direct their energies toward productive and pleasing, rather than painful and costly, expressions of hope.

Finally, the bettors who stretch forward and pull the rail as their picks approach the finish line are not usually deluded about the efficacy of this behavior in prodding Lucky Lady along. This mistakes an *expressive* behavior for an instrumental one.[37] Expressive gestures are common: people kiss the picture of an absent loved one or tear up the letter of rejection from the journal. For all that, they do not believe that the picture is the person or that the rejecting editor is paid back in kind by the tearing up of the letter. Expressive behavior often involves a symbolic representation, but is for that reason coherently *meaningful*, not magical: I show what I feel for *you* by kissing your image, or I reveal what I feel like doing to *you* by doing it to something you own or something by which you are represented. In Lucky Lady's case my behavior works somewhat differently: it expresses what I hope for *her* to do by a kind of representation – I would have Lucky Lady dig in her hooves and thrust herself forward. It is not, however, that I believe my mimicry will make her do so. It is as if, when I am expecting guests, I not only repeatedly look out for them, but actually go out to stand on the landing, as if I were in the act of greeting them. I need not believe that my standing out there will cause them to arrive.

Expressive gestures in cases of hoping are expressive precisely because they display or even rehearse behavior that instances or mimics what is hoped for. They exert energy in embodying what the hoped for scenario might be like, or how it might take place, thus helping us to prepare in feeling as well as action, causing us to remember or to decide what we wish to do, or enhancing our enjoyment of the awaited event. Hope that causes us to tip our hand or rehearse our moves in these colorful but sometimes useful and often enjoyable ways is hardly a danger. These expressive behaviors are not magical thinking but embodied imagination. This may be one clue to why rituals and ceremonies can be potent, and why ritualized and ceremonial interactions may be significant as reparative gestures aimed at affirming or restoring hope. They can imaginatively embody the dignity, value, membership, or authority of persons or a group who have been denied dignity, value, membership or authority. South Africa's Truth and Reconciliation Commission took the unprecedented step of inviting public testimonies from victims of violence during

---

[37] See Rosalind Hursthouse, "Arational Actions"; see also Goldie, *The Emotions*, ch. 5.

its prior apartheid regime, thus staging the exercise of public voice by many of those who were previously rendered voiceless by politics and law. A public apology, as Patricio Aylwin made when newly President of Chile in 1990, from a stadium that was once an illegal detention and torture center, embodies the public acknowledgment of the violent past and the hope that a decisively different future begins here and now. A ceremonial dedication can redefine the meaning of a physical space, creating or defining a monument that acts as a token of the hope of enduring memory of people lost; its physical reality is imbued with a meaning that aims to make and keep them somehow present even though it can never bring them back.[38] The ability to imagine and to embody imagination seems profoundly intertwined in the human capacity to hope.

It remains true that the beliefs on which some of our hopes rest are faulty, making hopes that rest on them "false" or "misplaced." Yet the mobilization – cognitive, emotional, practical, and expressive – that hope represents is not for that reason itself dangerous, irrational, or something to view with skepticism or condescension. One certainly may hope in vain, and we often do. Many hopes, very small and very great, trivial in importance and of the greatest importance, simply never see the realization of what they seek. But they might have done so, and done so *because* hope made a difference. The ordinariness, persistence, and efficacy of hope are perfectly captured in an image created by Lu Xun, Chinese writer and intellectual of the early twentieth century: "Hope can be neither affirmed nor denied. Hope is like a path in the countryside: originally there was no path – as people are walking all the time in the same spot, a way appears."[39]

Losing Hope, Killing Hope

"In the camp," Delbo insists, "you could never pretend; you could never take refuge in the imaginary." The crushing reality of the place, the pain, the exhaustion, the cold, that would later congeal into the hardened skin of memory,

---

[38] For a number of essays explaining and assessing the South African TRC's nature and purpose, see Robert I. Rotberg and Dennis Thompson, eds., *Truth v. Justice.* The Argentine government may turn the former Navy School of Mechanics, a torture center during military rule from 1976–83, into a museum; see Larry Rohter, "A Struggle With Memories of Torture Down the Street."

[39] Vera Schwarcz, "The Pane of Sorrow: Public Uses of Personal Grief in Modern China," 144. Schwarcz repeats this quote from Simon Leys, *The Burning Forest* (New York: Holt, Rineholdt & Winston, 1984), 223.

prevented her and her companions from fantasizing that they were someone or somewhere else.[40]

The witness who sings this song during his interview tries to explain what a "destiny" like Buchenwald has meant for him: a loss of continuity with the future. Instead of linking episodes, and that part of his nature experiencing them, into a unified continuum, his venture into memory makes him feel like a creature removed from its cocoon too soon. . . . "So there's no tomorrow, really," observes the interviewer to this witness. "No, there isn't any," he replies. "If you think there is, you're mistaken."[41]

Unfortunately the baby cried out, and they seized it. "And this was the last time I had the bundle with me," Bessie K. recalls, in a numb and almost trancelike voice. . . . I wasn't even alive; I wasn't even alive. I don't know if it was by my own doing, or it was done, or how, but I wasn't there. But yet I survived."

. . . "The way I felt," she admits, "I was *born* on that train and I *died* on that train."[42]

Hope serves us well for the most part, and can provide us balm or nourishment even when it can produce little else. There is a special poverty of spirit, sometimes an unendurable emptiness, in the loss of important hopes. There is a sickening cruelty in the actions of some who deliberately, or even knowingly, diminish the ordinary but sustaining hopes of others. The foregoing quotations from Lawrence Langer's study of oral Holocaust testimonies archived at Yale University provide stark instances of what it is like for basic forms of hope to be extinguished. To understand the curbing or extinguishing of hope, it is helpful to recall the aspects of hoping that are also hope's points of vulnerability: the *futurity* of what is hoped for; the *desirability* of what is hoped for; the real *possibility* (non-zero probability, less than certainty) of what is hoped for, in the estimate of the one who hopes; and the *efficacy* of hope itself, its dynamic tendencies to attend to or be attuned to what is hoped for in a way that tilts us toward making it so. Hope fails or dies when there is no longer a living sense of any open future at all; when we have ceased to desire certain things, or anything at all; and when we cannot believe in even the barest possibility of what we desire. In the absence or the waning of any of these three conditions, there is no basis for the fourth, the mobilization of hope in thought, feeling, expression, and activity. But things can also run in the other direction: it seems that a catastrophic loss of a sense of agency or

[40] Lawrence Langer, *Holocaust Testimonies: The Ruins of Memory*, 4.
[41] Langer, *Holocaust Testimonies*, 173.
[42] Langer, *Holocaust Testimonies*, 49.

control can lead to hopelessness, even if there remains some desire and some sense of possibility.

The loss of a future can be literal – as when one faces certain death, and is convinced that nothing lies beyond. Or it can be a sense of bleakness or blankness, which in some cases is a psychopathology but in others is a response to events so overwhelming, harrowing, and malignant that it feels, as it does to the Buchenwald survivor and to Bessie K., that one has died even as one survives. Both the illness of clinical depression and the forms of despair, even if survivable, that are spoken of in the narratives of many survivors of genocide or atrocity have in common not their occasion or significance, but a certain unintelligibility to others who have not shared in the experience. The alienness of being stripped of hope testifies to its foundational role in the human psychic economy.[43] To those "outside" catastrophic losses of hope, it is impossible to grasp how there can seem to be "no future," or how people with much life ahead can feel "it is over," or "I'm already dead."[44]

In the remarkable book *Descartes' Error*, neuropsychologist Antonio Damasio begins his essay on the connection between feeling and practical reason with the cases of Phineas Gage in the mid-nineteenth century and a contemporary man called only "Elliott." These cases illustrate broader findings that areas of the brain that are involved in our experiencing emotion are integrally linked to our abilities to connect reasoning practically to our behavior in situations in real life. Persons with brain injuries that destroy the integrity of certain brain systems linked to emotion also lose the ability to anticipate the future and plan accordingly. At the same time they lose a sense of responsibility toward themselves and others in a social environment, even to the extent of losing the ability to look out for their own survival in a deliberate way.

Gage, who suffered a bizarre accident, and Elliott, who survived surgery for a brain tumor, not only displayed flattened emotion, but became unable to observe social proprieties and moral precepts, which require a sense of future consequences and shared expectations. They could not even organize an effective plan for the day ahead, even though the purely mental operations of inference, planning, choice of means, and anticipation of consequences entirely in the abstract were not diminished.[45]

[43] Johanna Lesch, in "Hope, Agency, and Self: An Understanding of Its Human Position," writes of "foundational hope" as different from and more fundamental to psychic survival than ordinary hope.
[44] See Delbo, *Auschwitz and After*, 257–67, for an unforgettable exploration of this feeling.
[45] Antonion Damasio, *Descartes' Error: Emotion, Reason, and the Human Brain*, chs. 1 and 3.

These men, and others with similar injuries, could still think their way through life seen as an intellectual problem, but could no longer put that thought to work in life. While this research links global emotional deficits with global losses in effective practical reasoning, it strongly links emotion generally to *mobilization toward the future*, something that fits intuitively with a commonsense view that in feeling one is "moved." Hope, in particular, is an emotion that directly takes the possible realization of a future state of affairs as its object, and that naturally expresses itself in displays that either seek that state of affairs or imaginatively represent it as a spur to thoughts, feelings, and actions that might allow for its attainment. Loss of futurity can take the form of a death sentence, the extinction of particular future possibilities, or of experiences that damage or block the feeling of futurity that can carry us forward.

In contrast to global blocking of a sense or feeling of futurity, certain specific futures – certain possibilities – can be rendered conclusively, often painfully, inaccessible. Individuals may be or may become unable to bear children, may lose their eyesight in an accident, or may face a lifetime in prison without the prospect of everyday freedoms they might otherwise have enjoyed. Individuals and whole peoples have faced cultural destruction, the irreversible loss of ancestral lands and languages, and waning possibilities of reconstituting powerful and cherished ritual forms that embody who they are and where they have come from. Every life involves a progressive diminishing of prior possibilities at every point, even when some new ranges of possibility are acquired as others disappear. In this sense there may be different roles for hope and hopefulness developmentally and chronologically in human lives.

But relative to that inevitable, shifting human baseline, always culturally shaped in significant ways, there are circumstances that can close off certain futures for some people prematurely, arbitrarily, and unfairly. Actions and policies can create or allow conditions that destroy some people's futures maliciously, callously, or unjustly. To the extent that processes and circumstances that close up futures are the product of intentional action or negligence, the conditions of hope become one more socially propagated and distributed good of which people can be unjustly deprived. Given the importance of hopes to human beings, losses of hope, where the hopes are not unusual or extravagant, are appropriate matters for compassion. Given that some human beings are sometimes responsible, and even culpable, for unnecessary and unjust losses of hope for others, the destruction of hope is a moral matter. It is as much an occasion for repair, whether by acknowledgment, restitution, compensation, or other measures, as is causing the loss of wages or an arm.

Hope also requires desire. Human beings can lose particular kinds of desires for many reasons, and lose therewith whatever hopes might have been propelled by those desires. This is often a natural, and not intrinsically a bad, thing, as when people no longer hope for some of the stuff of their juvenile dreams. But some people's lives are shaped by impediments that render pointless or forbidden desires that are taken as normal for others. Slaves in the antebellum American South could not marry, or could not marry with legal effect and entitlements. Gay and lesbian citizens cannot in most places marry or found families today. People with certain disabilities used to be excluded from regular access to many facilities and spaces, and from consideration for forms of education and employment, that were, for no essential reason, structured – physically and otherwise – in ways that impeded their participation. Where desires are rendered pointless, and where this does not produce resistance and struggle, as it often does, certain hopes are put out of reach. And some lives are not furnished with access to ideas, representations, experiences, and information that would allow one to form certain desires at all. Again, this is true of all of us in some ways, but is unfortunately true for some of us in ways that others of us would find, correctly, intolerable. Some children live in neighborhoods where they do not see people in their own society who suffer from hunger and have no place to live; they cannot want their society to do something to change that, or hope that they can make a difference to such people when they grow up. They are morally limited in that way. Some parents do not know that their children need not die of diseases curable for pennies a day; they can hope their children do not die, but not desire, and thus hope and perhaps act, to get access to medical care for them.

Finally, a complete sense of helplessness, not just a feeling that there is nothing one can do, but the overwhelming feeling that one is incapable of whatever someone in such a situation might do, seems to render idle the openness of the future, the desirability of an object, and the possibility of its coming to be. A conviction of agency or of competence in a certain respect can be diminished in any number of ways. Sometimes it is better that it wanes, and along with it the hopes that it supports. It is not good to hope to be a sports star or an engineer if certain capacities or the ability to acquire them are simply lacking. Here the distinction between hope and mere wishful thinking has an important corollary: since hope tends to move us in some way toward the state of affairs hoped for, it can be self-correcting, other things being equal. The most effective way to discover that I won't make of myself a ballet dancer or a mathematician is to make the effort to acquire the skills or produce the performances that would qualify me as a ballet dancer or a mathematician, and to find that I haven't what it takes to go there. Wishful thinking, on the other hand, does not put itself to the test and has no inherent tendency to extinguish itself when it is mismatched with reality.

But again, there are the cases of those whose agency or competence is derided, destroyed, or prevented from developing: girls who are not allowed to be educated; boys who are not allowed to dance ballet; people with mental disabilities who are not allowed to do work and enjoy social lives of which they are capable. Lu Xun pictured hope as cutting a path where there had been none. But there can be a wall or a barbed wire where someone might have walked if the way had not been barred. The exclusion of people or whole groups from exercising forms of competence, and the denial and stereotyping that teach that some kinds of people cannot be competent in certain ways, can damage or pre-empt hopes if people themselves can be made to accept that verdict. It can even have a negative impact on hopes and efforts if people can be intimidated by the fear that it is true. It is fortunate that human beings often do not accept these judgments even when they are consistently or ruthlessly socially enforced. Often people's hope, based on a belief in their own agency, enables them to break or evade barriers. But we should always object to socially created barriers that are arbitrary, even if some individuals can surpass them.

Often people can be successfully discouraged, threatened, punished, and humiliated out of their hopes by persistently belittling their competence or thwarting their agency. At the extreme, agency can be summarily extinguished by death or truncated by mutilation, imprisonment, and terror, as by enforced ignorance and deliberately induced fear. Most of us have heard about the state of "learned helplessness," in which animals become disorganized and passive, and can eventually die from relentless, uncontrollable, and arbitrary electric shocks imposed in experiments.[46] It is enormously important that human beings have prodigious resources of imagination, invention, insight, and resistance that can open spaces of possibility and images of agency even under desperate conditions. But, as Charlotte Delbo's searing meditations on hunger and thirst in Auschwitz

---

[46] See Martin E. P. Seligman, *Learned Helplessness: A Theory for the Age of Personal Control*, for the later developments of this concept in application to human beings.

remind us, there are limits to the exercise of imagination under conditions of unbearable deprivation and brutality.[47]

Hope can wane and be lost through the curbing or blocking of any one of its constitutive conditions, through the loss or destruction of desire, belief in possibility, a sense of the future, or a conviction of efficacy. So, too, any of these conditions can be *caused* or *allowed* to wane, and they can be *intentionally*, *knowingly*, or *carelessly* undermined or destroyed. There is nothing insubstantial or metaphorical about the losses suffered when hope is gone. Every human life beyond infancy will necessarily suffer many such losses in its average course. This is no excuse for failing to acknowledge the wrong of destroying reasonable hopes unnecessarily, maliciously, knowingly, or carelessly. Some gross harms are intended precisely to create helplessness and humiliation of types that will destroy important hopes. Saturation bombing of civilian areas, torture, mutilation, massacre, genocidal or mass rape as an instrument of war terror – these are long-standing examples of strategies that serve to demoralize the enemy in war. As important, though less dramatic, are the grinding and cumulative effects of the everyday institutions and practices that discriminate against people or exclude them because they belong to groups that are "second-class" or despised. The costs of lost hope in a lifetime of frustration, slight, insult, humiliation, and exhaustion may be crushing in effect.

Hope, Trust, and Our Moral Understandings

The destruction of hope may be an intentional objective or may simply be welcomed as a predictable side effect of hostile or cruel actions. Yet, being wrongfully harmed in *any* significant way can threaten or damage hope. Any wrong, especially if it is a harm, and more so if the harm is serious, has collateral costs of a distinctively moral kind. Serious wrongful harm threatens literally to demoralize us, undermining the hope that lies at the living center of the sense of responsibility that makes us capable as moral beings. This is why every reparative gesture or practice must assess and acknowledge the human harms and moral costs of lost hope. Every attempt at repair must seek either to restore or replenish hopes destroyed or diminished, or to cooperate in the establishment of new hopes and a vision of the future that supports them.

---

[47] See Delbo, *Auschwitz and After*, for example, 70ff., 168, and 264.

Our moral relations are anchored in kinds of trust. We need to trust that the moral understandings we share with others are indeed worthy and credible understandings of how to live. I prefer to call this trust in our understandings "confidence" to distinguish it from the trust we must also have in human beings. We need to trust ourselves and each other to be responsive to moral standards that are presumably shared. It is this trust that grounds our normative expectations of each other, our expectations that we and others will do what we *ought* to do because of our presumed responsiveness to shared and authoritative standards. So to live together in moral relations we need *confidence* to some extent in the authority of our moral understandings, and *trust* in each other and ourselves to honor those understandings (or trust that when we fail, we will accept our accountability for the breach). Where does hope come into this story? Hope is embedded in, is in fact a condition of, both the confidence and the trust that constitute moral relations.

When we repose confidence in our shared understandings, we believe that the values and norms that we in fact live by really do tell us "how to live" in a normative sense. We believe that they tell us what is truly necessary or worthy for human beings in their common life. On a reasonable view of human understanding, though, we cannot escape recognizing the fallibility of our moral vision, and so a margin of uncertainty about our standards or the ways we apply them. Human beings' capabilities for reflection and criticism tend to guarantee that even if there are some individuals who can manage never to question the moral authority of the norms by which they live, there are no societies in which the reflective space is completely absent. This is so because moral authorities within societies are apt to compete with different interpretations of "our way of life"; because complex situations and dilemmas can arise that show that a society's values do not decisively answer all their practical needs; because circumstances of life impose changes on communities that offer them comparison with other ways of living; because there are inevitable inconsistencies between ideals, or between ideals and practices, or between the application of the same ideals in different practices. Our moral commitments are never reasonably seen as beyond question, and they are at times put in question by conflicts, dilemmas, and new challenges. But the stability of our ways of living requires the subscription and participation of most of us a lot of the time. This means that our confidence in the authority of our moral understandings is more or less hopeful. We want to lead worthy lives, and we incline to believe that our moral understandings guide us in doing so: we believe that they have stood up to practical tests and relevant reflection at least comparatively well, and will continue to do so. This conviction moves us: we are inclined to defend our values, to insist on them, and sometimes to sacrifice for them; we are often prepared to rebuke, punish, or even sacrifice others in the name of values we hopefully affirm.

When we trust others, and ourselves, to be morally responsible, we *expect* others and ourselves to comply with moral standards, and to accept burdens of accountability in light of these standards. This means that we trust people to attempt to fulfill what the standards require. As important, we also trust that when any of us fails to live up to standards he or she will acknowledge that they are rightly exposed to criticism, to negative and punitive reactions, to demands for accounting, and where accounting does not fully excuse them, to demands for repair. This trust in morally responsive and responsible conduct varies in its strength across situations and with respect to different persons. A good deal of this trust is nonetheless pretty robust, whether it is the specific and pointed trust we place in a friend to lend a sympathetic ear, or in a surgeon to perform a medical procedure conscientiously, or whether it is the generalized comfort and complacency we show as we drink publicly purified water from a household tap. This morally essential trust is shown in our living and acting upon *normative expectations*, expectations that people will act as they *should.* Our normative expectations often embody a strong anticipation of due care and compliance with standards – in other words, of responsibility – from others and ourselves. This is a significant part of what it means to be in moral relations with others; one moves through a shared world acting to a significant degree on normative expectations. One acts as if others are "good for it."

More significant, though, normative expectations, unlike other ordinary expectations, embody a sense of *entitlement* to what we expect, and not merely an anticipation of it. We show this sense of entitlement in the ways we typically think we have a right to react when people do not act as they should. We think we have a right to feelings such as outrage, indignation, or resentment (just as we think gratitude is due in the case of welcome behavior that exceeds expectations). These emotional reactions are themselves unpleasant, menacing, or punitive, and they dispose us to engage in behavior that is rebuking, punishing, or demanding of redress, with a sense that wrongdoers have earned such treatment. When we ourselves fail our own normative expectations, to the extent that we have a sense of responsibility we experience self-reproving and chastising feelings, and may be inclined to make ourselves "pay," in the forms of self-criticism, remorse, apology, and attempts to "set things right."

Normative expectations, then, are different from merely predictive expectations that are based on past regularities or general assumptions. When I say that "I expect you at six," I might mean I am *predicting* your appearance, inferring from your habits or from evidence about your behavior, including perhaps intentions you have expressed, what you in fact will do. There need be no assumption that you should do what I expect that you will. But when I say "I expect you at six," and my expectation is a *normative* expectation, then what I mean is that I am *holding* you to appear at six, that is, *holding you responsible* for arriving at six. The latter is the kind of expectation I have if I believe that your arriving at six is something you are *supposed* to do, because you have promised, for example, or because you know other people are counting on you to appear then. If you don't arrive by six and I blame, resent, or rebuke you, my expectation was a normative one: I thought you were supposed to be there and I assumed you knew that too and would be moved by a sense of responsibility to comply. In the grip of normative expectations we are not only set to look for behavior of a certain sort, but we are also set to demand compliance; if we don't get compliance we are inclined, other things being equal, to inflict a price or to demand redress for failure if the situation permits (which for the powerless it may not). With normative expectations we are set to make these demands even when we do not have a reason to be optimistic about compliance. In a normative expectation I expect something *from* you, and in that sense I'm counting on you for it, even when I lack reasons to think you'll do it, or even when I have reasons to think that you might not do it. These expectations can only be explained as expressing a kind of *presumption that is also an insistence* that people live up to standards.[48]

If normative expectations embody a kind of trust, then, it must be a kind of trust that isn't necessarily predicting that compliance is likely. How is that possible? When I trust someone for something, do I not rely upon that person, fully expecting (in the predictive sense) that he or she will come through? Some views of trust see it this way; they see trust as a kind of *confident* or *optimistic* reliance on another that assumes compliance

---

[48] This distinction is found in Anthony D. Woozley, "Injustice," 40–42. Martin Hollis distinguishes similarly between predictive and normative expectations, and rightly notes that normative expectations "hover uneasily between moral obligations and the local requirements of a particular society," and this "lets us speak of normative expectations under both moral and social headings." In *Trust Within Reason*, 10–14.

is likely.[49] If you trust someone, this view says, you are optimistic or confident in that you believe the behavior or performance you are relying on is very likely to be what you get. Normative expectations, on the other hand, seem only sometimes to embody strong anticipation of fulfillment. At other times, we expect something *of* someone without being certain, or even being doubtful, that we can expect them to do it. I think the best way to explain this is that normative expectations do embody trust, but that trust itself can be either more confident, when one relies on compliance one believes is somewhat or very likely, or more hopeful, when one relies on compliance that is possible but more uncertain. The fact that people *cling* to trust in the face of evident unreliability, for example, suggests that trust is sometimes hopeful, rather than confident.

If trust itself can vary from confident anticipation to uncertain hopefulness, then so too can our normative expectations embody different kinds of trust. Where we believe that people will do what they should because we believe they are indeed responsive to what is right, our normative expectations will be more confident. It is in these cases where violation of expectations is apt to produce not only corrective reactions, such as anger, challenge, or rebuke, but also forms of shock and incomprehension. Yet, there is another kind of case. Normative expectations can be trusting where they embody a *hopeful* attitude, one that includes a belief in the possibility of responsiveness, and a desire for responsiveness, alongside a demand for responsiveness even in the absence of reasons for optimism. In this kind of case, our attitude of normatively expecting something of others (or ourselves) "pulls for" correct behavior in the face of uncertainty, and possibly in the face of evidence to the contrary. When victims of an unjust system nonetheless cry out in indignation against it, they refuse to surrender their normative expectations even knowing that disappointment is predictable; they continue to insist upon what they cannot in the simpler predictive sense expect. But all of us live much of our lives on the basis of normative expectations that are uncertain of fulfillment, and some that are rather likely to be disappointed. That is what it is to be in moral (and for that matter, social) relations with others: we live with them and interact with them in a mode of sometimes confident, but always hopeful, expectation: we hopefully expect that we are responsive to and responsible for what our shared standards demand.

---

[49] See Jones, "Trust as an Affective Attitude," for such a conception.

Hopeful trust permits human beings a degree of buoyancy or resiliency in their moral outlook on others and in the ways they bear their own responsibility. Hopeful trust provides a way to continue to take ourselves and others seriously as moral agents, responsible for what we do, even under uncertainty. It buttresses our sense of our right to engage in corrective responses toward those who are not already predictably compliant. It allows us to reinvest in the force of standards that we believe are worthy when others do not agree or have grown cynical. Hopeful trust may explain how it is that people can cling to trust when there is no cause for optimism about the trustworthiness of those upon whom they rely.[50] In this it can be disastrous, but it is not necessarily so. It may be instead a speculative human investment that is answered in many cases by a saving return. It may sometimes, if Philip Pettit is right, draw out trustworthiness in people where it was not there before; if they are not entirely hardened or malicious, they may be moved to live up to one's trust in the form of acting responsibly.[51] It is a good thing that we are capable of hopeful trust, because in the case of trusting to people's responsibility, and so maintaining moral relations, we are destined to be frequently disappointed.

We can now see that *hopeful trust* is not only possible, but morally essential. To lose the capacity for hopeful trust is to lose one's grip on morality, for then we can only take up the demanding attitude of normative expectation – the attitude of holding others responsible – toward those whose compliance we have reason to confidently expect. The dynamism of hopeful trust is that it can mobilize our resources of thought, feeling, and expression toward the end of holding – and by so doing (hopefully) making – ourselves and others responsive to moral standards and responsible in living up to them. Through hopeful trust we see all those capable of responsiveness as responsible, as subject to morality's demands as we understand them, and as fair game for resentment, rebuke, penalty, and reparative demands. We keep alive our senses of responsibility, and morality as a real personal and social force, in the face of human failure and worse. Perhaps it was something like this that Kant had in mind when he wrote: "It is a vain affair to have good so alternate with evil that the whole traffic of our species with itself on this globe would have to be considered as a mere farcical comedy. . . . " Kant claimed instead that

---

[50] Thanks to Johanna Lesch for pointing this out clearly in "The Necessity of Hope in Human Life."

[51] Philip Pettit, "The Cunning of Trust."

we should believe in the capacity of the human race to be the cause of its own advance toward what is morally better.[52] I cannot say, however, that I believe, as Kant apparently did, in any human capacity with the "inevitable" consequence of moral betterment as a historical destiny.[53] That *would* be an "illusion of agency" too big for hope on a human scale. For moral hopes are contingent and destructible, as are other hopes.

Moral hopes, those hopes that fund our confidence in moral ideals and our trust in each other's responsibility, are not necessarily as grand as the hope that the human race is inevitably progressing. Moral hopes may be as humble as being prepared to give or accept one more promise, or to be entrusted with or to entrust yet one more fragile thing dependent on human care and effort. Human beings in desperate conditions may lose hope, including moral hope. They may lose the ability to believe in any future in which goodness or dignity are available, or may cease to find these ideas credible enough to desire their realization. Or they may be starved, terrorized, and exhausted into a powerlessness profound enough to close the horizon of moral responsibility.[54] Who knows that human beings could not come to forget what "good," "right," or "responsible" mean? Instead of removing the moral importance of hope to a transcendental plane, let us understand and respect the enormous role played by hope in the human lives we lead here and now. Let us accept an obligation to nurture, protect, and restore the hopes on which human beings and moral relations depend.[55]

---

[52] Immanuel Kant, "An Old Question Raised Again: Is the Human Race Constantly Progressing?" 141.

[53] Kant, "An Old Question Raised Again," 143.

[54] Tzvetan Todorov's *Facing the Extreme: Moral Life in the Concentration Camps* is a sustained examination of moral capability under the most extreme conditions; Todorov concludes that moral reactions are "eradicable only with the greatest violence," 39.

[55] I thank the audience at Fordham University for challenging comments on a short version of this chapter, and Victoria McGeer for sharing her work on hope and moral development with me. Brian Davies steered me to relevant portions of Thomas Aquinas.

3

Damages to Trust

In a scene in the David Mamet movie *House of Games* a confidence man, Mike, gives Dr. Margaret Ford, a psychiatrist who specializes in obsessive-compulsive disorders, a lesson in the "short con" at a Western Union office. When another man enters to receive money by wire, Mike strikes up a conversation, claims to be a fellow (former) Marine, and insists that if his money arrives first he will advance the other man the money for which he is waiting in order to return to camp. Before long, the Marine offers Mike the same help in return: he, too, is happy to advance Mike the money if his arrives first. Mike lets his pigeon off at that point, because the con is only a demonstration of a principle he is teaching the doctor. Mike is a "confidence man," he explains to Margaret, not because you – the mark – give him your confidence but because he – the confidence man – gives you *his*. It's the confidence man's simulation of trust in the mark that provokes trust in return. Mike is skilled in triggering trusting responses in people so that they are likely to do what he wants them to do. What he wants them to do, ultimately, is to give him their money. In the end, this short con is embedded in a longer one: Mike is setting up Margaret. He shares "secrets," seduces her, and ropes her into willing complicity, all with the aim of taking her money. He teaches Margaret that the trick to inducing trust is to give the other person "your confidence." This is exactly what he does with her in "revealing" to her the world of confidence games. Is there a difference between what the con man "gives" to the victim and what he gets back? Clearly Margaret, to her detriment, trusts Mike. Does Mike trust Margaret or does he just rely on her to behave in particular ways? What is the difference? The dark fascination of Mamet's movie lies in our anxious uncertainty over when trust is real and when it is a trick, and how anyone knows whether it is safe to trust someone else. For the most part, though, we do trust various people, institutions, and environments. It is difficult to imagine not doing so.

Whom must we trust? There are individuals each of us relies on to come through on agreements, contracts, and promises. There are also particular roles and relationships – sister, doctor, employee, teacher, and many more – that we tend to assume will conform to some general expectations in our society for relationships of that type. At the same time, understandings of some of these relationships and the trust they invite are also tailored to the particular histories between the individuals in them who adjust their expectations in line with their histories. Beyond this, though, in modern societies each of us relies upon a vast web of strangers to whom we might be vulnerable. For the most part, we do not think about any of them as we engage in activities the safety and efficiency of which depend upon their reliability. Yet each might do us harm or disrupt our plans. Martin Hollis says: "Every day is an adventure in trust in thousands of others, seen and unseen, to act reliably."[1]

What happens when our trust is violated? We all know something about personal disappointments, affronts, and betrayals – untrustworthy coworkers, unfaithful spouses, ungrateful children, and fair-weather friends. Someone's late arrival to an appointment might be no more than a passing annoyance. Repeated tardiness of a friend might cause a quarrel and lead to a request for promises of greater courtesy. Here negotiating terms within a relationship presupposes and draws on a reservoir of trust; without it, there is no point to spending time revamping expectations. A missed appointment can cause us to trim our expectations of someone or to decide not to hire him for a job; this doesn't mean we are likely to believe the same person will steal our wallet. These are local and limited interruptions or alterations in expectation. They do not require us to recut dramatically the fabric of trust. When we come to severe disappointments of trust, to betrayals and to cruel, indifferent, or destructive treatment, the stakes are higher and the damage is likely to be profound or lasting. To understand moral repair it is necessary to understand the nature and fundamental roles of trust in anything resembling a normal human life and, more particularly, in moral relations.

When wrong has been done, moral repair may have to deal with blows or damages to trust that result from wrongdoing. Moral repair may also have to deal with deep distortions in people's senses of responsibility that

---

[1] Martin Hollis, *Trust Within Reason*, 10.

lead to wrongdoing and to toleration of wrongdoing, making it painfully clear that some people cannot trust some others. Finally, moral repair has to deal with the profound importance we all place on whether others support us in our judgments of wrong and responsibility, whether others share or accept as fitting the powerful feelings that invariably accompany and express our judgments of responsibility, and whether others are prepared to take action as required to shore up, or to reconstruct our standards, our trust, and our senses of responsibility.

Trust: Motive and Focus

Philosophers like to distinguish trust from "mere reliance," where the latter involves only a prediction that one can count on something's occurring.[2] What one counts on in this predictive way can be, for example, a kind of action by a certain person. Can we not say that I "trust" him for the thing I know he will do, for example fidgeting during a meeting, just because he invariably does it? Of course we can say we trust a person in the predictive sense, just as we can say that we trust a nail in the wall for hanging a picture, the car's brakes for stopping the car, or a rope for climbing. We can say we trust the person, the nail, the brakes, or the rope, meaning that we believe there is a basis for predicting or planning on the outcome to which the performance of the person, nail, brakes, or rope contributes. But this use of "trust" loses an important part of what we mean in saying we trust someone when we think of that as an attitude or relation that can hold *distinctively* among people. The thought in distinguishing trust from mere reliance is that trust among people captures a specially *interpersonal* attitude or relation, a kind of anticipation that is distinctive to how a person looks at, and *can* look at, other people. The idea is that this interpersonal trust must involve expectations of others that attribute some kinds of awareness or motivation to them that a person, but not a thing, can have. Then it's not just a kind of mechanical regularity or impersonally predictable course of events that the person you trust does what you trust that person to do.

Many of us will also say we trust (and mistrust) pets and working animals, and find it natural to say that they trust (or mistrust) us. We don't say

---

[2] A clear summary of this search is provided by Karen Jones, "Trust (Philosophical Aspects)." A wider exploration of recurrent, and unsatisfactory, tendencies in thinking about trust is found in Selma Sevenhuijsen, "Too Good to Be True? Feminist Thoughts About Trust and Social Cohesion."

it, though, of all animals; we say it roughly of the ones with which we live, work, or interact in ways that we think of as recognizing and responding to each other's desires, needs, requests, or commands. Whether or not we are right to see some animals as trustworthy and not merely predictable – to that extent like people rather than like nails or ropes – it is clear that in trusting *people* we anticipate satisfaction of an expectation not just as a matter of course but as a matter of *response*. To what in our shared situation, and with what motivation, do we expect others to respond when we trust them? Is there a specific kind of awareness or motivation we expect that distinguishes trust among human beings from our merely relying on each other? And can we explain why it seems that Margaret trusts Mike, but he, the con artist, merely relies on her predictability? Here it is tempting to load a great deal into an account of trust, and so to moralize it, personalize it, or narrow it. Doing so can produce rich accounts of particular kinds and circumstances of trust, but will fail to comprehend in a single account all the varieties of trust there are.

Some accounts of trust emphasize that we are relying on another to be moved by good will toward us, and in cases where competence is required to perform as trusted, we are relying on the other's competence to perform. Since only those with a "will" can bear others good or ill will, reliance on good will can be distinctively directed at people rather than things or processes. Karen Jones, for example, has argued that trust is an affective attitude of optimism about the good will and competence of another in the domain of our interaction that creates an expectation that the other will be moved "directly and favorably" by the thought that we are counting on her.[3] Expectations of another person's direct responsiveness to my optimistic expectations of her fits *trusting relationships* among individuals who are directly aware of each other. These are also cases in which trust can be calibrated and customized in a detailed way if a trusting relation exists over time; we can then learn what we should and should not expect from particular others, and they in turn can learn what we do and do not expect of them. Often in trusting relations that extend over time one of the things we trust others to do is just this, to keep track of the particular expectations relevant to that relationship. But the picture of expecting you to be moved "directly and favorably" by the thought that I am counting on you doesn't translate well to our reliance on those countless persons, "seen and unseen," upon whom we

---

[3] This is Karen Jones's view in "Trust as an Affective Attitude." For a later view by Jones that goes beyond "three-place trust" and a basis in good will, see her "Trust and Terror."

indiscriminately and mostly unthinkingly rely to behave acceptably. It also does not necessarily capture the general sense of obligation people have to behave properly in any number of professional or social roles, independently of the specific desires and expectations of others with whom they deal.

Annette Baier's account of trust sees trusting as *entrusting* something to another's care.[4] Trust is accepted vulnerability in relying on the good will and competence of others to "take care" of something the truster cares about. Again, the account fits certain kinds of cases better than others. Entrustments, in which A trusts B to care for C, are an important kind of trusting relationship, but this structure is misleading as a picture of the scope and focus of much of the trust that constitutes trusting relationships. It fits well my giving over my dog to the kennel for four days care. What, however, do I entrust to my friend when I expect her to be honest with me, or loyal to me? It seems there are too many things to say here, and no list of them will suffice. Baier emphasizes that "care" requires discretion, so that its proper provision cannot be spelled out in advance. The problem here, however, is not only that one cannot lay out in advance all that will be necessary for competent care of what is entrusted; the problem is also that it is not possible to say specifically *what* is entrusted to her care when I trust my friend to be honest or true. The language of entrustment here is a misleading model; it is more accurate to say that I trust her *to be honest* or *to be loyal*, that is, to behave in ways that satisfy a general norm or standard that poses different demands and calls for distinct judgments in different contexts. Or again, what can we say we are entrusting to all others when any of us walks down the street without concern? Here there is not one norm presupposed but indefinitely many, any of which might be identified only in the breach or under threat, and each of these norms requires many things we cannot enumerate in advance.

In addition, the idea that trust requires you to respond to my reliance on you out of good will towards you, rather than for other reasons that are reliably motivating, asks too much. For example, Philip Pettit argues that part of the "creativity of trust" consists in the important dynamic whereby my reliance on a person prompts him to be reliable out of his desire to

---

4 Annette Baier, "Trust and Anti-trust" and other essays in her *Moral Prejudices: Essays on Ethics*. The "three-place" formulation helps Baier to bring out issues of competence alongside good will. Baier claims that trust may vary in its explicitness and that what is entrusted may be rather indefinite or abstract. I will suggest a different way of handling these "indefinite" cases.

keep the good opinion that my trust already displays.[5] One may also be responsive to trust out of concern for reputation, in pursuit of reciprocity, out of pride in one's role, out of fear of penalties for poor performance, or out of an impersonal sense of obligation, among other things. In cases of entrustment, the trusted person may act reliably out of any of these and other motives, or may act reliably out of regard for what is entrusted (a child, a pet, a painting), or out of prudence or independent moral concern (being trusted with a piece of information that can cause pain or harm). Other motives to care well for what is entrusted may weigh more decisively than, or in the absence of, good will toward the person who entrusts it. So the kind of motivation that might be of paramount importance in cases of intimacy and extended relationship – good will or regard for the feelings of the particular persons who are trusting in each other – may have no role to play in other relationships, or may not play the primary or the decisive role.

Trudy Govier offers another rich account of trusting that does not require relying specifically on the good will of the one trusted toward the person trusting. She sees trust as a complex attitude involving four features: expectations of benign behavior based on beliefs about a person's motivation and competence; an attribution of general integrity; an acceptance of risk and vulnerability; and a disposition to interpret the trusted person's actions favorably.[6] This characterization of trust captures well many situations of deciding to place trust in someone to perform a task or role under conditions of evident risk where one appraises another for that role. Choosing a personal assistant or a surgeon, accepting the authority of a teacher to evaluate work, relying on professional advice of a tax or investment counselor, or trusting elected officials or representatives, for those who do, might fit Govier's picture of trust. As an all-purpose characterization of trust, however, this picture requires too much of trust or some things of the wrong kind for many instances of trusting.

The behavior one expects in trusting need not be "benign," generally speaking, although it must be of the sort relied upon, and so desired, by the one trusting. If I contract with a hired killer, I trust him to kill the person whose death I have paid for; if I trust you to beat your wife when she challenges your (and therefore male) authority, I rely upon you to engage in violent behavior that deliberately inflicts pain. The expectation of benign behavior fits instead those cases where I trust people to do

---

[5] Philip Pettit, "The Cunning of Trust."
[6] Trudy Govier, *Social Trust and Human Communities,* 6.

things at discretion that could harm my own interests, or to behave quite generally in ways that do not harm or threaten anyone. Nor are assumptions of general integrity always necessary for trust in cases where we can rely on someone's being moved to respond, for example, by awareness of someone else's expectations in a particular scenario, like the generally unreliable rascal who may yet be trusted always to remember his beloved child's birthday. Responsiveness to the expectations of particular people out of good will toward them is the fact featured by accounts like Jones's or Baier's; where this fact obtains, general or all-purpose reliability is unnecessary. Unsavory characters can be trusted for diverse reasons to do either benign or unsavory things.

Do trusting relations lead to a disposition to interpret the trusted person's actions favorably, at least in the kind of circumstance in which they are trusted? Often, they do. Jones believes that trust, an emotionally weighted attitude, restricts the interpretations we are willing to place on others' actions.[7] This is a feature of certain emotionally invested kinds of trust, for example, that between friends or intimates in many cases. In circumstances of high and salient risk, however, we may and often should be highly sensitive to the slightest evidence of unreliability from credible sources. If someone in a position to know and no reason to lie reports malicious behavior of a well-liked babysitter, or if there are charges of fraudulent representations by an investment broker, trust is apt to decay very rapidly. If in some cases trust attaches us resistantly to saving beliefs, in others trust is rapidly extinguished or suspended even while beliefs about trustworthiness are sorted out. Finally, in trusting we do make ourselves vulnerable to others by basing our actions on their anticipated behavior and so exposing ourselves to upset, disadvantage, or in some cases danger or loss if they do not perform as trusted. But in so relying we do not always *view* ourselves as in a risky situation. In contexts of deep and serene trust, or in circumstances of merely complacent and unreflective trust, one never or at least rarely takes thought of one's vulnerability. This explains why disappointed trust in some contexts of deep or simply unreflective trust can be unnerving or shattering. It would not be so, or would be less so, if it had ever seriously occurred to us that we were at risk, and "accepted" it in the usual sense. Trust always makes us

---

[7] Jones, "Trust as an Affective Attitude," 12. Judith Baker discusses a kind of trust in friendship that requires firm belief in a friend even against available evidence, in "Trust and Rationality."

vulnerable to upset or loss from others we trust, but we may neither feel nor in fact be (on the probabilities) "at risk" from them.[8]

It is useful to have a family of analyses of trust that capture the distinctive features of different cases and contexts of episodes and relations of trust. It is also useful to have a general account that helps to sort and track differences among cases. Is there a genus that comprehends all these species of trust? Can a generic conception of trust embody a significant distinction between the kind of reliance that people place in each other and the kind of confidence we repose in things (and sometimes people) behaving in predictable ways? Richard Holton has suggested this view: trusting someone is relying on him or her to do something, *and* being ready to react to their doing or not doing it with "reactive attitudes," such as resentment and gratitude. In being ready to so react to people, we take up a practical stance toward them that P. F. Strawson called "the participant attitude," the readiness to respond to people, and only to people, with this distinctive range of reactions.[9] As Holton puts it: "when a machine breaks down we might feel angry or annoyed; but not (unless we are inveterately anthropomorphic) resentful."[10] Holton has identified a general condition that distinguishes trust from mere reliance, but it needs to be taken one more step. For Strawson, the "participant attitude" is a stance that we only take toward people in *holding them responsible.*

When I count on the delivery person bringing the morning paper by 6 A.M. because he or she always or usually seems to do so, but when no one has promised or guaranteed it, I am disappointed or frustrated when it does not arrive, but I do not (if I am reasonable) feel resentful or betrayed. I expect the paper delivery person to bring it by 6 A.M., but that is something less than trusting him or her to do so. What is the missing ingredient? I do not hold the delivery person responsible for satisfying my expectation. So my expectation, while based on a reasonable projection of regularities upon which I might well depend, does not dispose me to react reprovingly to its disappointment. I'm only prone to those reactive feelings that blame and punish (or that stroke and praise when expectations are exceeded or are fulfilled against the odds) when I rely on you to do what you *should.* I do not only expect *that* you will do it, I expect it *of* you. My expectation is a *normative expectation.* Normative

---

[8] See Pettit, "The Cunning of Trust," 208.
[9] P. F. Strawson, "Freedom and Resentment."
[10] Richard Holton, "Deciding to Trust, Coming to Believe."

expectations are not simply confident assumptions that people are likely to behave in particular ways; these expectations express instead a stance toward others that demands certain behavior *of* them, because it is what they are *supposed* to do.[11] Normative expectations of people embody a certain attitude toward them that is at once giving and demanding: we treat them as responsible and potentially responsive, and we are prepared to react negatively if they do not do what they should.

This means that *trust links reliance to responsibility.* In trusting one has *normative expectations* of others, expectations of others that they will do what they should and hence that we are entitled to hold them to it, if only in the form of rebuking and demanding feelings. One can have normative expectations of others without relying upon them; we then hold them to account regardless of whether we expect them to do what they should or whether we predicate our actions upon their so doing. And one can rely on others without acting or feeling as if they are responsible for the fulfillment of expectations. But when we rely on people, anticipating that they will fulfill our expectations, and the expectations are normative ones, we will believe we have cause for complaint, rebuke, and even punitive responses when they fail because they have not done what they *should.*

I propose, then, that we think of interpersonal trust generically as a kind of reliance on others whom we expect (perhaps only implicitly or unreflectively) to behave as relied upon (e.g., in specified ways, in ways that fulfill an assumed standard, or in ways so as to achieve relied-upon outcomes) and to behave that way in the awareness (if only implicit or unreflective) that they are liable to be held responsible for failing to do so or to make reasonable efforts to do so. This generic characterization captures two elements shared by a wide variety of cases of trust: expectation of others to perform as relied upon, and the "participant attitude" toward reliance in which I am prepared to hold you responsible for doing what I assume you *should.* Yet it allows the focus of the expectation and the motive for compliance with it to vary. The *focus* of the expectation (what would be relevant to measuring its fulfillment) can be more or less specific, and can be identified in rather different ways. The focus of trust can be identified by a description of distinct actions (to bring a cake to the pot luck, to shut off the air conditioner when you leave); by designating a task (to take care of my dog for three days, to cover my morning class); by stipulating a consistent kind of behavior in context

[11] An early paper that draws this distinction clearly is Anthony Woozley's "Injustice."

(to be nice to Auntie Sally, to invest my money conservatively); by reference to a role for which there are standard assumptions (to behave acceptably as my pilot, therapist, teacher, lawyer) or where there are mutually understood expectations that have developed in the particular relationship (friends, spouses, relatives, co-workers); or through reference to a specific or general norm (to perform conscientiously the duties of the office, to be honest or kind, not to lie or steal, to treat others as ends in themselves or as you would be treated). The focus of trust for a stream of daily encounters with unidentifiable individuals is that people "behave themselves."

This characterization of trust as reliance upon someone and being prepared to hold that person responsible leaves *motivation* open, as we may be moved in many ways to do what we know we are responsible for doing. Normative expectations invoke different kinds of norms. With different kinds of norms or with norms in different contexts, the reasons we suppose that people have to satisfy those norms include good will, reliable good character, conventional probity, pressure of community expectations, aspirations to solidarity, desire to please, desire of good repute, prudence, and fear of opprobrium or sanctions. There can also be sad or perverse reasons that allow us to rely on some others, such as their abject dependency, servility, or needs to preserve self-deceptive pictures of who they are. Our trust in the satisfaction of normative expectations can rest on different understandings of other people's interest in satisfying them, and perhaps do not have to rest on any very well-defined prior understandings. Sometimes people strike us as trustworthy, and we may think we need a reason to suppose they are not; we may simply figure "they're good for it," or "she looks o.k. to me." By keeping motivation open we keep open the space to distinguish more or less reasonable and wholesome forms of trust in specific cases or in particular environments or relationships, without excluding some of the more precarious, twisted, or less wholesome ones at the outset.[12]

This is not to say that motivation doesn't matter in defining what it is to trust in certain cases or kinds of relationship. I believe it is better to make particular kinds of motivation a part of *what* is trusted in, rather than a part of the definition of *trust*. I trust close friends not only to do certain things, but to do them out of concern and regard for me. While I trust my dry cleaner with my clothing, I do not generally expect her to

---

[12] Baier is sensitive to these unsavory reasons for being able to trust; see "Trust and Antitrust," in *Moral Prejudices*, 120–29, on tests for trust.

perform her tasks with particular concern or regard for me, but with the
responsibility to handle the clothing competently because this is reasonably expected by all her customers, of which I am one. Some roles and
professional relationships involve mixed forms of trust that make them
emotionally and morally complex for this reason. We can have mixed
kinds of trust in, for example, our physicians or lawyers (and also our
dry cleaners, shopkeepers, and delivery persons if we have long-standing
relationships with them); we expect them to be competent and to be motivated by recognition and commitment to fulfilling their professional or
occupational responsibilities, but we also often think – or want to think –
that they have personal concern and regard for us, and will be moved by
it. We might say then that in particular cases, trust can be a four-place
notion: A trusts B to do X with motive M. There are kinds of relationships,
especially those of deep feeling and extended commitment, in which we
trust others to have a certain set of motivations in connection with us that
we do not suppose they have toward all or many others.

   Finally, this characterization of trust allows us to see some instances of
trusting as more cognitively dominated by assessments of reliability, and
others as more affectively loaded with optimistic or hopeful attitudes.
Our investments in trust may be more calculative or more emotionally
colored, although these do not exclude each other. It is possible for someone to be emotionally disposed, for example, to see the best in another's
action in part because he has proven himself so flawlessly reliable in the
past. This is the kind of trust we sometimes speak of as "earned," and
it may be no less emotionally colored for that. Whether trust is more
cognitively or affectively based, there is also a gradient of confidence.
One may trust either believing more or believing less in the likelihood of
satisfactory performance, and also feeling more confident or more hopeful about it. Hopeful trust is reliance on someone to behave responsibly
where that outcome is seen as not much more than possible, or at least
very uncertain, but it is still one's reliance on someone else doing what he
or she should. Hopeful trust can be given in the hope that the giving of
it will activate someone's sense of responsibility. Reliance may be placed
in someone with the thought that even an unlikely prospect may yet feel
the pull of acting responsibly, for example, when stakes are high and
another's reliance is salient. Or it may be given because there is nothing
left to do but trust under grave uncertainty. Victoria McGeer argues that
it can be rational to trust hopefully, because "responsiveness to another's
positive view of our competence and potential . . . is a deep and fundamental feature of human psychology" rooted in our own development

of human agency under the hopefully trusting eyes of others.[13] Hopeful trust is not a marginal phenomenon; it is at work in the sense of responsibility of any one who has not been dulled into cynicism or crushed into defeat by others' (or his or her own) gross irresponsibility or evil. This point will be important for understanding the urgency of some moral repair.

The basic shift in conceiving trust as "reliance with responsibility" unburdens the account of requiring specific motivations while providing a unifying factor that distinguishes trust from mere reliance: the truster's expectations are normative expectations.[14] The truster relies upon the one trusted not only as one likely to do something, or as one wanting to do something out of positive regard for another or concern for another's reliance, but also as one responsible for behaving in the way relied upon. We can always tell, and we often need to tell, a richer story about thick mutual understandings, about how particular motivations matter, about specific entrustments and their assumptions of competence, or about how coolly predictive or warmly affective are particular cases of trust. The role of normative expectation in trust is essential to understanding trust violations and tasks of moral repair. Before turning to that, it also helps us to identify yet another kind of trust that is basic, pervasive, and hugely important to the everyday lives of human beings. Violations of this kind of trust are unnerving and, where extreme, can be devastating to a basic sense of safety and stability.

Default Trust

Not all trust is captured by the kind of episodic or extended interaction that I have called "trusting relationships," including entrustments. In these cases, individuals trust other individuals for satisfactory performance, even if the specification of that performance cannot be given completely or in detail in advance. When individuals enter trusting or entrusting relations with businesses or institutions, however, another kind of trust begins to appear. Even in cases where I deal directly with individual representatives of institutions, I will still usually be relying on a larger network of unknown individuals who I nonetheless tacitly suppose, unless something

---

[13] Victoria McGeer, "Trust, Hope, and Empowerment."

[14] Russell Hardin notes the problem of running together an account of trust and of trustworthiness, thus reading back into an account of trust, for example, those morally valued dispositions that might make someone trustworthy. See "The Street-Level Epistemology of Trust."

goes wrong, are doing all the things they are supposed to do to render me the services on which I depend. I give the bank teller my deposit, but I rely on the institution's competence and fiduciary responsibility, and the system of regulation that ensures and enforces its compliance, and the responsibility of whoever ultimately oversees that system to see to it that my money goes and stays where it is supposed to. The cast of individuals responsible for satisfying my expectations of adequate performance within and by institutions is something over which I have no control and it changes over time in ways of which I am unlikely to have any knowledge. Another kind of trust is revealed here. It is that unreflective and often nonspecific expectation that strangers or unknown others may be relied upon to behave in an acceptable and unthreatening manner. These others can be those encountered randomly (passersby); those unseen and unidentified whose actions could harm us through causal chains and over time and distance (food processing workers, air traffic controllers); or those encountered transiently in various roles where, from our point of view, the occupants are replaceable and we are relying on them to perform a function (assembly-line workers, airline pilots). There is a sense in which, in myriad activities of daily life, we trust "people." We trust *that* they will behave as they should. Sometimes it seems that what we trust is the reliable good order and safety of an environment.

How nice it is for us the more we can do so. Some of us who have the good fortune to live in the safer parts of orderly societies in peaceful times are able to float down a stream of largely unreflective unconcern with implicit confidence that people will behave as they should in countless contexts.[15] We do not and need not enumerate to ourselves all of the people and all of the ways of behaving upon which we are relying in getting on with daily life undisturbed. In roughly orderly but socially divided societies, ones where people live very different and unequally safe and secure everyday lives, many of us are able to enjoy a substantial amount of unreflective unconcern at least within particular social spaces, for instance in a neighborhood, a community, a club, or other safe and welcoming space. Sometimes when people refer to their "communities," either as networks of people or as geographical locations or as both, they capture this sense of the place where one feels relatively safe. This is not because one believes one is utterly protected, but because one believes one knows what to expect and from whom to expect it, and one knows

---

[15] See Jones "Trust and Terror," on the idea of "basal security" that terrorists know all too well how to undermine.

what is normal and what is out of place. One knows, in a word, what to expect and whom to trust.

This practical outlook of ease, comfort, or complacency that relies on the good or tolerable behavior of others is the form of trust I call *default trust*. I call those spaces and circumstances in which it is enjoyed, to whatever extent and in whatever ways, *zones of default trust*. It is the unreflective and habitual background, in those zones where it operates for individuals, for specific episodes and relationships of trusting and entrusting. Success in trusting relations can confirm our beliefs in the integrity and good will of others generally, and so can fortify default trust. But it is also the case that undisturbed default trust, especially when broad and deep, can constitute a "climate" in which specific trusting relationships of many kinds seem normal and ordinary; robust default trust within a work environment, for example, is likely to foster the willingness of individuals to work cooperatively and to rely on others.[16]

What I am calling default trust might seem like mere comfort or habit, but the occurrence of negative reactions of indignation, resentment, and betrayal when default trust is disrupted or disappointed is the signal that our reliance is trusting, and that it assumes others' responsibility and not just their predictability. We may resent rude treatment by a waiter, but we may also resent generally bad service on an airline when schedules are disrupted and information is unavailable or confusing. In the latter case the lapses are not directed at us, nor do we necessarily know exactly whom we blame; individual employees are likely to be exposed to the indignation of the unhappy customer who feels irresponsibly served, whether or not they are in control of the situation. We might say that in this, as in many cases of even more diffuse default trust, we did not rely on X to do A and Y to do B, and so on (although we might have some beliefs of this kind), but rather that we expected "reliable, courteous, and orderly service" of the airline, which is not just a particular group of unnamed individuals but a mode of organization that is supposed to train and enable whatever individuals are filling organizational roles to perform effectively to the end we rely on. Crime victims may become furious at responding police officers who were "supposed to protect them," as well as at the unidentified assailants who actually did them harm; this reveals a tacit (and often unrealistic) reliance on unknown others who are believed to have responsibility for

---

[16] On trust as a "core social motive" with review of the social psychological literature, see Susan T. Fiske, *Social Beings: A Core Motives Approach to Social Psychology*, 23–25, and on possible cultural differences in propensities to trust, 543.

keeping public order. A crime victim might further blame the judge who released the assailant on bail after a previous offense.

With default trust we can often identify individuals to hold responsible *after the fact* of violation, and precisely because trust implies responsibility we are likely to search for someone or some others to whom to attribute it. Yet this identification after the fact often underscores that what we relied on was really the good order or safety of an environment. Before the fact we were trusting not A, B, or C, but were (probably unreflectively) trusting *that* we were safe walking down the street in broad daylight, *that* we would enjoy a pleasant dining experience, or *that* we would be conveyed without excessive aggravation to our destination. Default trust must often take the form of trusting *that* an acceptable state of affairs will obtain, rather than trusting *someone in particular*, or even many persons, or even whatever unidentified persons happen to be in a particular set of roles. Diffuse default trust may have a two-place structure of "trusting that. . . . " But because trust entails responsibility, we will look in serious cases for particular parties to bear the responsibility and to be the target of reactive responses. Whether we can say in advance whom we would reproach were default trust to be violated, we are prone to respond in just the same reactive ways to upsets of commonplace assumptions of "acceptable" or "normal" behavior, or of reasonably orderly environments and procedures, despite the absence of prior relations with or presumptions about individuals. In fact, the attitudes are likely to move us to find individuals at whom to direct them. Whether reactions are mild or acute and transient or lasting, they are of the kind that reveal that our reliance presumes responsibility.

On the positive side, in trusting relations with specific individuals, reactions of gratitude, admiration, and esteem signal that trust is met with superior performance or entrustment with special care or competence. Reactive attitudes are not only negative markers of responsibility, but are also positive ones. They flag behavior beyond what would be normatively expected, and express to others our sense that it either exceeds what norms require or meets normative expectations under conditions that are particularly demanding. I am not ordinarily grateful for a friend's hearing me out on a matter that disturbs me, but I might be grateful if I know she is distracted by her own difficulties, or I suspect that I am tedious in my hand-wringing, or know that a certain kind of discussion – this kind – typically bores her. Positive feelings of approval, respect, esteem, or admiration can also flow toward the consistency, fluency, or wholeheartedness of people's reliability, even where the behavior really is just what they ought to do. After all, a lot of us do what we ought only fitfully, grudgingly, clumsily, sullenly, or mechanically. We are grateful, too, when we are treated better than we deserve, as when we are treated less harshly than was due. So, too, it is with default trust. We respond with positive reactive feeling not only to those in trusting relationships, but also to strangers who are unusually courteous, helpful, or caring in the ordinary course of things, and more so when we find ourselves rendered vulnerable (by a fall, fainting on a bus, a lost wallet, a bag of groceries dropped in the street) among such strangers, and need to rely on those who might well feel no special responsibility to tend to us. If we did not normatively expect this level of concern and support from them, we hold them responsible in the rewarding form of a positive credit.

There will be zones of default trust for some or many people in any social order with minimal stability.[17] Yet there are different global tonalities of trust in different social worlds, and differing levels of default trust in different situations within the same social world for a given individual. There are environments or conditions where a usually operating default position of trust has been shattered for most people. Situations of siege warfare, bombardment, civil unrest, mass violence, or endemic terrorism can drastically alter the sanity or scope of default trust for most of a population. More commonly, however, default trust *within* societies is unequally distributed, often dramatically unequally distributed, as are most other socially produced goods. In settings where particular groups of people are slighted, dominated, oppressed, stigmatized, or exposed to violence on the basis of their sex, race, caste, religion, sexual practice, economic disadvantage, political beliefs, and the like, large zones of social life will not permit those people the ease of default trust that others routinely enjoy, and specific areas of social interaction may require them to be wary or extremely cautious. The social field of normative expectations is typically neither uniform nor level, and the levels of risk in relying on people to behave in ways one considers them responsible for behaving aren't either. Lucky are those whose social worlds allow them to operate over the wide range of ordinary encounters from a position of default trust that is broad and deep. A measure of social comfort might be the degree of fit between one's normative expectations and how routinely one's ordinary social life is organized to satisfy those expectations over a

---

[17] See Govier, *Social Trust*, both on sociology experiments in disrupting utterly commonplace expectations in everyday settings, 21–22, 108–11, and on "lower-trust" societies, ch. 6.

wide range, thus enabling robust default trust. A definition of social privilege might be the relatively high degree of this fit some groups of people enjoy compared to other groups, and the dedication of disproportionate social resources and mechanisms of social enforcement to maintain this fit, and to provide the advantages and pleasures of routine and sweeping default trust.

If we are among the privileged or the fortunate (and social privilege is a potent form of good moral luck), our zones of default trust in our social worlds will be broad and deep, as we find that it requires no special vigilance or elaborate measures to avoid many types of harm in the general run of life. All of us know that, even in those orderly societies in relatively peaceful times, we may suffer occasional insults and chance violations that can be serious, and even disastrous or fatal. To that extent there are places in healthy default trust where confidence gives way to hopefulness. Many of us who are fortunate, however, do not know enough to *feel* fortunate, or may simply take for granted, that we do not expect to be insulted by passersby because of our wheelchair, ethnic dress, or skin color; to have a professor comment on our figure instead of our term paper; to be raped on a date or when doing prison time under the state's exercise of criminal "justice"; to be ridiculed or beaten up regularly in school; to be exposed to a drive-by shooting; to be tortured while in police custody for a minor offense; or to be kidnapped by security forces for arbitrary and secret detention. Members of some groups are *normatively vulnerable* to violence, hostility, insult, and disregard. State regimes that rule by political terror see to it that their citizens know that their physical safety, their civil dignity, and their civil rights are not secure. For some, zones of default trust may shrink to almost nothing, leaving them to rely on a few others to whom they entrust their very lives. These facts, and not only violations of trust, bear importantly on some tasks of moral repair.

Violations of Trust

Violations of trust and the damages they inflict are of many kinds with vastly differing degrees of severity. The most obvious damage inflicted by violated trust might be to whatever one entrusted to another or trusted the other for. Since we trust others with everything from holding our place in line for our convenience, to the safety of our children or our lives, unreliability or incompetence (or worse, maleficence, indifference, or carelessness) can result in our losing things of some value or of the greatest human importance. If we have relied on someone and suffered losses because of that person's unreliability, we deserve an accounting, an apology, and perhaps appropriate compensation. When what is lost is your child, your sight, or your life, compensation will be inadequate or impossible. Yet even in cases where there is no way to make right or compensate for what is lost, there are still forms of satisfaction in having failure acknowledged, responsibility taken, and sincere apology and assistance offered, and we are due these gestures by those responsible. The failure of those responsible to satisfy in any of these important dimensions, and of others to join or support one in seeking this satisfaction, gives a basis for further complaint. Persistent denial of wrong, or of the repair that is owed to another who has been wrongfully harmed, does more than add insult to injury. I will return to this failure to repair or satisfy.

Seeing trust as reliance with normative expectations provides a framework for identifying other kinds of losses and damages that trust violation inflicts. Many serious violations of trust, and some less grave ones, in trusting relationships raise questions about continued or renewed reliance on particular individuals: can we and should we continue to depend on others who have shown themselves undependable? The nature of both the offense and the relationship are decisive factors in answering that question when trusting relations have been breached. Reliance in these cases can sometimes be reseated by clarification and negotiation, as when friends mend fences by agreeing explicitly upon what they can expect from each other. Or, once there has been a violation, the trusting party may simply limit reliance or stop relying on another. This may amount simply to a prudent, if sometimes inconvenient, restructuring of expectations, but it can mean the loss of a relationship or of some of the goods one valued within it. Violations of default trust pose some of the same options, but may leave less room for choice and little if any for renegotiation of relationship. The costs in deciding no longer to rely on some kinds of institutions and environments can be great even where this decision is possible, and often it is not. One may have no choice but to continue to rely on some minimum of public safety, for example, to move about in daily life; but after a serious shock to default trust – for example, criminal victimization, medical negligence, or awareness of a terrorist threat – one's sense of risk may be intensified to an uncomfortable degree in doing so.

Violations of trusting relations and violations of default trust are not always separate cases. Just as success in trusting relations can enhance a general climate of trust, a breakdown in trust relations can cause a cynicism or suspicion about human beings that hedges default trust. And as a healthy climate of default trust in a certain zone of life might encourage investments of trust in relationships with other individuals, shattered default trust can raise doubts and fears about the trustworthiness of any particular individual. Skepticism about trusting individuals undercuts willingness to enter into trusting relations and confidence in entrusting something of value to their care, especially under conditions of low control. Consider two especially damaging kinds of cases that lie at the opposite ends of a spectrum of direct engagement: the unforgivable betrayal by an intimate and the terrifying injury done by a stranger.

Psychologist Beverly Flanigan speaks of the "frightful confusion and highly charged exhaustion" that follows a serious breach of trust by someone we love and rely on. Still, devastating breaches of interpersonal trust can be healed, and trust can be restored, under certain conditions. If both parties can agree about the nature and the seriousness of the violation, if the wrongdoer is truly repentant and reassuring, and the parties can establish a shared view of the "moral rules" that will guide their mutual expectations in the future, trust can be restored.[18] If any of these is lacking, the breach may be irreparable; it is then not only trust but the relationship itself that is insupportable. If the understanding, remorse, or renewed commitment are limited or shallow, the relationship may continue with its bases of trust subtly altered on one or both sides. Perhaps there is less trust, or a lack of trust, about particular matters thereafter, with expectations lowered or selectively disengaged. In cases of lesser intimacy, in friendships or working partnerships for example, reconfigured trust may be the way to salvage and even solidify a continuing relationship. In the worst case of damaged trust among intimates, however, it is not only the violated relationship that is shattered but a whole nexus of the injured person's beliefs about himself, his judgment, his understanding of a shared history, and even the nature of "people," "the world," and "right and wrong."[19] These are cases where individual violations of trust have been due to terrible injuries or stunning betrayals, and therefore may compromise, at least in some ways or for some period of time, not only trustingness in relationships but certain kinds of default trust as well.

[18] Beverly Flanigan, *Forgiving the Unforgivable*, 62.
[19] Beverly Flanigan, *Forgiving the Unforgivable*, 23–29. Many writers refer to R. Janoff-Bulman's *Shattered Assumptions: Towards a New Psychology of Trauma* in connection with this devastating impact on one's view of the world.

Howard Zehr, a restorative justice advocate, describes criminal victimization, which may be experienced at the hands of total strangers, as "a violation of trust in our relationships with others."[20] Seen in more detail, crime destroys feelings of autonomy and security: "Someone else has taken control of our lives, our property, our space. It leaves victims feeling vulnerable, defenseless, out of control, dehumanized."[21] Victims of crime express needs for information, recognition, and safety as well as material compensation or redress, and the former needs have much to do with regaining a sense of trust in themselves, others, and the world.[22] It is striking, as Heather Strang notes in canvassing empirical studies of crime victims, that "there is evidence to suggest that victims may often see emotional restoration as far more important than material or financial reparation."[23] Especially important are the victims' needs for the acknowledgment of wrongdoing and of the reality and magnitude of harm that has been done by the wrongdoer, desires for explanation of an offender's action, and (to some people, surprisingly) for apologies.

For crime victims, one of the attractions of restorative justice programs that allow for direct but mediated (and always consensual) conferences with criminal offenders is the opportunity to confront the harmdoer directly. Some research, while hardly conclusive, suggests that motives for participation, such as being able to question, inform, and express feelings to the offender, and to receive answers and expressions of feeling in return, including acknowledgments of responsibility and apologies for harm, weigh as heavily as seeking penalties or material compensation.[24] The meanings of conferences for victims (and offenders) are no doubt complex, but one function of these meetings may be to render the harm focused and concrete for both. For the offender, this can make the victim and the consequences of harm more real; for the victim, meeting with the offender may also help to transform a violation of diffuse default trust into a more manageable instance of harm for which another particular human being is accountable.

---

[20] Howard Zehr, *Changing Lenses: A New Focus For Crime and Justice*, 29.
[21] Zehr, *Changing Lenses*, 25.
[22] Zehr, *Changing Lenses*, 25–29.
[23] Heather Strang, "Justice for Victims of Young Offenders," 287. See also Heather Strang, "The Crime Victim Movement as a Force in Civil Society."
[24] John Braithwaite, *Restorative Justice and Responsive Regulation*, 52, and Zehr, *Changing Lenses*, 193ff. Walter J. Dickey, "Forgiveness and Crime: The Possibilities of Restorative Justice," includes a striking transcript of a conference between a rape victim and her assailant.

Victims of war crimes and human rights violations (or the families of those who have died) may have similar needs, although the relevant kinds of acknowledgment fall upon governments in some of these cases. Many women who were kidnapped and held forcibly in sexual slavery by the Japanese army in the Second World War – survivors now old, and sometimes frail as a result of the physical brutality of their captivity – have refused monetary compensation because it does do not come with acknowledgment of the role of, and an official apology from, the government of Japan.[25] This should not be seen as minimizing the importance of tangible compensation, which can be vital to demonstrating the sincerity of an acknowledgment and apology, as well as truly or desperately needed by victims.[26] Rather, it should be seen, among other things, as the victim's opportunity to clearly place responsibility and so reclaim self-trust and dignity, a moral status that demands consideration from others. Perhaps it is also an attempt to begin to restore a sense of trust that individuals and institutions are responsible, if only after the fact of injury. When victims seek the punishment of offenders, they may be motivated not only by an abstract desire for justice, but also by the desire to solidify a sense of their own security and to see their societies as protective and responsible, thus reconstituting conditions for some kinds of default trust.

In cases of serious wrongdoing between intimates and between strangers, whether criminal or not, there is this common denominator: a shattering of *control*. Flanigan says: "What is out of control is your sense that the moral boundaries of your relationship can any longer be mutually defined with the person who harmed you. Out of control, also, is any likelihood of resurrecting the dreams and hopes about the future as you imagined it."[27] Zehr says that victimization violates "our vision of ourselves as autonomous individuals in a meaningful world."[28] At stake in serious wrongdoing is our sense that we expect, act, and hope in a human world that promises some stability and so some control through our own choices. Our sense of control in that human world, however,

[25] See Elazar Barkan's discussion of the "comfort women's" case in *The Guilt of Nations: Restitution and Negotiating Historical Injustices*. For detailed follow-up on the unsuccessful legal and political maneuvers, see Keisuke Iida, "Human Rights and Sexual Abuse: The Impact of International Human Rights Law on Japan."

[26] Brandon Hamber discusses the failure of the post-apartheid South African government to deal adequately either with promised material reparations or the larger context that might make them meaningful to victims, in "Reparations as Symbol: Narratives of Resistance, Reticence and Possibility in South Africa."

[27] Flanigan, *Forgiving the Unforgivable*, 79.

[28] Zehr, *Changing Lenses*, 29.

does not come from an experience or a conviction that human beings are *absolutely* predictable or benign or that we can ever largely control the conditions of our vulnerability to others. For human beings, trusting in people, seen and unseen, at varying depths for various things, is one of our central ways of feeling in control. Our ability to act out of belief in others' and our own reliability unburdens us of conscious anxiety and impossible vigilance; it allows us to anticipate, to plan, and to predicate outcomes on what we ourselves and others are expected to do. Is it possible to live without this fallible but resilient human feeling of control that trust provides? What would that be like?

Survivors of extreme trauma seem to offer us a glimpse into the state of human beings living among others with default and interpersonal trust that is shattered or severely limited. Jonathan Shay is a psychiatrist who has worked since 1987 with combat veterans who suffer from severe, chronic post-traumatic stress disorder (PTSD). In two remarkable books, Shay explores the injuries that occur under such circumstances as irresponsible leadership, involvement in atrocity and desecration of the dead, arbitrary and untimely separation of soldiers who have experienced combat together, the thwarting of the expression and sharing of grief and rage, or a failure to provide meaningful communal rituals of return. He describes these injuries precisely as "psychological and moral" ones that involve the destruction of social trust.[29] As he explains it: "Social trust is *the expectation that power will be used in accordance with 'what's right.'* When social trust is destroyed, it is not replaced by a vacuum, but rather by a perpetual mobilization to fend off attack, humiliation, or exploitation, and to figure out other people's trickery... "[30] The results of shattered trust can be lives in which people cannot sustain employment or relationships, or lose the ability to move about publicly without distress. People are exposed to horrifying misuse of power when they experience violations by others that are threatening to life and integrity, especially under conditions they cannot escape. Importantly, trauma can also result when people are themselves drawn or forced into situations where they engage in or are complicit in terrible violations of others that they cannot forget or repair, such as engaging in or condoning atrocities.

It is not only trust in others that is catastrophically damaged by the experience of extreme trauma, such as violent attack. Extreme threat and injury also affect trust in *oneself*. Susan Brison, in her moving account

---

[29] Jonathan Shay, *Odysseus in America: Combat Trauma and the Trials of Homecoming*, 33.
[30] Shay, *Odysseus in America*, 151. Emphasis in the original.

of the aftermath of her own sexual assault and attempted murder, reports that "the autonomy-undermining symptoms of PTSD reconfigure the survivor's will, rendering involuntary many responses that were once under voluntary control," such as memory, proneness to startle, or loss of desire due to fear.[31] Ordinary and previously pleasurable or relaxed activities may become fraught with unease, anxiety, or terror. Experts in trauma agree that experiences of helplessness and terror can lead to severe difficulties in trusting others, oneself, and many aspects of a world that appears benign, even protecting, to other people. The effects of extreme trauma due to captivity and dehumanizing violence can also, it now appears, have effects that extend over generations.[32] In cases of betrayal, serious injury, or extreme violation, it may be neither possible nor desirable that the injured person attempt to renew reliance on those who have inflicted the grievous harm. But the restoration of working trust in other individuals and in human environments may be possible, and it is essential to normal life. Political mass violence – war, terror, genocide, massacre – may be the hardest case in which to restore default and interpersonal trust, yet there is a feature even this hardest case of mass violence shares with other cases of broken or damaged trust. It concerns what happens in the wake of wrongdoing, and it can make a great difference, or all the difference, in whether significant trust can be reclaimed.

When we recognize that we are wronged and as a result trust is damaged or shattered, trusting expectations play yet another role. We are likely to trust that others will recognize the wrong for what it is and will responsibly acknowledge it. In the case of those who have done the wrong, the expected acknowledgment involves taking responsibility and demonstrating willingness to apologize and make amends to the harmed person and perhaps also to a community whose order is disturbed. In the case of others who are not themselves the wrongdoers, we trust that they will intervene to stop wrongdoing if they can; that they will respond to victims with honest recognition of the wrong and the harm done them; that they will address the offenders with reproach and demands for accountability; and that they will validate the victim's entitlement to redress by joining the victim in seeking it, or seeking it on the victim's behalf. This is the expectation that "justice" in the most intuitive sense will be done, or at

---

[31] Susan Brison, *Aftermath: Violence and the Remaking of a Self*, 79–80.

[32] On effects of trauma, see Judith Herman, *Trauma and Recovery: The Aftermath of Violence – From Domestic Abuse to Political Terror*, ch. 2, and Shay, *Odysseus in America*, ch. 16. For a massive compendium of studies on multigenerational trauma, see Yael Danieli, ed., *International Handbook of Multigenerational Legacies of Trauma*.

least will be attempted. It is the expectation that wrongdoers will "pay" in any of several currencies: in the acknowledgment of their fault, the acceptance of deserved punishment, or the making of amends. To the extent that we expect proper conduct of others, we also expect reliable support from others for the practice of holding each other responsible for how we behave. Holding each other responsible *is* proper conduct, and it is conduct that is necessary to keep our practices of responsibility going. Failures of some to act responsibly trigger expectations of responsible corrective actions. These actions can come from those who did wrong or from others. Many of these expectations of correction are again premised on trust, because we are relying on others to respond correctively even as we know very well that many wrongs, including ones of shocking magnitude and inhumanity, go unaddressed.

Our expectations that people will be held responsible, called to account, and held liable for "making right" are themselves normative expectations that express our insistence that others do what they *should* in the wake of wrongdoing. In having normative expectations of any kind, we assume that we know which norms obtain as shared bases of judgment. In assuming this, we understand ourselves as members of communities of normative judgment; we trust ourselves to be qualified judges of what norms require, to know "what's right," whether the norms in question are those of poker, table manners, respect, or human rights. We further expect that others with whom we share these understandings will judge as we do. This sets us up for yet another form of trust violation, which occurs when we perceive wrongdoing but find that others fail to acknowledge or responsibly address it. If we perceive this and we are the wrongdoers, we may be emboldened by impunity, or ridden with guilt. If we are victims of wrongdoing who perceive this, we may be outraged, or crushed by the sense that no one cares and we do not matter. We may also lose confidence in our ability to be competent normative judges, or we may wonder whether the norms we believed to be in force do in fact still carry authority. Third parties play a crucial role in signaling to those wronged, to wrongdoers, and to each other that an action violates norms and whether or not such an action requires a response that reasserts the norms and recognizes victims and wrongdoers as such. We are social beings who rely on others to play by shared rules that can guide our expectations. We also rely on each other to stabilize our senses of entitlement and responsibility, including our responsibilities to address and redress wrongs.

Normative expectations underwrite all the forms of trust by which we guide ourselves through a human world that we anticipate, or at least hope, we can rely upon in countless ways. Our reliance on others who make up our human world goes through their presumed senses of responsibility: we rely on others (and even indiscriminately rely on unknown others, as in default trust in its zones of operation) because we assume there are rules and that others are generally responsible in complying with them and in seeking or demanding others' compliance or their amends. A condition of moral relationship is that we regard each other and ourselves in this way: as responsible beings responsive to normative boundaries, including those important normative boundaries we call "moral" ones (which are sometimes, but not always, sharply distinct from other social or conventional ones). The expression of that regard is embodied in our acting on trusting expectations on the one hand, in our proneness to react in rebuking or demanding ways to the violation of our trust when we or others are wrongfully harmed, and in our readiness to react to rebuking behavior with gestures of amends when we are wrongdoers. Trust is the ground of moral relations; our reactive responses to breaches of normative expectations by each other and by ourselves aim to keep us morally grounded.

Failure to receive confirmation of one's judgment that certain actions are unacceptable, that wrongs are worth correcting or redressing, that wrongdoers should be held to account, or that victims deserve reparative response is always disconcerting, and it can be destructive. It can lead to resentment and mistrust of those who seem to think that some people and some wrongs are unimportant, or to a chronic and isolating indignation or bitterness of those injured when serious wrongs are denied or trivialized. Between groups, communities, or nations, this bitter disappointment or smouldering resentment can be exploited by opportunistic political leaders, who can use it to kindle intergroup violence. For this reason it is important within and between societies to make sure that serious injustices and harms are not ignored even if it is inconvenient, costly, or shaming to acknowledge them. Lack of normative confirmation can also trigger confusion and anxiety in individuals about whether they are competent judges of right and wrong; they can lose conviction or self-trust in making these judgments. Or they can slip into a protective cynicism so that they see "the rules" as just things people assert arbitrarily for advantage; they "grow up," and see that the idea that wrongs must be addressed or that justice must be done is "naive," or that taking responsibility and making amends is for "fools" or "suckers." In either case, people's comfort and confidence in holding others responsible may wane or collapse, and so will those expressive reactions of outrage, indignation, or resentment that communicate our sense that others are out of bounds. In our own case, our susceptibility to feel shame, guilt, or remorse – those reactions in which we rebuke ourselves and join others who rebuke us – may weaken or disappear. Even if we continue to rely on others as a kind of prediction, the normative force of those expectations will fall away. If the expectations persist, they will lose the quality of demands to which we hold each other.

Normative isolation, confusion, and cynicism are unstable conditions that can erode or undermine people's senses of responsibility, defeating our sense that some things are owed by us to others. These conditions and their consequences can be contagious, since we look to each other to reinforce and validate our judgments and the demands we make on ourselves and each other to be responsible. They can lead to instability or decay, not only of reliance, but of normative expectations themselves. Failure to secure confirming judgment that normative expectations are violated can also lead to the discovery, or the concession, that the norms one thought were shared and authoritative are not. Norms may not be shared, if different individuals or different segments of a community believe that different rules are in play. Norms may not be socially author-itative if their violation ceases to command a widely seated or significant response because they no longer embody forms of conduct or relation-ship that a society or community values or that it cares to sustain.

Lack of shared normative ground means that expectations are not aligned, or that failures to fulfill expectations do not qualify as matters of responsibility. Then what you expect from me may no longer be some-thing I expect from myself, or may no longer be something you think you have a right to. In this state of affairs trust is impossible or is destined to be disappointed. Loss of authority of norms may occur unevenly in a community, as some are quicker to abandon the assumption that people should any longer be expected to act in particular ways. The "ways" can be as quaintly customary as ladies wearing gloves to work or as charged as black people averting their eyes and stepping aside when white people walk by, as in a once commonplace American code of racial deference. This brings us to one more part, and a crucial part, of the story about the normative expectations that structure our senses of responsibility and shape the nature of our trust and our reactions to its violation. This part of the story takes us into the territory of systemic distortions in responsi-bility and reciprocity that are commonplace in human societies, and are the source of serious and even appalling mistreatment of some human beings. Some normative expectations are morally unjustifiable, and need

to be not only defeated but uprooted and replaced. This too is a job of
moral repair.

Distortions of Responsibility and Objectionable Attitudes

Human beings hold each other to a bewildering array of norms of diverse
types: customs, folkways, rules, conventions, social practices, cultural
styles, institutional norms, moral requirements or standards, and such
morally loaded aspirational ideals as that of "good parent," "true friend,"
or "person of integrity." Throughout my discussion of trust, I have spoken
generically of normative expectations. These embody norms of diverse
types. In a certain kind of society I expect you not to arrive bare-chested
for dinner, but I also expect you not to assault me, and will see your doing
either of these things as going objectionably out of bounds. Aren't these
normative expectations importantly different, in that the first involves
a rule of social decorum while the second involves a moral obligation
not to willfully harm? They are different, but there are good reasons to
view normative expectation as a single kind that encompasses demands
of different sorts.

One reason is that trust among us spans many varieties of normative
expectation and, if we are trying to understand trust and its overall role
in human life, we need to see its full sphere of operation. We ought
not prejudge whether the success of trusting in some areas that are not
especially moral might carry over to ones that are, or that the reverse
is true. Our moral relations are woven through and expressed in our
social relations, and we should not expect people to keep separate ledgers
of reasons to trust or not to trust.[33] For that matter, there are reasons
to resist a sharp partition between all moral and all nonmoral cases of
norms, expectations, and obligations. It is true that there are cases that
seem unambiguously of one type rather than the other: restraints on
taking human life are moral, ones on the use of particular pieces of
silverware for different dinner courses are not. Yet in between there is a

---

[33] In a nine-year study of Hindu-Muslim violence in Indian cities, political scientist Ashutosh
Varshney found that cities with developed social, political, and economic integration –
with many ethnically integrated organizations, such as trade unions, professional groups,
political parties, sports clubs, peace committees – were less vulnerable to conflict.
Mahvish Khan, "To Keep Peace, Study Peace." While one may dispute the precise role of
trust in these settings, it is not unreasonable to think that many reinforcing cooperative
relations build a dense fabric of cooperation that both draws on trust and feeds back
into trust. Varshney's study is published in *Ethnic Conflict & Civic Life: Hindus & Muslims
in India.*

broad range of norms that structure mutual interaction and expectations so strongly or in such ways that to ignore or violate them has moral implications.

Rules of etiquette, for example, may seem like purely conventional stipulations. To the extent that rules of etiquette invest particular actions or modes of presentation with meanings such as respect, gratitude, tact, or deference, however, to abandon them may be to express an offensive, insulting, or provocative attitude to someone, to which that person might well take exception.[34] And to act in ways one has reason to anticipate will upset people's plans and feelings, or to proceed without concern for their serious embarrassment, discomfort, alarm, or resentment, can be, where other things are equal, careless with others or cruel to them, and these are moral matters. Naturally, one ought not to stand on convention when human life, dignity, or well-being is at stake; but often most of what is at stake in our interactions with others is whether we find we are treated with a modicum of tact, kindness, and respect. This can be readily achieved in many commonplace situations simply by sticking to some social formats that do not unnecessarily surprise, embarrass, or insult others. Many stories of bloopers by outsiders within unfamiliar cultural fields only serve to underscore that if you know the rules of play, and if there is no pressing moral objection to following them, you do no harm by following them. On the other hand, if you do not follow them, the harm you do sometimes may be reasonably considered under moral categories. Sometimes, of course, people have moral reasons to be tactless, rude, or unpredictable, but this exception really does prove the rule. In such cases it is the moral force of one norm (turning away or reproving a racist joke) that supersedes the possible moral fallout of violating another (chuckling politely at jokes that aren't funny, so as to spare the teller some avoidable embarrassment.)

Moral and social worlds and their norms are deeply intertwined in yet another way. Moral statuses, such as dignity, autonomy, or equality, and forms of recognition, such as respect or concern, are often embodied, expressed, and understood in terms of legal, institutional, and conventional social statuses and forms of treatment. What it is to "respect someone's autonomy," or to "treat someone with dignity" – or the

---

[34] Sarah Buss defends the view that manners, despite a considerable conventional element, are a way of directly acknowledging people's dignity by expressing respect, and that this is the essential function of good manners that is not merely conventional. See her "Appearing Respectful: The Moral Significance of Manners."

reverse – often takes the form of recognizing certain legal standing, allowing access to certain institutional or social roles, or holding someone subject to or exempt from certain social demands. Consider a vivid historical
example from Bertram Wyatt Brown's *Southern Honor*. Brown, writing of
the sexual politics of patriarchal marriage in the antebellum American
South, reports that while divorce was rare even where permitted, a wife's
infidelity was the most common and most successful ground in pursuing
divorce. Even so, the legislatures with the power to grant divorce were
inclined to disregard even flamboyant infidelity if the wronged husband
failed to display appropriate "manliness" in controlling his wife: "If the
husband could not control her, he was not to be awarded community
approval in the form of a divorce."[35] Wives ought not to stray, but husbands ought not to be spectacularly inept in preventing their doing so by
failing to be "manly." The example (even stripped of detail) lays bare an
intricate tangle of legal practice, moral understandings, and social expectations that jointly define each other within a web of normative expectations for people of certain classes at a certain time. Male legislators had
normative expectations of female chastity; of women as weak-willed and
in need of male protection and guidance; of men as husbands entrusted
with the discipline of wives on which society and family life depended;
and of their duty to shore up the patriarchal authority entrusted to each
man in his household by granting divorce in some cases and refusing it
in others. Men and women were supposed to have the corresponding
expectations of themselves, other men, and other women. All of these
were embedded in an "ethics of honor," a system in which social status, law, and moral values were combined. The example, while quaint,
demonstrates the usual intricate interplay of social and moral life.[36]

We are social beings whose senses of responsibility are inevitably config-
ured around social arrangements that express and enforce moral assumptions. Especially important for our senses of responsibility are norms that
define *relative* status, not only how individuals of a kind are to act and
to be treated, but how individuals of some socially specified kinds are to

---

[35] Bertram Wyatt Brown, *Southern Honor: Ethics and Behavior in the Old South*, 298–307,
quoting from 308.
[36] See Margaret Urban Walker, *Moral Understandings: A Feminist Study in Ethics*, for extensive
examination of the reasons that morality is not, and cannot be, modular with respect to
the rest of social life. See also my essays "Seeing Power in Morality," "Ineluctable Feelings
and Moral Recognition," and "Human Conditions," in Margaret Urban Walker, *Moral
Contexts*. For purposes of the current discussion, it is enough to emphasize the complex
interaction of diverse kinds of social norms, especially those that express relative statuses.

act toward and be treated by some others. Different statuses make for some different normative expectations; different relative statuses make for asymmetrical but corresponding normative expectations. Some not only are entitled to superior power or greater access to authority than others but are entitled to superior power or access to authority *over* others, and those over whom they have power are supposed to recognize the legitimacy of this arrangement. Most of us are prepared to defend some version of the dominion of adults over children, or of the competent over those mentally incapable of managing their affairs. But many societies have also endorsed and enforced the rule of free over slave, male over female, elder over young adult, higher over lower caste, white over black, well-born over low-born, rich over poor, and so on. Many societies today continue to enforce some of these social hierarchies and even the most "egalitarian" still reverberate with them. The different and asymmetrical normative expectations that these hierarchies once demanded – in the form, for example, of reflexive assumptions about cognitive or social authority that favor men over women, white over nonwhite, the "respectable" middle classes over the poor – continue to play out in behavior, often less than consciously.

Where social hierarchy is a consciously maintained system, its stability requires that individuals experience their rightful expectations and responsibilities very differently, that new members of society learn these asymmetrical rules of engagement, and that all be prepared to assent to their legitimacy and to aid in their enforcement. Even where social arrangements are grotesquely distorted or unconscionable from an (ulterior) moral point of view, they claim *normative* (social and moral) legitimacy for their members, presenting their ordering of relationships as "what's right." People's expectations and senses of responsibility are trained and pressed to fit their very different social places. Some degree of coercion and violence is commonplace, and they are always necessary, in hierarchically structured societies. But to reproduce a *social order* requires that normative expectations bear a good deal of the weight. As Laurence Thomas points out, systems of hierarchy, domination, or enslavement are "expectations-generating power arrangements" that operate to a significant extent on a basis of trust.[37] People must be able to trust each other, and themselves, to play their roles, adopting and responding to the normative expectations that fit them. They must also trust each other to assert and enforce those normative expectations the structure requires

---

[37] Laurence Mordekhai Thomas, "Power, Trust, and Evil."

individuals to have. In these cases, people are trusted to behave in ways that elevate the interests or authority of some arbitrarily over others, or that expose some kinds of people to subordination, exploitation, exclusion, violence, or marginality in important spheres of public life.[38]

The social field of normative expectations in many human worlds is neither uniform nor level for all players, and opportunities for forming or sustaining trusting relationships or enjoying default trust are likely to be very unequally distributed as are other socially produced goods in societies with sharp differences in social and moral status. Those of lesser status may, for example, have no basis for a normative expectation that they will be treated with routine respect in many everyday transactions, that they may address or interact with others of higher status as peers, that they may move freely in some public spaces without danger of insult or assault, or that they may engage in behavior seen as normal or innocent for some others without seeming provocative, menacing, suspicious, or outrageous instead. One response to this situation is a more or less willing adaptation by those who receive bad treatment. They may form what are called "adaptive preferences," coming to expect and feel comfortable with the treatments to which they are almost inevitably subject, trusting others to behave "as it must be" and being willing to play their roles in return.[39] Thus they become complicit, although not really freely so, in the system that demeans and oppresses them. The obedient wife or compliant slave might have little experience of alternatives. In another kind of case, a person might believe her subjection unjust or cruel but believe that pressing for a different situation is too risky or dangerous. In this kind of case it is unclear whether we should continue to speak of adaptive preferences; we should rather speak of an adaptation, despite preferences to the contrary, to a reality that is judged impossible or too risky to change or escape. Adaptation then takes the form of accepting existing arrangements and trying to manage them, perhaps trusting that by doing so one can avoid an even worse fate. But holding on to normative expectations against the grain of one's social world can be difficult.

If people of despised or subordinated groups hold on to normative expectations of decent treatment or social parity to any extent, they will discover that these expectations are rarely met. Worse, if they express their aberrant expectations, claiming regard others are not prepared to

---

[38] See Iris Young, "The Five Faces of Oppression," in *Justice and the Politics of Difference.*
[39] Martha Nussbaum discusses this phenomenon in *Women and Human Development: The Capabilities Approach,* 111–60; see also Amartya Sen, *Development as Freedom,* 62–63.

extend to them, they will be greeted with indifference, ridicule, contempt, or violence by those who see them as ignorant, foolish, arrogant, or dangerous precisely for feeling entitled to these expectations. The human will to resist injustice runs deep, but to live in ongoing protest against one's exposure to indignity, subordination, exclusion, or violence is a heavy load to bear. It is difficult to sustain normative expectations in the face of predictable violation, but especially so if one receives little confirmation for one's responses of resentment and outrage at bad treatment or insult. One is apt to be worn down or defeated without this support. Individuals of exceptional conviction may be able to keep these expectations alive as a kind of demand even as they are destined to be repeatedly disappointed or punished for their failure to accept their lot, and if they are courageous they might actually express their insistence on better treatment. The image of the enslaved Frederick Douglass turning violently on the overseer to establish that he would not be whipped is indelible.[40]

Most of us, regardless of the strength of our convictions, will need some community of moral judgment that provides a reference point and a rallying point for our refusal to accept vicious or demeaning norms and the demeaning treatments they justify. We need this community to keep alive our sense that what is accepted is nonetheless unacceptable. Physical or normative isolation under conditions of indignity or mistreatment are especially defeating, for they cut off the resort to a confirming community from which individuals can draw strength and conviction. When people's societies offer them only a social place that devalues them or disregards their interests, those people must band together within to shore up their sense of legitimate expectations of something better. Support from outsiders can also be a moral lifeline, as when movements for human rights internal to societies are endorsed and supported by a wider or international order.

If systemic abuse or widespread wrongdoing tests and sometimes crushes the ability to maintain trust and hope in victims of wrong, so can wrongdoers and bystanders become hardened, brutalized, or desensitized to the wrong that they do or tolerate. They, too, lose or bury the forms of responsiveness and responsibility that would lead them to be troubled or moved by the suffering or humiliation of others. Schooled in the acceptability of violence or indifference to some others, or in systems of hierarchy and domination over them, those with power to hurt,

---

[40] Frederick Douglass, "Narrative of the Life of Frederick Douglass."

disregard, or rule those who are less powerful may never learn to see them as human beings fully like themselves, or indeed as fully human beings, as the histories of sexism, racism, colonialism, homophobia and xenophobia reveal. Repeated convulsions of ethnic massacre, genocide, and purges of political enemies in the past century also exhibit the ways that neighbors and compatriots can become demonized or dehumanized with astonishing swiftness and deadly effect.[41] Still, those who need to keep others in inferior or subordinate places, rather than simply to command or destroy them by application of force, must rely on their social inferiors to cooperate to some extent out of a sense of responsibility, and they must in turn trust them to do so. At the same time, relationships that deny the basic human equality and dignity of their participants will place both oppressor and oppressed in the position of combining trusting reliance with varying types of manipulation through deception or coercion. Those with power often deceive themselves that their inferiors in fact see them as superior and deserving of obedience; in fact they know that they can rely on force to secure obedience in any case. Those in subordinate positions may learn how to feign subservient attitudes as well as behavior, or to remain inscrutable to their dominators. But in fact they may have no place to hide when the more powerful choose to demonstrate their true superiority, that of superior force and violence. What results is a form of distorted relationship that combines trust in kinds of responsiveness and reciprocity that are not symmetrical (you owe me food and I owe you obedience), and regard that is highly selective (I prize your modesty and domestic virtue but forbid you to develop your abilities through education), with purely manipulative behavior and the threat of force.

Relations of trust are ones of reliance with an assumption of responsibility. In them, we rely on others from within a "participant attitude," as Strawson referred to that way of being in "ordinary inter-personal relationships" that shows a readiness to hold ourselves and others responsible. Strawson contrasted the participant stance with another way of approaching other human beings he called the "objective attitude." From within the objective attitude we view a person as a possibly predictable entity "to be managed or handled or cured or trained; and perhaps simply to be

---

[41] Jonathan Glover's *Humanity: A Moral History of the Twentieth Century* catalogues and analyzes many of these episodes in a sustained reflection on how our "moral resources" can be corrupted or defeated with catastrophic results. Jean Hatzfeld's interviews with Rwandan *genocidaires* in *The Machete Season: The Killers in Rwanda Speak* are a deeply disturbing study of this deadly mobilization.

avoided."[42] In the fully objective attitude we regard the wills, attitudes, and motives of others entirely as bases of prediction that support *our* own ends for them. In doing so, we cease to treat their relationship either to their own ends or to us as one of responsibility, something for which they are required to account. And in the fully objective attitude we do not require ourselves to account *to them* in terms of responsibility. To the extent that we do this, we cease to see them as participants with us in the practice of "holding each other responsible." We may see ourselves as responsible "for" them, protecting what we think are their interests, and perhaps accounting to others for the job we do. Or we may view them entirely as entities we need to control for our safety, amusement, or convenience; we may use, manipulate, trick, or simply manage them. But insofar as we do this, we refuse to meet them in the plane of mutual responsiveness to normative expectations and reciprocal accountability for our responses.

If we have been able to understand the nature of trust as involving a participant attitude to reliance, we can also understand deviations and distortions in trusting relations as involving an "objective" one. The difference between participant and objective attitudes is a way to see, for example, the difference between Mike the con artist and Margaret the eager "accomplice" with which we began. He manipulates her feelings and behavior to his ends; he might be impatient or frustrated if his plans don't work, but he won't *blame her* for failing to meet his expectations (although he might pretend to), any more than he will blame the toaster for burning his toast. This difference is also a way to understand the operation of many "ordinary inter-personal relationships" between persons unequally placed in many social worlds. The essentially manipulative objective attitude describes some parts of socially legitimated relationships that are not reciprocal in the plane of responsibility. While the con artist relies for control on artifice and finesse (and, ultimately, exit), continuing relations of hierarchical power are typically backed by the established possibility of penalty, punishment, or violence. In some respects, these socially legitimated (although not truly morally legitimate) relations lie somewhere between control by threat of main force and the artful manipulation of the con man. They also lie somewhere between situations in which some human beings control and care for immature and incapable others and relations among persons that are roughly reciprocal and that aim at mutual and transparent normative expectations.

---

[42] Strawson, "Freedom and Resentment," 79. On the objective attitude, see 79–92.

Strawson saw the objective attitude as legitimately applied to those who are immature, incapable, or deranged, where it is unfair and point-less to hold them responsible and visit on them responsibility-imputing reactive attitudes such as resentment, indignation, or hurt feelings (or for that matter, gratitude or admiration). He also saw that the participant and objective attitudes were not all or nothing, and that while "opposed," they are "not altogether exclusive."[43] Of the objective attitude he remarks in passing: "we *can* sometimes look with something like the same eye on the behavior of the normal and the mature. We *have* this resource and can sometimes use it: as a refuge, say, from the strains of involvement; or as an aid to policy; or simply out of intellectual curiosity. Being human, we cannot, in the normal case, do this for long, or altogether."[44] But being human and learning the complex codes of our cultures, we can in fact learn manipulative, unaccountable, and nonresponsive modes of relat-ing to certain others, or we can learn to be those others to whom some relate in these diminishing ways. In some social worlds, the legitimated patterns of relating, especially among those unequal in power, are likely to exhibit mixtures of objective and participant attitudes, attributions of responsibility on selective grounds and sliding scales, and asymmet-rical normative expectations. It is not surprising that institutionalized, hierarchical relations are often justified by claiming that those who are controlled or dominated have reduced abilities for self-governance and responsibility, rather like children or the mentally incompetent. Whether rationales for unequal terms of moral relation are benign or hateful, what they produce is often morally objectionable, even abhorrent. When these attitudes lead to violence, subjugation, undeserved harm, disrespect, or humiliation, moral repair must attempt nothing less than the task of reconstructing deeply sunk social attitudes and the political, legal, and institutional supports that sustain them.

Abandonment or Assurance?

Our bonds of trust with others are moral sight lines and lifelines. We have reason to expect we can rely on others, and we expect those others to acknowledge their responsibility. If they do not perform as relied on, we still have expectations that they will acknowledge fault or that others will join us in finding them faulty. Damages to trust, or the absence of trust where it should be, call out for assurance: assurance that we share norms,

---

[43] Strawson, "Freedom and Resentment," 79.
[44] Strawson, "Freedom and Resentment," 80. Emphasis in the original.

assurance that we can rely on each other, assurance that failures of reliability will be acknowledged and corrected, and assurance that systems and institutions will be restored to dependable working order. Not least, we require assurance that we count, if not to those who have violated trust, then to others who affirm our membership in a community that repudiates our mistreatment. The enemy of trust is the loss of assurance, not only through the disappointment of expectations, but through isolation or abandonment.

Individuals can be deliberately isolated in order to – in an apt phrase – "demoralize" them, like the political prisoner or hostage who is confined or tortured, or the child or adult who is held captive to domestic violence and terror. In extreme instances, whole populations can also find themselves isolated or abandoned when they are exposed to violence and murder as others stand by, either refusing to believe the evidence of what is happening or refusing to intervene. David Gewirtzman, a 75-year-old retired pharmacist, and Jacqueline Murekatete, a recent high school graduate, share an experience that they now together teach others about: he, a Polish Jew, survived the Holocaust by spending two years buried beneath a pig sty; she narrowly escaped death but lost most of her family in the Rwandan genocide when she was nine. Now in the United States, they speak together about the realities of genocide.[45] When genocide raged through their societies, turning some citizens into victims targeted for mass death, other governments did not intervene specifically to stop or prevent genocide, and their friends and neighbors either stood by or were actively involved in persecution and killing.[46]

These are horrifying and large-scale instances of a sadly common, indeed everyday, phenomenon: some suffer undeserved harm, injustice, or terror and others turn away, do not intervene, or join actively in the disrespect, violence, or persecution. Where injustice and evil have not been prevented or arrested, there is still the opportunity after the fact to stand with the victims of injustice, insisting on acknowledgment, redress, and repair. In some cases of horrific political violence, as in the Holocaust

---

[45] Corey Kilgannon, "Something in Common: Horror: Survivors Describe Evils of Genocide."

[46] An outstanding account of this is Philip Gourevitch's *We Wish to Inform You That Tomorrow We Will Be Killed With Our Families: Stories from Rwanda.* The eyewitness account of Romeo Dallaire, the Canadian officer who headed the UN peacekeeping mission and failed to summon UN support, appears in his *Shake Hands With the Devil.* Holocaust accounts often conjure up the incredulity of Jewish citizens who found that their countrymen and neighbors either turned away from them or joined in when they were stripped of rights and rounded up for detention and slaughter.

or the genocide in Rwanda, there have been measures after the fact that attempt some form of acknowledgment or redress, however incomplete: trials, reparations, documentation, and memorials. "Repair" seems an ambitious category for catastrophic cases, but there are always ways for a community to signify condemnation of wrongdoing and respect for victims. Serious wrongdoing requires acknowledgment and assurance, rather than indifference, denial, or abandonment, if a significant level of trust is to be regained either in the wrongdoers or, more commonly and urgently, in the larger community. Apologies, documentation, or commemoration are among those respectful gestures even where little else can be done. Often much more is needed.[47]

In many cases, nonetheless, victims suffer both the injury of wrongdoing and the further insult of abandonment by those from whom they seek confirmation of, if not redress or compensation for, their injury. Failures of wrongdoers or others in a supporting community to acknowledge the fact of wrongdoing and injury, and to confirm the victims' deservingness of repair, are themselves *additional injuries* to trust and hope. These additional wounds themselves in their turn create needs for acknowledgment and repair and further obligations of wrongdoers or others to respond.[48] Thus are injuries compounded and histories of injury produced when wrongdoing is ignored, denied, or inadequately addressed. Histories of injury and insult can occur between individuals, or between nations, or between groups. Without at least the acknowledgment by others of serious wrong and the need for repair, or without a clear demonstration of concern for the suffering and loss of victims, victims and the families of victims can fall prey to bitterness or despair. In bitterness, one insists on what is right but with a sense of futility and alienation; in despair, one gives up on insisting on what is right. In either case, trust has been destroyed not only in the wrongdoers but in a community that fails either to recognize wrong or to value victims.[49]

[47] Trudy Govier discusses the central role of acknowledgment in "What is Acknowledgement and Why Is It Important?"

[48] The idea of the "second injury" or "second wound" occurs in the therapeutic literature on victimization and trauma. Janoff-Bulman, *Shattered Assumptions*, 147, cites Martin Symonds: "The 'second injury' to victims," in Symonds's *Evaluation and Change: Services for Survivors* (Minneapolis, MN: Minneapolis Medical Research Foundation, 1980). See also Danieli on the "conspiracy of silence" in *International Handbook of Multigenerational Legacies of Trauma*, 4–6.

[49] Sue Campbell's perceptive discussion of bitterness links bitterness to defeat of the hope that others will respond to the recounting of one's injury. See her *Interpreting the Personal: Expression and the Formation of Feelings*, 167–72. See also Lynne McFall, "What's Wrong With Bitterness?" on the importance of bitterness as moral protest.

There are many places – local, global, and in between – from which acknowledgment, confirmation, assurance, and gestures of repair can come, and all such attempts carry the potential for establishing or restoring trust. It should never be thought too late for a gesture of responsibility that confirms trust was violated, even where this can only happen among descendants of wrongdoers, bystanders, and victims, who share those long histories of compounded injury, and who may yet need to learn both to trust and to be responsible to each other.[50]

---

[50] Papers that were precursors of this chapter, exploring kinds of trust and the relations between trust and reactive attitudes, were given at the Catholic University of Leuven, Belgium, Washington University, Arizona State University, Michigan State University, Queensland University of Technology, and the 2000 Summer School on Ethics and Politics of Care of the Netherlands School for Research in Practical Philosophy. Audiences at all of these sites offered challenging observations for which I am grateful. I especially thank Victoria McGeer for crucial advice that led to this chapter in its present form.

4

Resentment and Assurance

Resentment is a kind of anger. With this much, everyone agrees. It is also widely agreed that anger we call "resentment" predicates some kind of wrong at the hands of other human beings, and that it is in some way a defensive emotion in its operation or its manner of expression. Resentment is both a reaction and a signal. It warns or threatens someone who is perceived as having crossed a line or done something unacceptable. It shows them that we have noticed that, and it shows how we are now disposed toward them. Someone insults you; you say "I resent that." You mean that you take it as an affront or offense to you, and you are "calling" the offender on it, issuing a challenge, putting the person on notice, possibly on notice of unpleasant or retaliatory action in return. Once resentment is expressed, it can mean that further confrontation is about to ensue, or that payback is on the agenda, or that you won't be speaking to the offender again, short of an excuse, explanation, or apology. But can't I resent the fact that it rained on my picnic, or that you are taller than I am, or that my neighbor drives a nicer car than I can afford? Here no one seems to have done anything wrong, and in the case of rain and relative height, it's not clear that any responsible party has *done* anything at all, much less *to me*. Dictionaries say to resent is "to feel or exhibit annoyance or indignation."[1] That's a broad definition that encompasses anything that is cause for irritation. Yet the term has an important lineage in moral thought, where it has been used to identify a very basic and natural response that ends up being tuned to norms and

---

[1] This definition, from *The Merriam-Webster Dictionary* (New York: Pocket Books, 1974), is typical.

being the bearer of one of the defining messages of life among social animals: you're out of line.

Adam Smith, in *The Theory of Moral Sentiments* first published in 1759, saw resentment as "given us by nature for defence, and for defence only. . . . It prompts us to beat off the mischief which is attempted to be done to us, and to retaliate that which is already done; that the offender may be made to repent of this injustice, and that others, through fear of the like punishment, may be terrified from being guilty of the like offense."[2] These are the "remote effects," useful and indeed necessary, of a natural feeling that reacts to injury immediately in a very disagreeable way. Resentment is "harsh, jarring, and convulsive" for the one who feels it, and it prompts "mischief," that is, punishment, to the offender. Resentment is not attractive, and Smith views it as a feeling, the expression of which immediately inspires disgust, fear, or aversion in others, at least until they can find it properly based on injustice, "actions which tend to do real and positive hurt to some particular persons."[3] Smith is nonetheless keenly aware how broad our unreflective responses to "pain" in fact are. Not only do we share them with other animals, but we visit them even on "inanimated" objects that cause us distress: "We are angry, for a moment, even at the stone that hurts us. A child beats it, a dog barks at it, a cholerick man is apt to curse it." Smith believes that "the least reflection" corrects this "animal" sentiment; if the natural consequence of resentment is to punish, to visit pain in retaliation for pain as a rebuke and a warning, then "what has no feeling is a very improper object of revenge." We are prone to act as if even a stone, and, for that matter, what gives pleasure or pain generally, might be held to account for harming us, just as we are prone, Smith says, to resent external actions and their effects when it is in fact reasonable only to react so to what people intend. This "irregularity of sentiment," our responses being ready but rough and even unreasonable in their targets, works well on the whole, Smith thinks.[4] It is after all a terrifying world in which our mere designs and inner feelings – rather than our actions – would expose us to judgment and rebuke, and it is a safer world in which we learn, by being exposed to responsibility for unintended but harmful consequences of what we do, to care about the happiness of our fellows. Smith sees resentment as a chastising anger that

---

[2] Adam Smith, *The Theory of Moral Sentiments*, 104.

[3] See Smith, *The Theory of Moral Sentiments*: on the remote effects, 40; on the jarring quality, 44; on prompting mischief, 41; on provoking aversion in others, 43; on the proper target of "real and positive hurt," 104.

[4] On the irregularity, see Smith, *The Theory of Moral Sentiments*, 125.

can easily be indiscriminate, but that has a necessary and proper function in social life. Its irregularity is not as important as its indispensability. He is realistic about the fact that anything that pains us may provoke the agitated and retaliatory response of anger that he calls "resentment." Yet he sees that what is interesting to understand about "that animal resentment" is the central moral role it plays when its raw material is disciplined through the virtue of justice.[5]

A slightly older account of resentment, no doubt known to Smith, is Joseph Butler's. In a selection of sermons published in 1726, Butler seeks to understand for what end such a passion is part of our nature, that we might sort out its presumably positive "God-given" role from its abuses of malice and revenge. In his sermon "Upon Resentment," Joseph Butler contrasts "sudden anger," an instinctive reaction to opposition, hurt, or harm, with "deliberate anger or resentment." Resentment he then describes in this way:

> The natural object or occasion of settled resentment then being injury, as distinct from pain or loss; it is easy to see, that to prevent and to remedy such injury, and the miseries arising from it, is the end for which the passion was implanted in man. It is to be considered as a weapon, put into our hands by nature, against injury, injustice, and cruelty. . . . [6]

Anger, then, moves us to strike out against hurt and violence generally, including sometimes that hurt or harm which is wrongful; but resentment proper rises to combat actual or looming injustice; it is "connected with a sense of virtue and vice, or moral good and evil."[7] It is that "indignation raised by cruelty and injustice, and the desire of having it punished", which anyone *ought* to feel, and which Butler clearly thinks people mostly will feel. Butler viewed deliberate resentment, when neither groundless, extravagant, nor vengeful, as "one of the common bonds, by which society is held together; a fellow-feeling, which each individual has in behalf of the whole species, as well as of himself."[8] It is that by which "Men are

---

[5] See Smith, *The Theory of Moral Sentiments*: on animal resentment, 141; on the virtue of justice, 105.

[6] Joseph Butler, *Butler's Fifteen Sermons Preached at the Rolls Chapel and A Dissertation of the Nature of Virtue*, 76. A companion essay, "Upon Forgiveness of Injuries," argues that this naturally designed "remedy" for deficiencies of wisdom and virtue is a painful one whose satisfaction in revenge defeats its own aim of diminishing human misery. Even so, it is only the "excess and abuse" of resentment in malice and revenge, and not the emotion itself, that is to be avoided, 81.

[7] Butler, *Butler's Fifteen Sermons*, 74.

[8] Butler, *Butler's Fifteen Sermons*, 75.

plainly restrained from injuring their fellow-creatures by fear" when virtue would not suffice.[9] Butler, it appears, saw anger as taking different forms depending on its occasion and the reflectiveness of the one in whom it occurs. He does not deny that "sudden anger" may be the unthinking response to pain or harm that is in fact a wrong, nor does he deny that "resentment" proper can in fact rise toward others who cause "pain and inconvenience" only. But he labels the latter case among the "abuses" of resentment, and describes it as "monstrous." Like Smith, Butler sees that anger is the genus, but the species "resentment" needs to be understood and defended as our natural and indispensable equipment for moral life, sorted both from its purely natural defensive function and from occurrences based on erroneous judgments that bring this morally important kind of anger to bear where it does not belong. As in Smith, Butler's proper resentment serves justice by equipping us with enough "severity" to levy deserved punishment and inspire fear in would-be wrongdoers.[10]

These classic accounts of resentment are wonderfully rich and perceptive, but they are not the accounts of resentment most widely cited today by philosophers. A striking and dramatic account of resentment to which many philosophers now refer is that given by Jean Hampton in her co-authored dialogue with Jeffrie Murphy, *Forgiveness and Mercy*.[11] Hampton's account has shifted decisively away in some respects from the tradition that Butler and Smith represent. Gone is the idea that resentment is a "fellow-feeling"; resentment is about injuries to oneself, and resentment is an anxiously self-defensive response distinguished from "impersonal" indignation. Where Butler and Smith both saw a clear functional value for human individuals and society in our capacities and even our propensities for feeling resentment and sharing it, Hampton sees resentment as shabby, misguided, and prone to be self-defeating. In her individualistic and agonistic account of resentment, beings acutely aware of their "value and rank" are moved to anger by injuries to themselves that challenge their presumed standings, and are mobilized in fearful defense of the self-esteem these standings underwrite. Hampton paints resentment as a fearful and anxious defensive reaction based on dubious views that one's own human worth actually can be diminished by others' actions. This view has now become widely accepted and cited in discussions where resentment is a topic.

---

[9] Butler, *Butler's Fifteen Sermons*, 78.
[10] Butler, *Butler's Fifteen Sermons*, 77.
[11] Jeffrie G. Murphy and Jean Hampton, *Forgiveness and Mercy*.

My story about resentment is considerably less self-referring than Hampton's, and seeks to revive the important insight that resentment is among our most basic social emotions – the ones that attune us exquisitely to the extraordinarily diverse norms that structure shared life for very intelligent social animals. Resentment is a versatile and economical emotion that serves us in the negotiation of shared lives pervaded by *norms* and the *expectations* to which they give rise. Shared life requires mutually recognized boundaries and fairly reliable expectations based on them. Responses that both target violations that seem to threaten the authority of norms and that prompt violators to reconsider and to beware, or responses that signal the need for this sort of corrective action, are thus important. Resentment plays this sort of role.[12] Occasions of resentment are in fact more numerous and more varied than previous philosophers' discussions would suggest. What best explains the extent and variety of possible occasions for resentment is that resentment responds to perceived *threats to expectations based on norms* that are presumed to be shared in, or justly authoritative for, common life. In some cases resentment also responds to experienced *threats to one's standing* to assert or insist upon those norms.

Possibilities for resentment are many because the field across which intelligible resentments range is as broad as that of the behavior to which norms are taken to apply. There are norms for table manners and modes of dress and address, for eating and sleeping and having sex, for styles of life and every social interaction, as well as for justice and decent treatment among human beings. Human beings are indeed "normative animals," in Christine Korsgaard's phrase.[13] That is why resentment plays such an extensive role in our reactive repertoire. Resentment is an accusing anger. Resentment registers anger at violations that might threaten the authority of norms, or that put in question one's standing as a competent judge of operative norms. It targets others' intentional acts as the source of threat and tends to impugn the violators' motives and attitudes. As P. F. Strawson argued, resentment is a "reactive" attitude attributing responsibility.[14] But at the same time, as I will explain, resentment not only sends a message but invites a response: it seeks assurance from offenders or from others that they can be (or can again be) trusted to reaffirm and respect the

---

[12] See Frans de Waal's *Good Natured: The Origins of Right and Wrong in Human and Other Animals*, especially chs. 3 and 4, on responses in nonhuman social primates that look very much like gratitude, indignation, etc.

[13] Christine Korsgaard, *Sources of Normativity*, 47.

[14] P. F. Strawson, "Freedom and Resentment."

boundaries norms define, boundaries that offer protection against harm or affront, as well as the security of membership and reliable expectations in a community of shared normative judgment.

My account is in some ways in the spirit of Butler's. I endorse Butler's insight into the social and expressive aspects of resentment, his characterization of resentment as a "fellow feeling", and his understanding of its use as "a weapon" to warn and admonish wrongdoers. I take these points further and develop them differently. I hold that resentment extends to injuries or affronts to those one takes to be one's fellows, but that the fellowship is not exclusively a moral one. Resentment instead operates routinely to target threats to norms of many different kinds that are presumed shared and are seen as threatened by violations. Resentment can arise in response to an injury to someone with whom one feels a prior sense of connection, but the experience of resentment can also forge a sense of fellowship where it had not been felt before. This potency inherent in resentment is double edged. It can enlarge our sense of commonality in ways that are humanizing or in ways that are, or can become, malignant. Resentment can also be spurred by a perceived threat to one's sense of belonging with others in a community of judgment that shares standards. What is at stake in resentment is both the security of membership in a community of shared values and the comfort and protection it affords; this security, and our need for it, goes well beyond matters of morals and of justice to our senses of identity and order. These are things human beings require and they will react forcefully to what threatens these things. As Butler suggests, they will often threaten in return those who seem to threaten them. When Butler speaks of resentment as a "weapon" against injury, injustice, and cruelty, however, he not only draws the defended territory too narrowly – to encompass only moral wrongs – but he is too confident about our equal entitlements to bear and brandish emotional "arms," and to respond to threat with counterthreat. He is also sanguine that the effects of our doing so are likely to be uniform, or as we intend them to be, regardless of our situations and, in particular, our social positions in them.

My account is also in some ways in the spirit of Adam Smith. I like Smith's feeling for the broad and rough function of our natural anger at what hurts or harms us; he is unperturbed by the "irregularity" of our natural responses, which do not confine themselves neatly to their most reasonable occurrences. Sometimes we do resent it when the rain ruins our picnic, and human beings can feel resentment at those who are prettier, or smarter, or taller than they are. But as both Butler and Smith recognize, insofar as resentment naturally tends to (although it often does not result in) aggressive and retaliatory action, resentments of the rain or of someone's superior height are out of place, for there is no boundary to be marked or lesson to be taught in such cases by this always somewhat menacing emotional signal. My account, however, makes a particular kind of sense of some misplaced resentments. If resentment is centrally about threats to norms, then misplaced resentments can be seen as reflecting an improbable or erroneous, but not necessarily irrational, view of matters like the weather or the uneven distribution of certain valued natural attributes. This is an aid to understanding. To resent someone's superior height or intelligence is to view the differential in these respects between oneself and them (or even between them and other human beings generally) as somehow *unfair*; to resent the rain's spoiling your picnic is to view the rain as if it had been delivered by choice on your picnic by a careless or unfriendly *agency*. Some people actually have beliefs like this, but most of us don't. Those who don't are quickly able, as Smith said, to see that while frustration, annoyance, irritation, or exasperation may well be understandable, these are case where resentment does not fit, at least if we continue to talk about resentment as an anger that goes to a sense of being *wronged*.

People can, however, resent a process, which is something people design and carry out; and people can resent states of affairs, such as being paid too little, which is also something that results from the choices and actions, as well as the indifference or inattention, of other human beings. When I resent my neighbor's having a car that I can't afford, the case is more interesting. It might be that I resent the fact that he makes so much more money than I, even though *he doesn't deserve it*. If so there's a norm lurking in there somewhere pretty close to the surface. But if I resent him because seeing his fancy car ruins my day as I get into my humbler one, then unless I think he bought the car in order to make me feel bad, this case is perhaps more like that of the rainy picnic – why should things happen that make me feel bad? In cases like that of the neighbor, however, it is most likely that attitudes – envy, frustration, dislike, and feelings of failure – are tangled together in a somewhat inarticulate mass with beliefs about who deserves what and how the world, or even just my world, should be. Some of our resentments are inscrutable because our beliefs and feelings are both opaque and confused.

My analysis allows us to ask the right questions about these cases, and so to identify points of confusion. My analysis is also more helpfully revealing about misplaced or unjustified resentments that are not trivial or fanciful.

I diverge significantly from those earlier authors in taking much more seriously than they do resentments that rise to perceived breaches that are not matters of injustice or immorality but which threaten the norms that nonetheless make social life secure. These cases are too routine to be just "irregular" in Smith's sense, much less "monstrous" in Butler's. People do resent loads of things that others do that are not in any obvious way, or in any way at all, moral matters. But they are ones that bear on social order, on who is judge and enforcer of that order, and on who can feel at home in it.

I begin my discussion with Hampton's colorful and influential contemporary view, using limitations in Hampton's account to draw out features of my own analysis. To be clear at the outset: I don't take Hampton (or Butler or Smith) to be attempting an account of necessary and sufficient conditions of resentment, nor do I attempt one. I take it that Hampton's account, as does my own, aims at a "normal form" characterization of a syndrome of feelings and expressions that in certain kinds of contexts is likely to be identified as resentment. I believe the grammar of the terms for emotion is somewhat rough and loose. This means that not much is settled simply by butting intuitions about individual cases against one another. Our vocabularies for emotion are not so neatly regimented, and whether someone is willing to call one scenario or another a case of resentment is not as significant as the reasons why we are inclined to describe cases that way or some other way. I want to achieve in the way of description a characterization that usefully covers the *widest* class of common cases and sheds light on why contested examples cause disagreement. In the sphere of explanation, I want an account that makes sense of the roles played in our shared lives by the experience and expression of the emotion, and why this sort of emotional reaction is so common.

Aside from a clearer understanding of what resentment is, though, in the end we want to know when resentment is justified, and when it deserves to receive the satisfaction that it seeks – reassurance that the norms threatened are indeed authoritative and that the resenter is indeed a member in good standing and a competent judge within the community that takes these norms seriously. We want to know when we ourselves, or others in response to us, should take our resentment seriously and whether and how we or they should respond. It might seem that resentment is justified only when the norms it rises to defend are morally necessary or, at any rate, morally acceptable ones, and that we should take resentment seriously only in those cases. In cases where norms are not morally significant or even morally acceptable, on this view, resentments should be ignored, corrected, or admonished. This looks like a pleasingly simple approach. It is actually not as simple as it seems, and it is not, I think, the wisest approach. The questions of when resentment is justified and when we should take it seriously are distinct, and require separate thought. Each question is more complex than it appears. We have reason to care about deep resentments and more especially about widely diffused resentments even when they are *not* well founded.

Resentments can signal fissures in the social body and breaks in people's attachments to it and to each other. Resentments are not only revealing of normative commitments and presumptions of community and membership, but they are also attitudes that press us toward aggressive and combative responses. As a result resentments can be exploited with disastrous results. While resentments on my account signal perceived threats to normative order and membership, they can also be used as a basis for identity and order, defined by what "we" are *not*. Smith saw resentment in one person as naturally repulsive to others, but resentments can also attract those who feel alienated from a normative community and who are looking for others who are alienated in similar ways. But in order to get to these conclusions I need to tell a different story about the nature and operation of resentment.

Getting Resentment in Broader View

For Jean Hampton: "Resentment is an emotion whose object is the defiant reaffirmation of one's rank and value in the face of treatment calling them into question in one's own mind."[15] On her view, resentment serves as at once a protest and a defense. The occasion of resentment for Hampton is "being wronged," which is not only being damaged or hurt, but being wronged in a way that "insults" or is "disrespectful of" one's worth, however that is conceived (for example as relative or absolute, fixed or variable).[16] "Resentment," she says, "is an emotion which reflects their judgment that the harmful treatment they experienced should not have been intentionally inflicted on them by their assailants insofar as it is *not* appropriate given their value and rank."[17] A resentful victim of wrongdoing is thus *angry* – more particularly "defiant" or "battling" against the lower standing imputed to him or her by the culpably disrespectful

---

[15] Murphy and Hampton, *Forgiveness and Mercy*, 59–60.
[16] On insult and disrespect, Murphy and Hampton, *Forgiveness and Mercy*, 44, 52.
[17] Murphy and Hampton, *Forgiveness and Mercy*, 54.

harming. But at the heart of resentment Hampton sees something defensive in another sense; she believes its angry defiance reveals a *fear*. It is a fear that the offender is right to think that the victim's worth *is* as implied in the insulting treatment, or that it is *permissible* to lower the victim in rank by means of such an action ("putting her in her place").[18] So resentment combines *anger* and *fear*.

Hampton draws a distinction between resentment and indignation, claiming that indignation is an impersonal anger at a challenge to "someone's value," which threatens a standard of value, whereas resentment is personal anger and defends the self "against the action's attack on one's self-esteem" and is "normally an emotion experienced only by the one who has been harmed."[19] One's self-esteem is threatened by the possibility that the action has revealed that one is, or has now been made, lower in rank or value than one was or had assumed one was.

So, for her, the occasion of resentment is being culpably wronged. The constitutive belief in resentment is that one's deserved or true rank and value have been impugned or imperiled. The feeling of resentment embodies anger at insult and its implications, and fear that one's status is lowered or one's diminished status is revealed. The aim of resentment is to defend and protect self-esteem.

But Hampton's view of resentment is narrow in several ways. I begin with her view in order to get resentment into a broader context. First, consider Hampton's limitation of resentment to reactions in defense of oneself when it is oneself who is wronged. This seems implausibly restrictive, for we commonly enough speak of resentment at the way others are treated or looked at, and it is not that these others must be ones with whom we have personal connections or prior identification. One can, looking on, resent a sales clerk's rude treatment of a shabbily dressed person, the condescension of a teacher to a girl in a physics class, or the self-congratulatory attitude of a wealthy political candidate discussing problems of "the poor," when these actions involve or refer to strangers or groups to which one does not belong. Further, the distinction Hampton makes between supposedly impersonal indignation and allegedly personal resentment is unconvincing. Diners whose suppers are badly served or employees who fail to receive their anticipated bonuses may be the very

---

[18] Murphy and Hampton, *Forgiveness and Mercy*, 57–58.

[19] Murphy and Hampton, *Forgiveness and Mercy*, 56. See 56, n. 16, for Hampton's comment that there are exceptions that prove the rule. Another account that makes injuries to oneself the core of resentment is William E. Young, "Resentment and Impartiality."

type of the indignant individual. So indignation is quite commonly a reaction to injuries to oneself taken very personally indeed, while resentment can just as well take the cause of others to heart. Resentment and indignation, in fact, may not be distinct emotions; in the modern but older usage of Butler or Smith, the two are not distinguished and the terms are used interchangeably, as when Butler speaks of resentment as "the indignation raised by cruelty and injustice." But even without settling the precise nature of the difference between indignation and resentment, I think there are enough examples to confute the alignment of resentment and indignation respectively with what is "personal" and "impersonal," or what concerns "self" and "other." No doubt to resent something is to "take it personally," but the sense in which this is true remains to be spelled out.

Hampton wants to see resentment and indignation as distinct but parallel, with resentment as the personal version and indignation as the impersonal version of angry *fear* at wrongdoing. But this doesn't seem to work either, for straightforward cases of indignation don't seem to be marked by the fearfulness that Hampton associates with resentment. The indignant person is characteristically the picture of confident or unreserved righteousness. For that matter, not all cases of resentment seem to involve fear. A gentleman spoiling for a fight may coolly brandish his resentment at an insult as a provocation to a contest – a duel, say – he has little fear of losing. A dominating husband may resent and expressly avow resentment of his wife's wage-earning, confidently and correctly surmising that the fact of his resentment will cause her to quit her job.

Yet the term "resentment" seems tinged for many people with associations of someone cringing or sulking in gnawing and roiling anger that is tamped down or turned inward, as if out of fear. I have no doubt that Nietzsche's memorable creation of the image of *ressentiment* – a kind of seething angry envy of the powerful by the powerless, who must nonetheless hang back in their despicable weakness – has had an impact, and not only on philosophers. But it is well to remember that Nietzsche is not talking about resentment in any commonplace sense. He coins a novel term of art to advance an imaginative scenario in which morality itself emerges as a kind of brilliant trick of the weak, who remain nonetheless despicable in their weakness. The fictional Nietzschian drama is propelled by what we would more usually describe as *envy* of the superiority of the strong.[20]

[20] See R. Jay Wallace, *Responsibility and the Moral Sentiments*, 246–47, for a succinct discussion of why Nietzschean *ressentiment* is not the same as resentment. Nietzsche's own discussion is in his *Genealogy of Morals*.

I will return to some ways that resentment can be inflected by envy or fear, as also by disgust or bitterness, and to some reasons why resentment is apt to be differently inflected for those in positions of relative weakness. But the examples given of the insulted but confident gentleman or the successfully dominating but irritated husband, as well as a very broad array of cases of *resentment at offense*, suggest a different explanation of what prompts resentment. What is central to resentment on this explanation is a perceived *threat*, whether or not one has reason to fear what is threatened, and whether or not one in fact does fear it. A threat suggests a prospect of damage to or loss of something valued, and people can get *angry* at the suggestion that someone is inclined to act in a way that might damage or get in the way of what they count on or deem important, even if they have no fear of heading off the threat. The sometimes in-turned or tamped quality of resentment in many cases may have more to do with the position the resenting one is in: one is not always in a position to give forthright expression to one's anger at a perceived threat. The nature of the *display* of this kind of anger is sensitive to the *position* – situational, emotional, social, institutional – one is in to show how one feels, or to anticipate a desired response to that display.[21]

Another questionable claim in Hampton's account is that resentment is a strategy aimed at defending self-esteem (or self-respect, terms she uses interchangeably in this context). This seems to require that a resenting person has some modicum of self-esteem to defend. She says "the ability to feel resentment following a wrong-doing depends upon one's having enough sense of one's own worth to believe that the treatment is inappropriate and worthy of protest."[22] Similarly, Jeffrie Murphy, her interlocutor in *Forgiveness and Mercy*, holds expressly that resentment defends one's self-respect, and that proper self-respect is essentially tied to resentment, so that "a person who does not resent moral injuries done to him ... is

---

[21] Many emotional expressions are sensitive to position in this way, and this is one of the complications of tracking the grammar of emotion concepts. One innovative and searching discussion of the issue of identifying emotions and of emotions commonly identified is Sue Campbell's *Interpreting the Personal: Expression and the Formation of Feelings*. Campbell argues that expression individuates feelings, with the important consequence that public uptake controls possibilities of expression. See also María Lugones's essay "Hard-to-Handle Anger" on the communicative dimensions of anger and the difference it makes whether one expresses anger from a position of social strength or one of oppression or marginality. For my discussion of the expressive, position-sensitive, synergistic character of emotions, and the contributions of the specifically feminist literature, see Margaret Urban Walker, "Moral Psychology."

[22] Murphy and Hampton, *Forgiveness and Mercy*, 55.

almost necessarily a person lacking in self-respect."[23] Yet there is a lot of everyday evidence that people need not hold themselves highly, indeed need not respect or esteem themselves at a basically decent level, to be great resenters. Self-abasing flatterers, cringing self-despisers, and miserable sell-outs, or people beaten down or those consumed with self-hatred of their powerlessness, such people are quite capable of resentments, including resentment of those to whom they self-abasingly bow, or of others who maintain dignity or integrity under circumstances similar to their own. Unless one wants to award the honorific "self-respect" to anyone who won't bridle at *something*, it seems resentment need not imply self-respect in even a modestly positive sense. On the other hand, while resentment is possible and common for those who fail to respect themselves, those who enjoy robust self-respect may be magnanimous, or respond with confidence or determination rather than resentment, even when they are themselves treated ill or are the object of neglect or undeserved indifference. It does not seem, then, that self-respect is either necessary or sufficient for experiencing resentment when threatened, or even when injured or affronted.

Finally, it is questionable to narrow the response of resentment to harmful and insulting treatment intentionally inflicted. This description calls up vivid images of abusive or disrespectful treatment that it would make one wince to observe, as well as to suffer. Cases like this surely merit resentment if any do. But this identification of occasions for resentment with damage and injury both pushes aside the pervasiveness of resentment in everyday life, and tends, misleadingly, to moralize it. Resentment is often provoked by the good, generous, fair, or even simply decent treatment of others, when the resentful one feels convinced that she would not have fared as well, or perhaps remembers an instance in which she did not; or when she thinks that it is she and people like her, and not those others, who are entitled to the treatment or rewards in question. And there is also the familiar case of charged and evident resentment felt in response to those perceived as exceeding their places, prerogatives, and authority, those who are "uppity," "arrogant," or "too big for their britches." These instances seem to illustrate that it can be just as threatening to see some others claim respect and receive good or dignifying treatment as it is to see oneself shown to the lower rung of the status ladder. More surprising, perhaps, is the extent to which resentment arises at the behavior of others that simply upsets established patterns and expectations. My objection to

[23] Murphy and Hampton, *Forgiveness and Mercy*, 16.

Hampton's view is not that she has not identified, and explored insight-fully, the ways resentment results from perceived injuries that are insults to status (her "rank and value"). My objection is that she has ignored the broader field in which being demeaned by being treated below one's status is *one* kind of occasion for resentment, which can be placed within a more general account.

Resentment and Threat

Resentment is best explained as a defensive response of anger (and in some, but not all, cases fear or other negative feelings) to others' inten-tional actions perceived as violating boundaries defined by norms and threatening the authority, or the resenter's presumption of the authority, of those norms in so doing.[24] Sometimes the violation is an actual injury. Without slighting in the least how much actual injury matters, even in cases of injury it is not only the harm caused by it but also the sense of *wrongfulness* of the behavior causing the harm that is characteristic of resentment. In this, resentment is distinct from other kinds of anger that may arise from frustration or thwarting that need not issue from another human agent, or that can be directed at human agents whose motives we do not impugn. The wrong is defined by some supposed rule or stan-dard, a norm. The constitutive belief is: they *should not* have acted in that way. P. F. Strawson points out that the pain may be as unpleasant in a case where someone treads on my hand accidentally as when one does so out of contempt, but it is that latter case that is grounds for resent-ment, because of "the very great importance we attach to the attitudes and intentions toward us of other human beings."[25] But before we get so far as attitudes and intentions, notice how various are perceived wrongs to which resentment is a response.

Resentment is occasioned not only by *harms* and *losses*, as when one is assaulted, cheated, made to suffer, or forcibly relieved of one's goods, but also by cases in which some ride free or manipulatively profit in excess ways from roles, systems, or cooperative practices in which others comply without extra profit; call these *exploitations*.[26] Resentment can also be provoked by someone assuming a position or being treated as entitled to

---

[24] I thank William Galston for pressing me to clarify the point that it's not the violation only, but the sense that the violation is a threat that is central to my account.

[25] Strawson, "Freedom and Resentment," 75.

[26] Jeffrie Murphy includes unfair advantage in his description of resentment in Murphy and Hampton, *Forgiveness and Mercy*, 16.

a status that disturbs a presumed status ordering; call these *improprieties.* If the disturbance makes the resenter's position or status lower or less valuable than it had been or that he or she believed it to be, we might call these *demotions.* Then there are cases in which one endures treatment beneath one's proper status – *slights.* Finally, resentment is often enough prompted by rule-breaking, norm-violating, or simply behavior seen as "out of bounds," even without evident profit to the violator or harm or expense to others; call these *offenses.* These are things "not done," or "unacceptable." Harms, losses, exploitations, improprieties, demotions, and slights may be my own or others, and may inspire resentment on my own or on others' behalf. Offenses may be apparently victimless social fouls.

The category of offenses is vast, but significant not only for that reason. It reveals something about what can occasion resentment, and so about what can be at issue in it. People seethe and prickle with resentment at those who laugh too loud, speak too freely, or fail to say "please" or "thank you," or utter other conventional formulas; at fashion fads, the piercing of body parts (now, other than ears), and weird haircuts;[27] at the yelps of other people's children, at people's sitting closer on a bench or bus than they must; and the list goes on and on. One explanation of many of these "offending" occasions, which is given by William Miller, is the enormous social importance of "disattendability." This is explored so acutely by sociologist Erving Goffman, who notes that what is ordinary, routine, and normal generates "normative expectations" to which we hold people accountable, if only in the medium of such negative feelings as disgust, alarm, pity, contempt, embarrassment – and, of course, resentment.[28] Cases of offense or affront are revealing, for what we see in them is not a harm or injury in the usual sense, but an occurrence construed as a threat

[27] Alan Gibbard pointed out: "Weird haircuts...make people angry, regularly and normally," although "our anger is mistaken," in *Wise Choices, Apt Feelings: A Theory of Normative Judgment,* 187. Yet it would seem if this kind of "offense" really is "regular and normal" that there is some description under which it is not *just* a mistake.

[28] William Ian Miller, *The Anatomy of Disgust,* 198–99. Miller doesn't mention resentment in this passage, although a good deal of what he says about the social valence of disgust and contempt are relevant to resentment as well. Civil disattendability shades off rather too readily into norms of "respectability" that load hierarchical social arrangements, sheer prejudice, and socially sanctioned contempt for and exclusion of certain groups or their "ways" from specific social locales. See Iris M. Young, *Justice and the Politics of Difference,* 136–41, on the oppressive force of "respectability." See also Susan Wendell, *The Rejected Body,* on the situation of those with some kinds of disabilities who are not disattendable to the "normal."

to either a norm or a familiar pattern imbued with some prescriptive force by the perceiver.

In all cases of resentment it seems we are angry because (we think) we or others are injured or because we are (we think justifiably) affronted by the actions of some who have gotten out of bounds. Someone has made free with what we thought were the rules, crossed boundaries we supposed intact, ignored claims we believed authoritative, or rendered idle or ridiculous our hope that things will go on in any of the many ways we believe they should. The sense of threat in resentment, as Strawson claimed, tends to assume the agent's apparent malice or indifference; we suppose he or she might have shown the good will, attention, due care, respect, or understanding that would have led to proper behavior. In many cases the proper will, care, or attitude is what we both believed was due and expected to be shown; in some, our normative expectations are more hopeful than trusting, and we expect people *to* do the correct thing even when we do not have the expectation *that* they are likely to do so. In all cases, we must think that those we resent *could* have behaved properly when they did not. As Strawson noted, resentment is a feeling that impugns the agent and imputes responsibility, and so culpability, for some kind of wrong.

Resentment arises to meet a threat. The perceived violation of the presumed norm must suggest the need for, or a prudent concern for, defense. It suggests this to someone in particular on a particular occasion when a norm is transgressed; the reason why the violation of a norm is found to be threatening need not be the same in every case. If a norm is thought to be very central and important, overt violation or noncompliance might strike one as revealing that the violator is malicious, impudent, or shockingly careless. The violator may be seen as worse than irresponsible, and may appear to be deliberately testing limits or making a bold display, something that requires to be checked. Even if the norm concerns nothing earth-shaking, one may still worry about the potential of careless transgressions to lead to progressive disorder in some area where good order is comforting. People resent sloppy table manners or modes of dress. If the norm's authority is in question, or if failure to respond decisively may seem to put it in question, violations may seem to require clear rebuke lest the norm lose what force it has. Improper or indecent dress touches sensitivities in many people about the general state of mutual courtesy and respect among people sharing public spaces. Where the authority of the norm is a high-stakes matter, any hint of impunity of violators may seem to need a sharp and decisive response. The argument most ardently and angrily offered against amnesties for political violence is that a "culture of impunity" invites the view that some of society's most basic protective norms are not taken seriously.

Individuals may also be differently sensitive to the transgression of norms or especially sensitive to the transgression of particular norms. Individuals may be more rigid or authoritarian in general, or more worried about or passionately committed to particular kinds of order. Finally, when one resents another's going out of bounds, one is presuming, in effect deriving one's own authority to pass judgment from, the shared recognition of the norm in play. For this reason, violations can also threaten the resentful perceiver's sense of authority and competence as a judge of what "is done" or "goes" or is acceptable "among us." If one's resentment at transgression is not shared or its eliciting violation is not recognized by others as such, there is reason for the resenter to worry whether the shared standards are as she believes, or whether it is she who is somehow out of step. There is also resentment that is defiant in its understanding that the norms widely shared are wrong, or that they exclude or demean one; but if one is uncertain about whether one is "defensive" or "paranoid" in resenting some of the conduct of others, one is uncertain of one's place as a judge.[29]

In cases of direct injury and insult, one is perhaps less likely to be wrong in the judgment that something unacceptable has occurred, although actions are always open to reinterpretation of motive and meaning. The case of offenses, however, is again revealing and instructive. In the case of offenses, many a resented behavior is seen as "out of bounds," not only in the absence of any actual injury, and even when the behavior is in no apparent way "aimed" at the one who resents it, but also when ill intent by the agent is undetectable by reasonable observers. These are the cases in which as onlookers we feel inclined to say to someone wrought up with resentment, "What's it to you?" This question is exactly the right one, for it requests an interpretation that specifies at least the transgression (what is wrong here, which may not be obvious to others) if not the faulty attitude it may seem to embody. One common resentful response, however, is also apt: "Who do they think they are to . . . ?" This goes to the heart of the

---

[29] Feminists and race theorists have explored forms of "outlaw" and uncertain anger extensively. For a selection, see Marilyn Frye, "A Note on Anger," in *The Politics of Reality*; Alison M. Jaggar, "Love and Knowledge: Emotion in Feminist Epistemology"; Elizabeth V. Spelman, "Anger and Insubordination"; Naomi Scheman, "Anger and the Politics of Naming"; Diana Meyers, "Emotion and Heterodox Moral Perception: An Essay in Moral Social Psychology"; Lugones, "Hard-to-Handle Anger."

matter of resentment. The offender is taken to be "thinking" that he or she is exempt from some requirement he or she must or ought to know applies. Resentment carries this implication of a faulty attitude on the actor's part.

This is a danger inherent in resentment. We may not have independent reasons to believe people bear us ill will or are indifferent or careless when we find that what they do threatens our sense of a prevailing order, but it is very easy, and it seems very common, to translate one's own sense of threat back into a presumption of fault or malice in the intentions of others. Resentment embodies a sense, or an implicit and presumptive imputation, of fault that can be difficult to dislodge, and one gripped by resentment may be far more disposed to *find* fault in others than to question whether his or her own resentment might be misplaced or exaggerated. And it is also true that when people resent hearing "foreign" languages spoken, or encountering people of racial or ethnic groups other than theirs in their neighborhood, or seeing evidence of gay and lesbian households, there is usually a prior belief that some kinds of people aren't to be trusted or accepted to begin with, and the fact that people like that are intruding where they don't belong is additional evidence of their inappropriate presumption or aggressiveness. Those who are already resented are likely to arouse yet more resentment for behaving as if they don't know – and shouldn't they? – that they aren't the kind who belong or whose ways of living are unacceptable.

Whether or not it is correct in particular cases to infer that an agent's attitude is faulty, the central matter of resentment is an injury or affront that is threatening in disappointing expectations, or dimming or dashing hopes for others' conduct that in some sense we think we had a "right" to.[30] The best explanation of that "right" is the belief in an operative norm of *some* kind, although *not* necessarily a moral norm. The huge category of resented offenses alone suggests that resentment should not be "moralized." What threatens is the *license* taken by some with what others of us take to be the operating understandings, limits, or rules. In the case of injury or cruelty, for example, the sense of threat is urgent because actual harm is the result of an offender's failure to abide by or to be restrained by a norm, and more such harm might be forthcoming.

---

[30] Wallace, in *Responsibility and the Moral Sentiments,* develops a somewhat similar view about resentment reflecting expectations, in the context of developing a view of responsibility with affinities to Strawson. See especially ch. 2 and app. 1. My own view of normative expectations as more or less trusting or more or less hopeful were developed in Chapters 2 and 3.

Or, if someone receives treatment inappropriate to his kind in a system carefully arranged around appropriate responses to kinds of people, that rankles but also threatens those faithful to that system: where will this breakdown of order lead? This is as true when a murderer goes free on a technicality as when a member of a despised racial group is treated with respect.

The threat prompting resentment, made fully explicit, is of *license with impunity*. The transgression announces a possibility that is at least annoying, often alarming, or even fearsome, a possibility that might persist unless something forecloses it. So the fact of the transgression puts in question, even threatens, the confidence, trust, assurance, or hope that has allowed one to be unconcerned about such injuries or affronts, or unburdened by their unsettling implications. This is the sense in which we "take personally" what we resent. It is not that what we resent necessarily is an injury or insult *to us*, or even an affront aimed specifically *at us*. Rather, transgressions against boundaries cause us concern when they announce the possibility of something we might have to reckon with, or a factor that throws us uncomfortably out of our normative expectations, moral and otherwise, or undermines our ability to assert with confidence what and where certain social, moral, or interpersonal boundaries lie. In that threat lies a *potential* for fear, as for other negative feelings, that can flavor resentment or compound it.[31]

Resentment is itself a "weapon" (using Butler's image) – an unpleasant, accusing, and potentially threatening response – when expressed overtly at the offender. When apparent to others, it is also, to continue the image, a kind of "call to arms." Where there is opportunity and ability to get transgressors back within bounds, or to impose some corrective action on them, or at the very least to summon support from others for a clear repudiation of what transgressors have done, resentment may be relieved as threat is diminished. It is something at least if the rules and

---

[31] Pamela Hieronymi, "Articulating an Uncompromising Forgiveness," argues: "*resentment protests a past action that persists as a present threat.* . . . a past wrong against you, standing in your history without apology, atonement, retribution, punishment, restitution, condemnation, or anything else that might recognize it as *wrong*, makes a claim. It says, in effect, you can be treated this way, and that such treatment is acceptable. That – that claim – is what you resent. It poses a threat. In resenting it, you challenge it. If there is nothing else that would mark out that event as wrong, there is at least your resentment. And so resentment can be understood as a protest" (546, emphasis in the original). Hieronymi nicely unpacks the "statement" that an injury makes, but fails to expand the analysis to threats to the authority of norms more broadly; her account of resentment, like many others, takes an injury to one's self to be the necessary occasion of resentment.

boundaries are reiterated, even if the individual offenders go unpunished and are no longer trustworthy. It is better, of course, if we can be assured that the punitive treatment (formal or informal) of transgressors serves as an informative and possibly deterring example to others. It is best of all if those who have broken the rules can actually be brought to reaffirm their subscription to them. Yet often the opportunity or ability to correct offenders or to inflict reprisals on them is uncertain or unavailable. Worse, sometimes repudiation is not forthcoming from any others, or from enough others, or from others with authority: they, or those who matter, don't care. Then the threat of license with impunity is fulfilled. In such cases, there is a basis for resentment at transgression to turn disgusted, bitter, envious, shamed, or fearful.

Resentment can be *disgusted*, for example, in a case where one has ceased to be surprised at certain goings on, and has given up any thought that one can forestall their occurrence or defend against them.[32] Consider the situation of a lone female office clerk in a welding shop who has failed to become inured to pin-up calendars and continuing sexual insults and challenges. Though she no longer rises to the bait emotionally she might still disapprove of her co-workers' conduct. She might, without any longer experiencing resentment, continue to disapprove of her co-workers' conduct and continue to believe that the norms that define it as rude, insulting, and hostile are valid, and that her co-workers know very well that what they do is at least some of these things. But if she still *resents* these goings on – if she still gets angry about the wrong these goings on inflict on her, or on women, and does not merely shrug and think "it's not supposed to be that way, but who can do anything about it?" – her resentment reveals that she continues, quite precisely, to "take it personally." The wrongfulness of her co-workers' behavior gets a grip on her and moves her emotionally and motivationally in the direction of her own hostile display – a kind of accusing anger that puts her in the expressive position of rebuking them. Her resentment, whether recognizably displayed or masked, *is* that rebuke.

Even if she feels resentment, of course, she might not show it. While resentment disposes her to show her anger in overt and confrontationally angry displays, actually showing anger in her situation may not be a sane or safe option. She may know this leads to escalation or attracts reprisals. She may then find her anger takes the form of a withdrawal or recoil in disgust

---

[32] Norvin Richards pointed out to me the important possibility of disgusted resentment, where one resents what one nonetheless fully expected.

from the situation. She might begin to experience her co-workers to some extent as a kind of noxious substance in the environment, rather than as fully fellow agents who can and should be confronted with their knowing misbehavior; she may also experience self-disgust at her own sense of powerlessness or her failure to recruit others to negative judgment or rectifying action. Her resentment may mingle with disgust, or disgust may simply replace it. Her resentment itself may move her in directions that in turn provoke other feelings that either modify the expression and course of the resentment, or perhaps cause resentment to give way to other, less stressful, costly, or defensive feelings, where active resistance isn't going anywhere.[33]

Bitter resentment might similarly involve scenarios in which one cannot stop blaming some others for failing to supply at least a community of confirming judgment, if not actual protection from injuries or affronts that one cannot or will not "learn to accept." Sometimes people are supposed to accept the treatment they protest, and sometimes they are supposed to accept the futility of protesting that treatment. People are called "bitter" who can't seem to do this. They can't stop complaining, and others see them as stuck in accusation that is not (in the eye of the beholder) going to change anything. Those who find themselves increasingly isolated, justly or not, in their accusation may find resentment acquires a brittle or hardened quality, less an accusing display than a kind of stifled protest that already anticipates it will be ignored or refused by others.[34]

Resentment may mingle with *envy* when one repudiates what others do, but at the same time wishes one had the power, nerve, or panache to get away oneself with what they do. This is the variation on resentment that Nietzsche's *ressentiment* captures and inflates to mythic proportions. But while envious resentment (or resentful envy) is real, it would be a

[33] The interaction and synergy of emotions in context is a topic that deserves more treatment, especially as it may highlight the rather loose grammar of concepts for emotion and some consequently fuzzy individuation of emotions. When does one emotion precipitate another, or modulate another, or emerge as a kind of transformation of another? Contempt, for example, might come about in some instances as a transformation of resentment when being mobilized in anger becomes exhausting. One might start resentful and then (as in the hostile sexist work environment) become resentfully disgusted, but finally become disgusted to the point where one depersonalizes and objectifies the unruly offenders. Then a kind of contemptuous revulsion might emerge that sees its objects as trivial or low, not as something to defend against and call to account so much as something to scorn or recoil from.

[34] Two insightful discussions of bitterness are found in Campbell's *Interpreting the Personal*, pp. 167–72, and Lynne McFall's "What's Wrong With Bitterness?"

mistake to think that all resentment involves envy. That would be to deny that anyone ever burns with anger at offense or wrongdoing without actually, perhaps secretly or unconsciously, wishing that one could get away with what wrongdoers do, or could themselves have the attributes that make wrongdoers capable of violating norms. Where is the envy when one resents bad service in a restaurant where everyone is badly served? Do I envy someone with terrible table manners, or a neighbor whose dog barks all night, even as I resent their behavior or negligence? Many people associate resentment with envy, I believe, not because resentment involves or implies envy, but because envy of another can easily lead to resentment, if the train of thought slips from "I wish I had what she has" to "It's not right that she has what she has" or "It's unfair that she has what I do not." If it really *is* unfair, for example, that I got the raise and promotion that you felt you had earned and I had not, then there is likely to be envy and resentment both.

Resentment might trigger *shame* when one wants to rebuke someone's behavior by showing the anger one feels at its impropriety but finds one lacks "the nerve" to do so because one is too timid or prudent or ingratiating. One might then see oneself as something – a coward, a toady, a brown-nose, or pussyfooter – that one feels it is lowly to be. Shame accompanying resentment is more poignant, though, where one is invisible or so negligible in others' eyes that the protest one's resentment reveals is beneath the notice or concern of others. When one's anger at wrong or offense is ignored, sloughed off, or laughed at, one is either discredited as a judge or not seen as someone with enough status to embody communal authority. It is easy to see how shamed resentment could breed envy: the miserably treated servant might rather be the tyrannical master, if those are the only positions available in certain social worlds. But it would be dangerous to assume that those oppressed or slighted necessarily yearn to turn the tables; often, they want to overturn those particular tables and stand on level ground in future relations.

On my account of resentment, when people cease to resent things they once resented it reveals some kind of resignation, a kind of "normative surrender." This might involve ceasing to believe that a norm is valid, or losing expectations that a valid norm will be honored and letting go of a personal stake in that norm. It might involve losing conviction that one is in a position to assert shared norms, or at least certain ones, with any effect. Yet people can continue to resent certain behavior even as they recognize that their normative investment is neither shared nor enforceable (at least locally), for example, someone of a despised and powerless group who still seethes with resentment at disrespectful treatment. Where resentment abides, it preserves and expresses a personal "normative stake," an insistence on the validity and importance of a norm, a repudiation of the prevailing situation of dereliction or insouciance, and so a continuing normative protest of what exists in favor of what should be. They continue to take it personally.

Resentment can also be *fearful*. The association of resentment with fear is common, as noted above, and with reason. Fear comes in with resentment especially in cases of standing or passing vulnerability and inadequate or unreliable defense. When one does not expect one's resentment to constitute an effective accusing and restraining signal, one might be as much afraid as angry at ill treatment. Worse, in some weak positions, one might fear that one has invited additional harm or threat for having *shown* resentment – a kind of anger – in response to the original harm or offense. Fearful (and perhaps disgusted or bitter) resentment can involve *second-order fear*. It is bad to be injured or affronted, so to be under threat of, even in fear of, further injury or affront because what protected you from it is destroyed, ineffective, or in doubt. It is worse to see no way to re-establish the security the norm was supposed to provide, for now you are afraid that you are going to have to be afraid, to live in fear, without assurance or protection of a community of shared boundaries that one's fellows are willing to assert and enforce both with you and for you. Second-order fear is understandable in continuing situations of weakness, including situations of continuing subordination by role or status. Members of oppressed, stigmatized, or despised groups are vulnerable in such ways that are ongoing, across many social situations and encounters. Second-order fear might be one of the conditions in which resentment assumes a "roiling" or "gnawing" quality, an accusing anger that can't, because it must not, get "out" expressively.

Resentment that is fearful feeds on exposure to injury in virtue of one's demonstrated vulnerability, or exposure to affront in view of the apparently negligible importance or authority of one's expectations or hopes. Yet I have argued that even resentment that is *not* fearful turns on a sense of *threat*. This suggests an explanation of why some injuries to others can excite resentment whether or not one "identifies" with those injured or offended. Indeed, it explains why the perception of another's being injured or affronted can sometimes *prompt* identification with that person that was not there to begin with. In some cases the breach of bounds that reveals the vulnerability of others causes us to recognize that we, too, are exposed; and so, that we have something in common with them. If what threatens us is license with impunity, then those upon whom objectionable action is visited are not the only ones threatened, for the offender who will go beyond bounds could be a future menace or a dangerous example to others. In the case of victimless offense to presumed standards, the authority of the standards we rely on is jeopardized, and our confidence in proceeding on the basis of these standards, or even a hope that these standards will be respected, is undermined. In other cases we may feel our group membership threatened, either because we are no longer sure that our community is one with operative standards we can accept or respect, or because we feel defeated in our attempt to grasp and apply standards that are operative. Is a community that harbors or tolerates this sort of thing really one I can call *mine?* Or, is my competence as a judge or the authority of the standards that I assume are common put in question here? Am I "out of it"? There are significant resentments of alienation and marginality, in which one's protest simply places one outside serious consideration: one is an old fogie, a wacko, a malcontent, a whiner, a bitch.

Resentment as Moral Address

To come back to the central point, whether or not resentment is further driven or infused by other feelings, it is a kind of *accusing anger at something done.* The anger is directed at the doer of what is out of bounds with the implication that the doer knows, or ought to know, better. Does the anger of resentment have an aim? If expressions of resentment carry a message of protest, rebuke, or demand (expressed verbally in such forms as "I resent that" or "How dare you/he/she?" or "There ought to be a law"), what satisfaction does resentment seek? To ask this question is to assume that some emotional responses have not only an etiology in certain perceptions, but also an expressive point or communicative direction. Resentment seems to be one such emotion. Hampton claims that in resentment the victim "would have it" that *rank and value* are not lower or lowered, because that is on her account what is threatened. Butler and Smith seem to think that resentment seeks or threatens the punishment of the offending party in order "to remedy or prevent harm."[35] On my account what resentment calls out for is *assurance of protection, defense, or membership* under norms brought into question by the exciting injury or affront. What can assuage resentment of actual *injury* is renewed trust

[35] Murphy and Hampton, *Forgiveness and Mercy*, 57; Butler, *Butler's Fifteen Sermons*, 74–76.

or hopefulness that people including oneself will be defended or protected, and that there will be some serious effort to see that a wrong
is "made right" by at least receiving a remedy. What reassures us in the
face of *affront* is confirmation that our sense of boundaries is shared; it
is those who offend who are up for negative appraisal, rebuke, or exclusion, not we who will be ignored, ridiculed, or silenced. Now, to whom
are resentment's rebukes or demands expressed?

I have already mentioned Strawson's famous paper on resentment and
other reactive attitudes. Strawson considered resentment a "reactive attitude," and these attitudes, it has been pointed out, are a kind of *moral
address*: they are expressive not only because they reveal something going
on in the one who experiences them, but because they are a kind of communicative display that sends a message and invites a kind of response.[36]
They address those at whom they are directed, and often others, bidding
them to recognize the existence or the possibility of a kind of relationship, the kind in which parties are responsible to each other. In the case of
resentment, the appeal or invitation for assurance of protection, defense,
or membership can sometimes be addressed *to the offender*: The angry
display "sends a message" to the offender about the unacceptability of
the offender's behavior. This sort of case is what Butler and Smith had in
mind, and it seems to be the response now characteristically read as indignation, overt rebuking anger. But the assumption that one's accusing and
reproving anger and the possible reprisal it portends will be effective supposes one is in a position to accuse, reprove, and threaten the transgressor
in turn. Many of us in many situations are not in this position. Especially
where one with reason to resent is vulnerable, resentment could be the
wrong message to address to an offender where the offense displays ill will
or bold indifference (rather than neglect). There, the victim's vulnerability might cause expressions of resentment to have exactly the wrong sort
of effect: a provocation to further aggression, bad treatment, ridicule,
or contemptuous flouting of rules. Nonetheless, resentment expressed
by a vulnerable individual might in some cases be an unexpected and
unsettling message to the offender, signaling a surprising willingness to
strike back.[37]

---

[36] See Jonathan Bennett, "Accountability"; Gary Watson, "Responsibility and the Limits
of Evil"; and Barbara Houston, "In Praise of Blame," on reactive attitudes as forms of
address. The phrase seems to be Watson's.
[37] Thanks to Michelle Mason for this point.

Insofar as resentment, like other reactive attitudes, can be read as a message or signal, resentment's anger is not unwisely addressed to others who are not the offender, but who might be in some position to reaffirm standards and so ratify the resenter's judgment. They might act in defense of the victim, in the form of intervention or reprisal. They might seek to protect the victim (and perhaps others including themselves) from repetitions of the injury. These are the responses that create or recreate the basis for confidence, trust, or hope that the boundaries that include and protect us are as we believe and need them to be. Seen in this way, the "aim" of resentment is, ideally, to activate protective, reassuring, or defensive responses in some individuals, or in a community that can affirm that the victim is within the scope of that community's protective responsibilities, or that the resenter is in fact competent in grasping and applying the community's shared norms. The transgressor can reassure the wronged party, and also the community, by "getting the message": she might respond with acceptance of rebuke, with evidence of remorse or shame, and might offer apology or amends. Allies can reassure those injured or affronted by initiating or joining in confirming or corrective action. The sought-for "answer" to being "addressed" in the mode of resentment is "be assured, trust again" or "be assured, we judge as you do." This translates Kant's idea that we must be both "sovereign and member" in a kingdom of ends into the call-and-response language of reactive emotions.[38]

Commonly enough, however, resentment turns inward, festers or roils, and is not appropriately answered. That is why the association of resentment with the weak, with those whose vulnerability is confirmed by the fact of their exposure to harm, exploitation, demotions, and slights, is understandable. The weak will be in harm's way precisely because their weakness invites predation or indifference. Worse, they look forward to living with injuries and slights, and with the second-order fear of having always to be angry and afraid. A weak position – socially, whether structural or situational – portends that one's resentment is less likely to be "heard," or if heard to be answered. Alternatively, it is more likely when heard to attract reprisals or ridicule for its presumption rather than protection from what prompts it. The resentment of subordinates and victims can outrage their betters and tormentors when it does not amuse them. An expression of

<hr />

[38] Immanuel Kant, *Grounding for the Metaphysics of Morals*, 40 (in standard reference, 434).

resentment can invite ridicule from those in a position to disqualify as a judge the one resenting. Not everyone is in a position to brandish Butler's weapon; the likely results of doing so, at any rate, are not constant across situations or social positions. The seductive glimmer of truth about resentment in Nietzsche's account of *ressentiment* is that the weak might have to be "expert in silence, in long memory, in waiting, in provisional self-depreciation, and in self-humiliation."[39] Nietzsche was right to call this corrosively fearful anger "poisonous." Thwarted resentment can do damage. But it is easier to understand the nature and depth of the damage if we appreciate the degree to which resentment both expresses a sense of wrong *and* calls out to others for recognition and a reparative response. It is incomplete and misleading, but it is not simply wrong, to focus on resentment – accusing anger – as the paradigmatic response to wrongdoing. It is not wrong, because resentment is that expressive and motivating response that most clearly, when unimpeded, embodies both a rebuke to what has occurred and a demand for validation and support of that rebuke.

When Should We Care?

I have argued against limiting resentment to a response to *actual* injury, to specifically *moral* injury, or to injury to *oneself*. Resentment functions as a reactive attitude for those who believe themselves *or* others injured *or* affronted, whether in fact they are, and whether or not such injury or affront is morally objectionable. What is at stake in resentment is the mutual recognition of norms that define our society and our claims to membership in it. That is what begs to be examined when someone's resentment reveals a sense of threat. In particular cases resentment may be baseless, exaggerated, or misdirected, as other emotions can in some instances be. Even when it is, however, it serves as an extremely sensitive indicator and revealing expression of people's personal investment in what they understand to be, or what they believe should be, prevalent norms, and the security and identity people derive from believing that they know "what we do." It also reflects people's investment of certain social patterns with normative force.

Resentment is not pleasant, but it has an important role to play in social and moral life. Its expression calls attention to the ongoing definition and enforcement of the standards by which we live, our unequal authority to

[39] Friedrich Nietzsche, *The Genealogy of Morals*, 172.

define and enforce them, and the collective task of keeping vital our senses and practices of responsibility. Unexpected or, in the observer's view, improper displays of resentment highlight our disputes and misunderstandings about our standards and about the nature and membership of communities. For these reasons, the question of when we should take resentments seriously is not so easy. It is not just one question. There is the question of when resentment is justified, that is, when resentment should be acknowledged as reasonably based. Then there is the question of how we should respond to reasonably based resentments. There is also the question of whether and how we should respond to resentments that are not reasonably based, and to ones that are actually morally objectionable, such as the resentments of those who want to reassert the authority of unjust hierarchies among human beings by which some human beings deserve to rule over others or are safe in treating others with disrespect, indifference, or brutality.

The simplest story would be one rather like Butler's or Smith's: the only justified resentment is that which addresses injustice, and our response to it should be sympathy with the victim and rebuke to the offender. Once its fundamental interpersonal function of chastisement is understood, resentment can only be justified when it rises in response to serious moral wrongs, because these are human actions that require and deserve chastisement. We can admit the frequency of resentments in response to violations of norms that are not obviously moral norms, and recognize the reality of resentment predicated on norms that are contrary to what morality requires, but still judge that significant moral wrongdoing is the only kind of case in which resentment is *due*, and hence the only kind of case in which the claims and demands of someone's resentment should be answered, or affirmed, by others.

This view of things is not as neat as it appears. If the only resentments worthy of being answered with reassurance and reassertion of norms are ones occasioned by the violation of important moral norms (roughly Butler's "injustice and cruelty"), that still does not tell us when resentment is proportionate or disproportionate. One may be too resentful, or experience more resentment than seems due given the offense. Thus someone who would only be satisfied by seeing the person who assaulted him hang, and the rape victim who would be satisfied by nothing less than castration of the rapist pose the problem of limits and proportion. They are clearly justified in resenting their offenders (at the very least), but it is not clear that they are justified in the degree or intensity of punitive attitude and its corresponding demand. Resentment in response to serious moral wrong may also be undying or unyielding. The one wronged may not be willing to forgive, to forget or to be satisfied by any reparative activity, including repudiation or punishment of the offender and compensation or other efforts at satisfaction by the offender or the community. To assess whether the resenter's position is unreasonable in its demand, intensity, or relentlessness, even when it is reasonable in the fact of its moral accusation and objection, remains necessary.

It is surely correct that resentment of serious moral wrong, experienced or expressed by victims or others, requires a response. If what resentment calls out for is reassurance of the authority of norms and of the membership of victim or resenting onlooker in a community that takes these norms seriously, then responses are called for that aim at this reassurance. In the ideal case, the offender should reassure the victim and the judging community with responsibility-taking, remorse, or shame at the offense, and apology and offers of meaningful amends. Whether or not the offender is able and willing to respond in the way due, the community owes reassurance in the form of acknowledgment of wrongdoing, perhaps sympathy for the victim, and the community's commitment to redress, for example, by rebuke to the offender, punishment of the offender, demands for reparative action by the offender, or attempts at repair by the community. For whether or not the offender is a party to repair, the community has interests in and obligations to make efforts to stabilize trust and replenish hope for victims and for others. Resentment at serious wrong, then, deserves responses from wrongdoers and from the community that claims to embody the standards violated. These responses need to affirm the authority of violated norms and to validate the victim's just complaint.

The victim's sense of injury and resentfulness, however, is not an infallible guide to the correct proportion or specific form of supportive or corrective action. As in systems of punishment, which are one way that communities institutionalize communal and individual responsibilities to respond and repair, there are considerations of consistency, as well as pragmatic, political, and moral constraints, that shape the ways a community can reasonably affirm standards and validate victims. The social censure, criminal punishment, liability to explain, compensate, apologize, and atone (whether legally enforceable or not) that are visited on wrongdoers are some avenues of affirmation and validation. The types and degrees of censure, punishment, and liability will inevitably need to be scaled and organized for some measure of consistency in line with practical, political, and moral limits. The moral limits on communally backed rebukes to offenders include ones that forbid indecent, inhumane, or excessive harshness. To be morally reparative, communal practices of correction should aim, where possible, to restore the offending individuals to responsible membership in communities; that is ultimately the most reassuring thing that can be done with or about wrongdoers, where that possibility is available. Communities certainly should avoid treatments of wrongdoers that are degrading and dehumanizing in ways that harden or brutalize the wrongdoers so as to render them unfit for morally responsible relationships. This treatment undermines the basis for renewing trust in and hope for wrongdoers.

Practices that rebuke should neither whet nor satisfy appetites in victims or others for disproportionate or inhumane penalties. A lively restorative justice movement in the criminal sector in many contemporary societies argues for the practical and moral superiority of social practices that emphasize responsibility-taking for wrongdoers and a sense of direct involvement in seeking repair for victims, whether this goes alongside punishment or replaces punishment. Practices such as victim-offender or group conferencing with wider networks of concerned individuals and community representatives suppose, in many cases correctly, the capacity for responsibility of those involved. The founders of VOCAL (Victims of Crime Assistance League) in Canberra, Australia, a leading area in restorative justice activity, explain that although their members, crime victims and crime victims' families, may have angry feelings, the aims of their organization are not essentially retributive. "They want a less formal process in which they can participate and their experience of victimisation be taken seriously; they want to be better informed about their case and to be treated fairly and with respect; they want material restoration and, especially, emotional restoration, including an apology."[40] These are common themes in all literature on restorative justice in a criminal enforcement context, and empirical studies of victim satisfaction lend support to the claim that victims are seeking to be recognized and answered by their communities and, in the best case, by those who have harmed them.[41]

---

[40] Heather Strang, "The Crime Victim Movement as a Force in Civil Society," 79.

[41] Two useful summary analyses of the emergence of these programs, and some evaluative research on them, are Russ Immarigeon and Kathleen Daly, "Restorative Justice: Origins, Practices, Contexts, and Challenges," and Mark S. Umbreit, Robert Coates, and Ann Warner Roberts, "Cross-National Impact of Restorative Justice Through Mediation and Dialogue." John Braithwaite, one of the founding figures in restorative justice thinking, provides extensive overview of theory and practice in *Restorative Justice and Responsive*

Yet there will still be wrongdoers who are already manifestly hardened and brutal, and so unresponsive, as there will still be victims whose resentment – or grief or outrage – will not yield to reparative efforts. There is clearly no simple answer to the question of when wrongdoers or victims are "beyond repair." It is useful nonetheless to understand what resentment seeks – normative affirmation and victim validation – for we can then give some form to the question of whether there is some reasonable reparative possibility, intended to replenish trust and hope, that the victim's and the offender's communities have ignored or rejected. Understanding resentments' demands (and, more broadly, the conditions of terror, outrage, despair, and grief that are also the results of serious wrong) can help to decipher the seemingly formless rage of some victims. It might also help us to identify with more precision some of the stakes for a community of normative judgment in what it chooses to do with, to, or about those who break rules with serious, even monstrous, damage to others. Understanding that resentment is not only about defending or avenging oneself, and grasping that it seeks the re-establishment of security, membership, and the authority of norms that unite and protect us in a community can lead us to look at what is missing from the victim's point of view. It also makes us reflect on when and why reacceptance of some offenders seems insulting, dangerous, or monstrous to victims and to others.

Jean Améry's *At The Mind's Limits* contains an extraordinary reflection on his "retrospective grudge" decades after the Second World War as a victim of imprisonment in concentration camps where he was tortured: "But to my own distress, I belonged to that disapproving minority with its hard feelings. Stubbornly, I held against Germany its twelve years under Hitler. I bore this grudge into the industrial paradise of the new Europe and into the majestic halls of the West. . . . I attracted the disapproving attention no less of my former fellows in battle and suffering, who were now gushing over about reconciliation, than of my enemies, who had just been converted to tolerance. I preserved my resentments."[42] Améry sees that his continuing resentment is condemned by moralists and

---

Regulation. See also Howard Zehr's influential book, *Changing Lenses: A New Focus for Crime and Justice,* and Dennis Sullivan and Larry Tifft, *Restorative Justice: Healing the Foundations of Our Everyday Lives.*

[42] Jean Améry, *At the Mind's Limits: Contemplations By a Survivor on Auschwitz and Its Realities,* 67. I thank Thomas Brudholm for calling my attention to this powerful and revealing discussion.

psychologists; that the West German government paid reparations (that are to date the most extensive reparations ever carried out to individual Holocaust survivors and to the state of Israel); that resentment, in his view, embodies "impossible" desires to nullify a wrong that is past.[43] Améry nonetheless defends his unrelenting resentment in moral terms, and his defense echoes some important features of the account I have given of resentment.

Améry's defense of his resentment reveals conditions under which intractable resentment can be morally justified, or at least it identifies the kind of reasons to which it is relevant to appeal in justifying it. With apology for simplifying so intricate and rending an account, I suggest that we might also read it as a lesson in how resentment over horrific injustice might nonetheless be *answered* even if it seems impossible or unconscionable to extinguish the resentment and the underlying outrage itself. Améry's resentment is not only or primarily resentment directed at brutal individuals who violently wronged him, such as the Flemish SS man Wejs who beat him on the head with a shovel handle for working too slowly in the camp. His resentment and his argument go to a moral failure by responsible parties and by the communities of judgment from which he as a victim expects and demands affirmation and defense of the reality and depth of his injury.

The scene of Améry's discussion is the decades following the end of the war, and Améry at one point calls his resentment "my personal protest against the antimoral natural process of healing that time brings about."[44] Time, without judgment and without reckoning, might "heal" wounds of wrongdoing for societies as a whole and for a new generation by allowing the vividness of horrors to wane. Even wronged individuals who have not been shattered beyond healing may sometimes find it possible to "let it go." Time, he warns, can cause a shared social concern that wrong must be addressed to fade. But what Améry protests is not the inexorability of time, forgetting, and (at least for some) the natural healing of wounds as such. What he protests is a failure of fellow human beings – past perpetrators and a judging community – to "revolt" in cases of grave injustice against that inexorable process by decisive moral action, what he calls

---

[43] Améry, *At the Mind's Limits*, 63–68. On the German Federal Republic's reparations, see the compiled documents and discussions in Roy L. Brooks, ed., *When Sorry Isn't Enough: The Controversy Over Apologies and Reparations for Human Injustice*, ch. 2; see also Elazar Barkan, *The Guilt of Nations: Restitution and Negotiating Historical Injustices*, ch. 1.

[44] Améry, *At the Mind's Limits*, 77.

"a settlement in the field of historical practice."[45] Beyond punishment of
specific wrongdoers, Améry wants the crime to "become a moral reality for the criminal, in order that he be swept into the truth of his
atrocity."[46] This truth Améry identifies as the *abandonment* and *loneliness*
he experienced in being tortured and marked for death, and which persists into the present. While he imagines that the brutal SS man might
have faced such a sense of abandonment before a firing squad, his lingering resentment is directed to that "multitude," the German people,
so few of whom showed even compunction about what was happening
around them nor remorse after it was brought, by external force, to an
end.

Améry pleads for an intervention that captures the moral outrage not
only of the killing and cruelty but of the mass complicity often present
in political violence. In the case of Nazi atrocities, he argues, the victims
were first abandoned to wrongdoing by their communities, and then, in
his view, abandoned in its aftermath by these and by the international
community in the tide of economic optimism of post-war rehabilitation,
the expediency of power politics, and the inexorable working of time
that ensures forgetfulness for generations that follow. Unsure what concrete practice might do the necessary moral work, he is sure that it will
involve "history become moral," a way of not letting the reality of, and
the responsibility for, those twelve years dwindle away.[47] He suggests as
an example that all cultural products produced during the twelve years
of Nazism be disowned and destroyed. He wants succeeding generations
to claim the shocking and shameful parts of history as they so regularly
do the glorious and elevating ones. Améry seems to recognize that there
is something futile in this quest, but that does not prevent his brief for
his resentments from making moral sense. It makes eminent sense if one
understands that resentment protests an inexcusable injury but also seeks
communal reassurance and validation. Even if his resentment can never
be satisfied, it does not mean that moral action of the sort he argues for
is not needed, even required, by the injury his resentment protests. Such
measures may not satisfy his resentment, but they could answer it.

Where victims feel forgotten and deserted, where their claims even
for the "moral truth" of their injury seem to meet with blankness, cheery

---

45 Améry, *At the Mind's Limits*, 77.
46 Améry, *At the Mind's Limits*, 70.
47 Améry, *At the Mind's Limits*, 78.

indifference, or suggestions that they are the ones who are out of line, or where this happens too soon even if it must happen in some degree eventually, there resentment persists as an unfulfilled demand. A case apt for comparison with Améry's essay is a short account of a childhood experience by Bernadette W. Hartfield. Hartfield tells the story (apparently set in the 1950s or 1960s) of being taken by a white family to a public swimming pool in Ohio and there being refused entry because she is black. Her first reaction is grief and rage (and incomprehension, because she had not encountered this blatant racial exclusion before, although she grew up in the south). When her hosts, initially sympathetic, begin to think she should get over it, her anger moves to include them; while they certainly would not endorse the racist policy, it becomes clear that neither do they think the incident "requires" continuing outrage. They in fact expected her, the black child, to be used to this sort of treatment and "not take it so hard." Like Améry, her anger goes not only to the indignity of a racist insult and exclusion, but to those others, in this case literally witnesses, who do not stand with the victim and honor the victim's outrage.[48]

Where the offense is so monstrous that it challenges the most elementary conceptions of decency and humanity, the proper response to the offense itself and the losses it wreaks is what we are more likely to call outrage and horror; we use "resentment" and even "indignation" to connote anger at wrongs and offenses that are not at the extremities. Yet even with respect to cases at the extremes, resentment is, as it seems to be in Améry's account, sensibly directed at those who seem to prefer quick and limited solutions or to leave all to the passage of time. In these cases, the resentment addresses, as it seems to do in Améry's case, not (or not only) the original wrong but the failure in its wake to undertake the due and demanding work of moral repair for the longer term.

Resentment here reveals that when one feels wronged or affronted one looks for the corrective, or at least a confirming, response that is due. If no response, or no adequate response is forthcoming, one's resentment is likely to feed not only on the wrong and the wrongdoer, but on the failure by others to support the victim in the demand for acknowledgment and redress, and the failure of a community that is supposed to embody certain standards to rise to the defense of either the victim or the violated standards. The victim feels victimized once again by this dereliction; the

---

[48] Bernadette W. Hartfield, "A Story of Anger Compounded."

witness to wrongdoing may feel affronted all over again by indifference both to what the witness sees and to the witness himself as a member of a presumed community of shared values who is in protest against an apparent violation. There is also the complicated case of the witness who is a bystander to wrongdoing, and who perhaps is not too eager to make much of a wrongdoing to which he or she may have some culpable or questionable relationship. Both Améry and Hartfield describe such cases.

The tragedy of large-scale political violence and of intergenerational historic injustice is that there are no clear measures of "adequate" or "proportionate" response and it is not an idle question whether there could be any truly adequate response. In these cases, though, what becomes important is that there is *some* morally effective response, and that the response is not perceived as expedient or cheap, given what the victims and heirs to such moral catastrophes have suffered. The task facing communities in the wake of these wrongs is to find some way to answer victims' just desire for validation and for a lasting grip on the moral truth of what they suffered, whether or not their individual resentments are satisfied. In the case of large-scale violence and historic injustice this is likely to involve not one response, but many forms of address, and it is likely to be, as Améry says, in the "field of historical practice." This means that repair is in the history we make and make sure is told, but it is also in a process we should expect to be intergenerational. The facets of the process include truth-telling, education, and commemoration that preserves the factual and moral truth, that reasserts the dignity of victims and sustains the rebuke to wrongdoers and bystanders, and that incorporates the shameful parts of communities' histories alongside their more welcome ones. These measures not only protest the original wrong, but rebel against the cruel possibility for victims that time will bury all wounds, even if no one works to heal them. This respects victims and a community of judgment, even if it cannot entirely satisfy their resentment, grief, and outrage.

What is essential in meeting the resentment of victims of injustice is that there be *clear practices of communal acknowledgment* that assert the *victims' deservingness of repair* and the *wrongdoer's obligation to make amends*, as well as *communal determination* to see that meaningful repair is done. Indeed, in some instances communal acknowledgment and validation may be reparative even when other forms of satisfaction, such as punishment of wrongdoers or material compensation for injuries, are not easily achieved. A question now widely debated at the opening of the twenty-first century concerns what legal, political, and social institutions and practices provide effective moral action in the wake of large-scale episodes of violence and oppression. Some mechanisms, of ancient and recent vintage, include: judicial prosecutions with due process based on specifiable crimes with legal consequences; amnesties that release wrong-doers implicated in a particular era or episode of political wrongdoing and violence from legal consequences; truth commissions that establish an official authoritative narrative of wrongdoing to provide victims and survivors with needed truths, and to stand against continuing lies and future denials; material reparations for victims that acknowledge the fact of wrong and deservingness of repair; moral reparations and satisfactions such as apologies, memorials, accurate history, continuing education, preventive measures, and legal guarantees. Not all of these are practically feasible or politically available in every situation, nor do these mean the same in different situations.

For example, Ruti Teitel explains that the production of an official authoritative truth has been essential under regimes of state violence that practiced widespread torture, extra-judicial execution, and disappearance that was organized for "deniability." Yet after the fall of communism in Eastern Europe, the unrelenting and cynical use of "official" histories and massive surveillance and record-keeping on citizens discredited officially produced truth. It was something to be attacked, stripped away, and exposed to daylight in such practices as "lustration," where secret police files and collaboration of citizens with the oppressive state apparatus were to be made available to those targeted, or to the public, or made common property.[49] Martha Minow examines the strengths and limitations of criminal process in dealing with political violence. Judicial process has the potential to reveal and document truth, but in some contexts will reveal only a painfully restricted portion of truth at considerable expense; and due process, if real, ensures that if the legal burden of proof is not met the guilty may not be punished or even authoritatively labeled as responsible.[50] The outpouring of debate on the particular contributions and limits of different processes of social and individual repair reflects increasing understanding that in the wake of wrongdoing there are different situations and multiple stakeholders to be addressed. The repair of wrongdoing and other social goods and obligations to citizens

---

[49] Ruti Teitel, *Transitional Justice*, ch. 3, "Historical Justice."

[50] Martha Minow, *Between Vengeance and Forgiveness: Facing History After Genocide and Mass Violence*. See also Teitel, *Transitional Justice*, on criminal justice in transition.

are competing priorities. There are also competing priorities within the field of repair itself. The recent wave of discussions at least shows that Améry's cry of complaint is not unanswered. Many solutions are being tried and sought in the field of historical practice, and many practices feature prominently the need to address the anguish, and the just anger, of victims.

What then, however, of resentments that are not reactions to serious wrongdoing? What of resentments that react to *right-doing* that breaches and threatens morally obnoxious norms? I will be brief here, but I think it important to rebut the idea that resentments without serious moral basis do not deserve our attention. First, resentments at threats to forms of order that do not raise moral issues are not irrational; they may deserve affirmation, respect, or sympathy. Once we understand that resentment is not simply about actual injury to one's person, but is also about one's security of membership in a community of normative judgment, we can see that some resentment responds to threats that are by no means trivial simply because they do not immediately involve moral values. Identity and belonging, and community and order that rest on legible norms and our shared grasp of them are extremely important to human beings. We all need homes and places. While our histories and identities are often attached to concrete habitations, geographical locales, and familiar objects, sacred and everyday, our histories and identities are also constituted and anchored by our grasp of how "we" live with each other. While most societies have incorporated group norms that are cruel and oppressive to some, so that norms are not to be valued independently of their content, human beings seek and need the "home" of shared expectations as much as they need a roof over their heads. Shared expectations are a roof over our heads, and a floor beneath us; they provide reasonable assumptions about when we are safe and where we belong.

This is not a small good. To lose this "cover" or "ground," to see it collapse or erode, threatens us with not knowing how to go on sanely and safely. Social and personal changes can produce forms of normative alienation and estrangement. There are resentments common to the aged, for example, where some see a world in which "nothing is like it used to be," and where some basic social rules have become quaint or even laughable. These resentments signify a feeling that one is without social shelter – literally "without," outside, at the margins, pushed to the edge of a community in which one is no longer certain of one's place. There are predictable resentments of institutional and social change, where participants who previously felt competent and in control are threatened with appearing foolish or stupid because they need to learn new things. The new things might include learning to interact with people whose presence and whose different ways were alien and reassuringly avoidable before. Insofar as we wish to respect persons, and to respect them particularly in the dimension of their responsiveness to normative reasons – to respect them as responsible agents who take care for others' reasonable expectations – we ought not to find it silly that people feel alienated in these ways. We should want to reassure them that they are not less valued, or less than one of us when rules change. We should want to do this out of respect, and also out of compassion. There is loneliness and abandonment not only in being treated brutally, but also in feeling quietly excluded or erased.

Finally, there is the case of resentment that arises when morally unacceptable and even grossly malignant norms are violated among those who mistakenly, but perhaps fervently, hold to these immoral norms as the right way to live. Resentment is a reaction to the violation of normative expectations to which one feels entitled, and one can feel entitled to hold to norms that are contested or discredited in one's larger community if one continues to believe that these are really the right ways to live. It can be very important to understand these resentments, especially when they represent a point of solidarity for groups of people who are willing to act aggressively, even violently, to secure a social order based on their vision of community. Elizabeth Kiss, discussing an upsurge of animosity and violence by skinheads toward Roma people, Jews, and foreign students of color in Hungary in the 1990s, explains:

"Everyone has his home," one skinhead insisted, "the gypsies should return to India and the Africans to Africa." Others argued that gypsies should be put on reservations. Mixed in with this swagger and bravado were more poignant statements, pointing to the desperate need of many of these young men to belong, and the way the fellowship of the gang was merged in their minds with a sense of pride in their nation. As one insisted, "They don't belong here. *We* belong here. *We* are the Hungarians." . . . Another commented that what drew him to the skinheads was "our togetherness. I mean you see a skinhead on the street who you've never seen before and you're together, you trust each other."[51]

[51] Elizabeth Kiss, "Saying We're Sorry: Liberal Democracy and the Rhetoric of Collective Identity."

Contests, even losing battles, over the identity and membership of communities are loaded up around senses of the just, the right, what makes us "us," what makes us safe and "at home," and these contests can have unpleasant, even explosive, results. They are the tinder that can ignite when the sparks of political rhetoric reach it. Opportunistic politicians can spring the "tribal trap," whipping up benign or dormant ethnic, racial, or cultural differences into ugly racial or nationalist politics, violent encounters between religious or ethnic groups, or genocidal fury, as we have seen throughout and at the close of the twentieth century.[52] This should warn us not to take the dividing line between "social" and "cultural" norms, on the one hand, and properly "moral" norms, on the other, in a way that places all the importance on the latter. All norms that contribute to community and identity are a focus of feeling that is potentially powerful. When resentments are broadly diffused or deeply embedded in social groups – or when some clearly adopt a politics whose purpose is to diffuse and embed them – we cannot be too careful. We should care.[53]

Resentment and Other Emotions of Rebuke

I have not meant to imply in devoting attention to it that resentment is the invariable, necessary, or uniquely proper response to wrongdoing, in either the narrowest moral sense or the broader one in which one

---

[52] Jonathan Glover's *Humanity: A Moral History of the Twentieth Century* is an impressive and depressing compendium and analysis of the tides of violence and inhumanity that marked the century past. On the Rwandan genocide, which Glover discusses briefly, the classic text is Philip Gourevitch, *We Wish to Inform You That Tomorrow We Will Be Killed With Our Families: Stories From Rwanda*. On the longer term and ongoing manipulation of senses of identity, affirmative and degraded, see Hilde Lindemann Nelson, *Damaged Identities, Narrative Repair*; on complex negotiations of identity, culture, and citizenship in contemporary societies, see Will Kymlicka, *Politics in the Vernacular: Nationalism, Multiculturalism, and Citizenship*; on the conscious and self-serving construction of "civilization" and "the state of nature" by Europeans with respect to nonwhite peoples, see Charles Mills, *The Racial Contract*; on the everyday reproduction of the lines between those who matter in society and those who need not matter to those who matter, see Jean Harvey, *Civilized Oppression*.

[53] Jean Hatzfeld's interviews of men in prison for their participation in the Rwandan genocide are stunning, not only for the workaday attitudes of the killers, but for the descriptions of a persistent flow of derogatory and hateful remarks and jokes stirring up resentment at the Tutsi minority against the backdrop of a history of periodic "ordinary" massacres that unfolded at a signal, without significant resistance, into the massive popular genocide of perhaps a million people. See Jean Hatzfeld, *The Machete Season: The Killers in Rwanda Speak*.

does wrong who transgresses norms. Disappointment, sadness, grief, and despair are common responses to wrongs that result in deep and permanent losses; terror, fear, and mistrust are also common reactions to violations that seriously undermine a floor of trust on which a large part, or some essential part, of everyday living rests. Sometimes revulsion, disgust, disdain, or contempt are the responses to those who go out of bounds. These last attitudes seem to lie at the limits of our responses to others whom we can continue to see as moral fellows; they can just as well be felt toward things that are not persons (the sticky residue that soils one's clothing in a public space) or can indicate a dismissal of others who are seen as outside one's moral fellowship (the "monster," "scum," or "garbage" people talk about when they liken doers of serious wrongs to something not human at all). It is not that resentment is more important than these. But resentment is a normal and extremely common response to perceived wrong; when it is in proportion and responsive to moderation, it is a functional response, and not one, as Smith and Butler knew, we could do without.[54] This is precisely because, unlike the other responses mentioned, resentment naturally (that is, where its expression is not tamped or impeded) reaches out in a demanding and at least mildly threatening display that might warn and correct wrongdoers. While people pull or shrink away from the disgusting, and they often cave or turn inward in disappointment, grief, or despair, people lash out or poke back in resentment. While people long for recognition of loss, they burn for recognition of wrong, and tend to flare out or glare out at others, making overt or implied demands for satisfaction.

I have used resentment to stand in for a distinctive family of cognate feelings, some gentler and some fiercer, that register a perception of something wrong and express a reproving attitude that invites corrective responses from wrongdoers or others. Disapproval, indignation, and outrage are other family members. The self-directed self-punishing emotions of guilt, compunction, and remorse are the members of this family that respond to cases in which one has, or thinks one has, only oneself to blame for something wrong. We punish ourselves with these "self-reactive" feelings, but they can also prompt us to take responsibility

---

[54] Primatologist Frans de Waal's close studies of apes led him to conclude that deviations from a "sense of social regularity" concerning how oneself and others ought to be treated and how resources ought to be divided trigger negative reactions of protest and punishment in our primate relatives. He says: "it is safe to assume that the actions of our ancestors were guided by gratitude, obligation, retribution, and indignation long before they developed enough language capacity for moral discourse." *Good Natured*, 161.

and make amends. All these emotions seem to aim at moving us in some corrective direction, whether we are victims demanding response, wrong-doers taking responsibility, or members of communities seeking to keep each others' senses of responsibility intact.[55]

55 This chapter evolved through many presentations at many places. At every one I have received challenging feedback that moved me to reconsider and recast my claims. I thank audiences at University of South Florida, State University of New York at Buffalo, Pennsylvania State University, Queens University, Dalhousie University, Syracuse University, University of Connecticut at Storrs, the Research School of Social Sciences at Australian National University, Arizona State University, and the Committee on Politics, Philosophy, and Public Policy at the University of Maryland. Special thanks to Peggy DesAutels, Robert Richardson, and Mitchell Haney, who steered me away from a mistake about resentment and fear early on; and to Norvin Richards, whose commentary on a colloquium version of the paper at the American Philosophical Association Pacific Meeting was especially insightful and helpful. Thanks to Karen Jones for asking me to clarify the connection between resentment and envy, and to Stew Cohen, who pressed for an explanation of resentments aimed at things and states of affairs rather than people and their actions.

5

Forgiving

When we forgive, it seems that we fasten down some injury in the past in order to leave it there behind us. Sometimes we want or need to leave behind the person who wronged us, too. Hannah Arendt, in a striking discussion of the topic, thought of forgiveness as a unique remedy for the "irreversibility" of human action. For Arendt, a human action, a performance that reveals something about "who" the actor is, enters a web of human relationships and intentions "where every reaction becomes a chain reaction and where every action is the cause of new processes" and so cannot be undone. The full significance of this fact will be seen. Arendt argued that the "predicament of irreversibility" is met by forgiveness, which is itself an action. Forgiveness alone, she thought, is the action that releases us from the "boundlessness"of another action from which we otherwise "could never recover." An otherwise endless and irreversible action is overtaken by another action with the peculiar power to forever set the former to rest.[1]

It does not seem, though, that Arendt fully pondered the implications of the irreversibility and unpredictability of acts of forgiveness. Forgiveness, too, will have consequences that reverberate indefinitely in ways that may exceed our foresight and our control. This is one reason why an account of forgiveness needs to capture that part of forgiving that looks ahead hopefully to an uncertain future and not only the part that

---

[1] Hannah Arendt, *The Human Condition*, ch. 5, "Action," quoting from 190, 236, 237, respectively. Arendt considers punishment an alternative to forgiveness, not its contrary; they both attempt to make an end to something that otherwise is "endless," 241. It is often pointed out that forgiveness and punishment are not incompatible.

looks to settle something in the past. There are conditions that make that hopefulness more or less risky, and understanding forgiveness as something of moral value involves understanding what conditions those arc.

The English-language philosophical literature on forgiveness is interestingly varied, but tends to frame questions about forgiveness in a particular way. Most philosophical accounts of forgiveness try, in the Socratic way, to say what forgiveness "really is," usually by trying to identify what goes on when someone forgives and what is accomplished when forgiveness is achieved. Philosophers know that different people have different ideas about what to call "forgiveness." Yet there is a tendency in philosophers' accounts to speak of "true," "real," or "genuine" forgiveness, or about the "essential," "central," or "necessary" elements of it. This can imply either that there is one real process that alone deserves the name, or that if there is more than one kind of forgiveness, one of them is the "best" or "truest" case of it.

I have come to find it odd to think of there being a single correct idea of forgiveness, in the way that there is a correct theory of the structure of DNA. Forgiveness is a variable human process and a practice with culturally distinctive versions. Psychologist Beverly Flanigan has studied forgiveness in our society by working with people who have suffered "unforgivable" injuries at the hands of those intimates in whom they had placed the greatest trust. Flanigan finds that different individuals, when confronted with wrongs that are especially difficult to forgive, see the task and point of forgiveness in different ways. Some aim at ridding themselves of resentment and hatred toward their offender, others aim at feeling neutral, still others want to retrieve some degree of trust in those who hurt them, and some seek reconciliation with their offenders.[2] Flanigan thinks that while forgivers do not necessarily share a definition of forgiveness, they do share in a process. The process has to do with the forgivers' restructuring of basic assumptions about life so that the likelihood of harm is built into a new orderly set of assumptions. I, too, think that forgiveness is a process of restructuring. However, Flanigan's psychological account, though insightful, does not capture the *moral* reconstruction that must be part of its role. That is my topic here.

[2] Beverly Flanigan, "Forgivers and the Unforgivable," 100. See also other studies in Robert D. Enright and Joanna North, eds., *Exploring Forgiveness*, by authors with expertise in mental health, social science, and criminal justice. For a general study of modes of accounting across cultures, see Ken-ichi Ohbuchi, "A Social Psychological Analysis of Accounts: Toward a Universal Model of Giving and Receiving Accounts."

I will begin by talking about three features of forgiveness that are commonly argued or assumed in philosophical discussions of forgiveness to be the "key" or "essential" elements. Philosophers speak of "overcoming resentment," "restoring relationship," and "setting a wrong to rest in the past" as essential marks of forgiveness. None of these features need be present in every case plausibly seen as a case of forgiving, yet any one of these three features can be crucial in a particular case to achieving the resolution forgiveness is seeking. We should think of forgiving in a flexible way, a way that shows why each of the three features favored by philosophers can matter in many cases, but that also shows why none of them is definitive in every case. This flexible way of seeing forgiveness should encompass the different kinds of passages a wronged person makes that have this character: from having a need and a right to grieve and to reproach the wrongdoer, the one forgiving achieves *a morally reparative decision* to release himself or herself from the position of grievance and reproach, and to release the wrongdoer from open-ended (but not necessarily all other) demands for satisfaction.

The key to this kind of account, however, is to keep in view what it is to *repair moral relations*, and so to see the dimensions in which the decision to forgive is something morally valuable, and even admirable. Forgiving is something we often (but not always) have reason to do, and it is something we have reason in many cases to admire as an achievement of some moral significance. We might be able to explain its moral significance by showing its role in moral repair, and to explain why we correctly admire it by showing why it is something challenging for the one wronged to take this reparative path in many cases of wrongdoing. It is not immediately evident that a single account of forgiveness can span the ordinary and the horrifying, the unsurprising and the unspeakable, the broken appointment, the infidelity, and the war crime. It might be, however, that all these cases share a common structure and so common possibilities – an offense, a victim's harm and suffering, threat to security of the victim and in some instances to a community, threat or damage to conditions of moral relationship among victim, offender, and others, acceptance of responsibility and fault by an offender, and the offender's release from further grievance by the victim. Even so, these cases are still dramatically unalike in the means and the costs involved in completing the process that leads from wrong to resolution, and in assessing the likely outcomes in the longer term. But so do cases of forgiveness in the "everyday" dimension differ from one another. What is important here is less to draw a bright line between "real" and "false," or "limited" and "complete" forgiveness than to understand the sort of achievement at which forgiveness aims, the difficulties attending it, the impact of circumstances on the likelihood of its success, and the reasons why we need it, value it, and sometimes admire it. So I begin with some definitions that I think are not complex enough, and do not allow for the variability of different kinds of cases.

Facets of Forgiving

Many philosophical accounts settle on one or more than one of three basic features in trying to identify what forgiveness is. First, forgiveness settles a wrong precisely as such in the past while releasing the future from its impact. Second, forgiveness overcomes or lets go of resentment or other "hard" feelings against the offending person. Third, forgiveness restores damaged or broken relations between those injured and their offenders, and perhaps relations among them and others. The second factor, "forswearing resentment," is the clear favorite among philosophers for the "key" factor, with the third, "restoring relations," lagging somewhat behind it. The first factor, fixing the offense as such in the past, is often in effect presupposed as the scene setting for forgiveness, more the occasion for forgiveness than part of its function. I agree that these three aspects of forgiveness are common and in many instances crucial dimensions of the process. Yet none is necessary in every case that we can recognize as forgiving. Any of these features might be unavailable or undesirable in some contexts, personal or political. I take up these components of forgiveness in the order of their popularity as candidates for the true or genuine case.

Forswearing Resentment
In forgiving, must we forswear resentment and other hard or angry feelings toward those who wrong us?[3] Although there is an important truth

---

[3] Accounts that feature letting go of angry feeling as constitutive of or an essential part of forgiveness include: R. S. Downie, "Forgiveness"; Martin P. Golding, "Forgiveness and Regret"; Paul Lauritzen, "Forgiveness: Moral Prerogative or Religious Duty?"; Joanna North, "Wrongdoing and Forgiveness"; Jeffrie Murphy and Jean Hampton, *Forgiveness and Mercy*; Norvin Richards, "Forgiveness"; Howard McGary, "Forgiveness"; Cheshire Calhoun, "Changing One's Heart"; Margaret R. Holmgren, "Forgiveness and the Intrinsic Value of Persons"; Paul M. Hughes, "Moral Anger, Forgiving, and Condoning"; Piers Benn, "Forgiveness and Loyalty"; David Novitz, "Forgiveness and Self-Respect"; Pamela Hieronymi, "Articulating an Uncompromising Forgiveness"; and Trudy Govier, *Forgiveness and Revenge*. There is ambiguity in some of these accounts, which speak alternately of giving up the "right" to such feelings, "overcoming" them, or "eliminating" them. Curiously,

captured by this idea, I don't think it can encompass the complexity of forgiveness. For one thing, this view supposes that all instances of wrongful harm prompt anger, or that feelings of anger and rage are always what impedes the ability to forgive.[4] Aside from anger, resentment, contempt, indignation, wrath, rage, hatred, scorn, and vengefulness, being harmed wrongfully can cause disappointment, hurt, heartbreak, sadness, despair, pessimism, mistrust, helplessness, and hopelessness; also disgust, anguish, shame, guilt, humiliation, fear, or terror. Many of these feelings are likely to occur instead of or alongside angry ones, especially when the wrongdoing or wrongful harm is serious. Should we then stretch the idea of forgiveness to cover overcoming all bad feelings occasioned by the wrong? If we do, arguing that the elimination of all such negative feeling (or giving up a right to it) is a necessary condition for forgiving in every case, this only makes it less likely that we will recognize many cases of forgiveness. Someone who otherwise wants to release himself and his offender from the sequels to a wrong may be able to do so conclusively in a determined and practical way without ceasing to experience many difficult feelings at the memory of the wrong.

Consider the common case of a spouse betrayed by infidelity who forswears further recriminations, denunciations to others, and withdrawal from intimacies of sex and companionship with his wife; he may go forward with their joined lives with good will and resolution that the past is past. But he may be unable not to feel many things when the memory of his wife's unfaithfulness is stirred; and there may be, for all his resolution, some vibrancy and hopefulness, some playfulness and silly freedoms that he will not recapture. It seems entirely reasonable to think that he has forgiven on the basis of his rejoining their relationship, and the attempts he makes not to let residual feelings of anger, sadness, and fear get in the way of this. Consider, too, the ways that survivors of violent crime or abuse are sometimes able to forgive assailants with generous and sometimes public actions that leave no doubt that they want to fix their terrifying injuries in the past. This gives us no reason to assume

---

Bishop Joseph Butler's, "Upon Forgiveness of Injuries," the ninth of his sermons, is a standard source citation for this view, although it is not in fact Butler's own view. Butler seeks to defend the probity of resentment as a "weapon" given us to curb wrongdoers, and argues only against "excess" or "abuse" of resentment that usurps a Christian, not affectionate, benevolence toward anyone as a fellow being. See both this sermon and "Upon Resentment" in Joseph Butler, *Butler's Fifteen Sermons Preached at the Rolls Chapel and A Dissertation of the Nature of Virtue.*

4 See Richards, "Forgiveness," and Hughes, "Moral Anger," on this.

that their inner lives are not still vulnerable to many types of emotional turmoil as a result of their injury.

Finally, consider victims of oppression, stigmatization, or terror who agree after a political transition to accept a modus vivendi for public life with those who are former persecutors or the beneficiaries of their persecution. A live edge of pointed just anger or continuing sorrow for things and people lost may accompany their honest agreement to go on in civility and cooperation without demanding that further accounts be settled, prices paid, or apologies tendered. Surely sometimes this digni-fied and considered form of letting go should to be acknowledged as forgiveness. Archbishop Desmond Tutu, who served as Chair of South Africa's Truth and Reconciliation Commission, created in 1995, in a tele-vised interview described forgiveness as abandoning a right to revenge or payback, saying simply that one can't let go of pain by an act of will.[5] A Cambodian reporter, in the audience when two top Khmer Rouge leaders, responsible for the deaths of hundreds of thousands of people, including most of the reporter's family, were received as defectors with limousines and bouquets, observed: "When I see them, it is difficult to forgive, very difficult" . . . It is just like waking me up when I see them. But we have to forgive and move on."[6]

The idea of relinquishing revenge or payback is closer to the truth but not quite there. The one forgiving must give up a right to revenge, but one might forgive and not give up the belief that it is right for the wrongdoer to accept his or her punishment. People can and do forgive those who have perpetrated crimes against them, without being inclined to insist on the remission of the criminal offender's legally prescribed punishment. Nor should we say that the injured person in forgiving gives up a right to demand any repair from the wrongdoer. One might forgive someone once that person had agreed to make satisfactory amends, and forgive because the prospect of amends allows one to reaccept the wrong-doer, or to lay down one's protest at injury, or to trust that in demanding

---

[5] Archbishop Desmond Tutu, interview with Bill Moyers. In his book, *No Future Without Forgiveness,* Tutu says that forgiving means "abandoning your right to pay back the per-petrator in his own coin," but also says that in forgiveness we declare "our faith in the future of a relationship and in the capacity of the wrongdoer to make a new beginning," 272–73. Jeffrie Murphy calls this view of forgiveness "less morally rich," because it does not capture the "change of heart that constitutes forgiveness as a moral virtue," in his *Getting Even: Forgiveness and Its Limits,* 15. My view does not attempt to describe forgiveness as a moral virtue.

[6] Seth Mydans, "Under Prodding, 2 Apologize for Cambodian Anguish."

amends one is not seen by the wrongdoer or others as excusing, ignoring, or condoning the wrong that was done. In such a case, one's forgiveness does not then release the wrongdoer from the task of making amends – although sometimes in forgiving we do declare further repair unnecessary. I will return to the important fact that forgiving is often *conditional*; it is often given on condition that certain circumstances hold, and perhaps the most common condition that opens the way for forgiveness is the offender's acceptance of responsibility and what that entails, including penalty, punishment, or amends to the injured party.

Uma Narayan says the forgiving party lets go of a right to what she calls a "sense of grievance," that would move the wronged person to keep after the wrongdoer with continuing reproaches and punitive attitudes and behavior.[7] This does not entail opposing all forms of punishment or relinquishing all right to amends still to be paid, nor does it mean that if one forgives, one never backslides or struggles with reproachful feelings or with their expression. It means that if one has forgiven, one then has a reason to reject and, even stronger, a *commitment to reject* backsliding into recrimination, anger, or mistrust, even if one cannot completely control these emotions. Avishai Margalit says "forgiveness is first and foremost a policy," a decision that the injury is no longer a reason for such actions as "hostile or cold behavior toward the person who caused the injury."[8] It may be that in particular cases such a policy cannot really be adopted unless negative emotions are extinguished, but that is not true in every case. In forgiving, one accepts that reproachful and punishing reactions are no longer *acceptable* responses to the offender, even if one cannot or cannot yet completely extinguish them. One might, for example, apologize for their occasional overt expression, and make efforts to bring them under control. Forgiveness as a moral commitment to a practical policy is also a conception that can extend to cases of forgiveness by groups, including peoples or nations, where forgiveness is more easily seen as a commitment to proceed without continuing demands for repair even though the individual feelings of members are not something one can fully assess or control.[9] There are complexities in the conditions – personal, interpersonal, and social – under which such a policy is practically

[7] Uma Narayan, "Forgiveness, Moral Reassessment, and Reconciliation," 169–78, especially 171.

[8] Avishai Margalit, *The Ethics of Memory*, 202.

[9] Peter Digeser, *Political Forgiveness*, 2, offers "a secular, performative notion of forgiveness" that is designed for public or governmental uses, and therefore emphasizes "action over motivation."

possible and morally advisable, and I will return to the difference between a practical policy that excuses, condones, or just "buries" the offense, and one that is adopted to further morally reparative ends.[10]

There is, of course, a great deal of difference between a kind of serene forgiveness untroubled by remaining despondent, hurt, angry, or reproachful feelings, and a kind of forgiveness that requires remedial self-control. We might say these are different kinds of forgiving that reflect people's different possibilities, temperaments, and histories, and impose different costs of self-awareness and effort. Would it *always* really be *best*, though, if we could achieve the kind of forgiveness that unburdens us of *all* anger or suffering? I'm not sure this is true. In some cases of very grave injustice or great destructiveness, forgiving without some residual feelings of grief and sorrow, if not of resentment, might seem too close to condoning, with the threat of dishonoring or cheapening something, or someone, with profound value for us. Cynthia Ozick says, of forgiving the murders of others, "Forgiveness can brutalize."[11] But it need not, unless we demand that it surrender feelings which can survive as a testimony and living memorial. Forgiveness has importantly to do with who bears the "cost" of the offense, and how it is absorbed, as will be seen in considering what it means to consider offenses "unforgivable."

Restoring Relationships

Let's look next at the idea that forgiveness is essentially about restoring relationships. Some writers emphasize the rehabilitation of relations as the central element in forgiveness, putting it alongside the end of bad feeling or treating the giving up of negative feeling as instrumental to the ideal goal of reconnection.[12] But this covers up important differences among situations. There might, for example, have been no relationship prior to the injury. When a crime victim has been unjustly harmed by a

---

[10] Prime Minister Hun Sen of Cambodia literally recommended this as the correct response to former Khmer Rouge leaders who had been responsible, directly and collectively, for one million deaths between 1975 and 1979: "We should dig a hole and bury the past and look ahead to the 21st century with a clean slate." Quoted in Seth Mydans, "Cambodian Leader Resists Punishing Top Khmer Rouge."

[11] Cynthia Ozick, in Simon Wiesenthal, *The Sunflower: On the Possibilities and Limits of Forgiveness, with a Symposium*, Book 2, 215.

[12] Accounts that primarily emphasize a relational achievement in forgiving include: Butler, "Upon Forgiveness of Injuries," in *Butler's Fifteen Sermons*; Aurel Kolnai, "Forgiveness"; Nicholas Tavuchis, *Mea Culpa: A Sociology of Apology and Reconciliation*; and Berel Lang, "Forgiveness." Jean Harvey, "Forgiving as an Obligation of the Moral Life," contrasts a "wide" (i.e. relational) account of forgiving with a narrow one, without claiming that the former is more genuine. Calhoun, Hampton, Golding, Lauritzen, Holmgren, North, and Benn include a significant relational aspect in their accounts.

stranger, the offense creates a relationship where there was none before. Part of the sense of outrage, resentment, fear, hopelessness, and shame of crime victims can be the sense that their life is invaded, that now they are bound in their life in a charged and exhausting fashion to someone who has no right to be there. This is also true of the families of victims, who can never forget, whether or not they forgive. Forgiveness cannot aim at the restoration of relationship here, unless this means restoring the fact that *no* relationship exists, just as no relationship existed before the crime. That, of course, is not a possibility, short of genuine, total forgetting, something presumably fairly rare among those who are very seriously wronged. Another case that needs to be taken seriously is one that many people are faced with, and struggle with. This is the case of forgiving those who have died or are permanently gone from our lives. In neither of these cases does the ideal of "restoring relations" capture the problem or its resolution.

In the case of those who are dead and gone it may be argued that forgiving them means we *would* reaccept them and restore the relationship with them were they to reappear.[13] This is doubtless often true, and we do say: "If only I could see her once again..." meaning that we would then forgive and be rejoined. This ignores, though, something distinctive about these cases. Many cases of forgiving the dead can be understood as special instances of conditional forgiveness. I mean by "conditional forgiveness" our forgiving someone on the basis of a particular understanding without which we might be unwilling to forgive. I imagine that people sometimes forgive unconditionally, but my guess is that most of the forgiving human beings do is conditional, if only implicitly so. One familiar form of conditional forgiveness is that we are forgiven by others on the basis of an expectation that we will not do the same kind of wrong again, at least to them. That is why it is common for people seeking forgiveness to offer assurances, even promises, that they won't do it again. That is why it is so often insisted that an offender's repentance is either necessary to forgiving or reasonably disposes us to forgive, because it gives a reason to think that this common condition of forgiveness is likely to be fulfilled.[14] This should lead us to ask in the case of forgiving those dead and gone whether in some cases the very impossibility of further relationship that is brought by death or final separation might not be the

[13] So North suggests in "Wrongdoing and Forgiveness," 503.

[14] J. Wilson, "Why Forgiveness Requires Repentance," argues that repentance is necessary; others, for example Murphy, Hampton, Tavuchis, argue that it is sufficient or sound reason for forgiving. See also Edward H. Flannery, in Simon Wiesenthal, *The Sunflower*, Book 2, 138.

reason it makes sense to forgive the one who will never return. It might be true that we might reaccept them were they to reappear, but it is also true that if they could appear again they might then misbehave or shatter us with their indifference. If we imagine being reunited with an abusive parent or a traitorous friend, why should we think they would behave any better? So we might be enabled to forgive in these cases precisely because those who have wronged us are never coming back.

One pressure on my closing accounts with those now unreachable is that I am left alone to take the measure of something that is done once and for all. The settling of one's mind and heart in these cases goes to someone whose "record" is complete. While for the living, it can be sensible, fruitful, or merciful to keep their records open, with the departed we do not get this choice. There remains only what posture of mind and heart we take up with respect to the record now closed.[15] *Because* now nothing can be changed save our own attitude to what they were and had done, how we dispose ourselves toward them can matter terribly to us, whether we decide to remember them with compassion or believe even our fading memories must contain a reproach. One thing among others for which people departed might or might not be forgiven is that they have left one stuck with precisely that choice, and this may be anguishing if we had longed for a sign from them that would have been a ground to forgive. If we take seriously the case of forgiving those dead or departed, and many people seem to do so, it seems that at least some ways of settling accounts without prospect of restoration should be seen as forgiveness, for in many such cases the impossibility of future relationship is not only compatible with forgiving but creates the condition for it.

What of the case where there existed a concrete prior relation between one wrongfully harmed and the harmdoer, and both remain available to each other? If the idea (or ideal) of reconnection has application, it should apply to this kind of case. Here restoration of relationship, or at least some form of reconnection beyond injury, is the paradigmatic "happy ending." In actual cases, though, reconciliation is precisely not an ending, but rather a continuation or a new beginning. Continuation of a breached relation may, in some cases, be neither an ending nor something happy even despite good faith efforts, and it may be so precisely due to the history of injury that required forgiveness. Even when

---

[15] Victoria McGeer examines Jane Austen's *Persuasion* as a story of problems and possibilities presented by lovers parted badly who encounter each other at close range many years later, in "Moral Travel and the Narrative Work of Forgiveness."

the wrongdoer is contrite, it may not be possible for the injured party
to reconcile while hard or despairing feelings remain intense, or while
the injured party is unsure of being able to control the expression or the
practical effects of bad feelings.

This is the important truth in the view that forgiveness involves overcoming bad feeling. The problem can also arise, however, from the end of
the one seeking reacceptance through forgiveness. For either party, persisting in or reconstituting a relation in which either must be a hypocrite,
a groveler, frankly false or self-deceived, or someone stunted, shamed, or
humiliated isn't forgiveness; it is condoning, resigning, or caving in for
the offended, or an unwholesome form of humiliation or deception for
the offender. In situations with this forecast, *if* there is to be forgiving, the
price of it might be precisely letting go of the relationship. One may
thereby release oneself and the other from additional harms, including
the harm of trying to maintain a relationship that will be demeaning or
depraving to the parties. And so, just as it should be seen as forgiving
when one can go on in good will without being rid of all negative feeling,
so too one should honor the forgiving that releases both injured and
wrongdoer from continuing or restoring a relationship that could only
demean or morally deform one or both of them.

This brings forward a central point: "forgiving," at least as we use this
to refer to something morally valuable and perhaps admirable, refers to a
process with moral effects, even as it has social and psychological aspects
and conditions. Everyone recognizes that *simply* being able to go on with
a relation, to function in it, is not forgiveness. The widely invoked dis-
tinctions between forgiving and condoning, and between forgiving and
forgetting show this.[16] If I forget, there is no longer even the occasion
for forgiving, and if I condone what you did, the wrong in it is covered
over rather than confronted, as it is in forgiving. For example, if I rejoin
a friendship marred by a callous betrayal by persuading myself that it
wasn't really that bad, or by going on in gnawing suspicion and mistrust
but finding myself too timid to demand an accounting, speak my mind,
and vent my sadness or anger, then this is not forgiving, but evading
or condoning.[17] In forgiving something is "set right" in a way that neither compromises, dulls nor buries the sense that a wrong was done. But

[16] The "problem" of finding what distinguishes forgiving from condoning is set by Kolnai,
"Forgiveness"; see also Hughes, "Moral Anger," on cases that fall between.
[17] Holmgren, "Forgiveness and the Intrinsic Value of Persons," gives an excellent account
of aspects of a process of forgiving, some of which are directed more at one's self, and
others more to the offender or the relationship.

neither must it leave the offender or the one forgiving, or their relationship, in a morally damaged position. What, then, is the "moral content" that distinguishes forgiving from condoning, or merely resigning oneself to letting go, or taking an exclusively therapeutic view of forgiveness as ridding oneself of negative feelings?

I think that to understand the moral content of forgiveness, we need to understand the content of moral relations. The damage forgiveness tries to work through or get beyond is being treated wrongly, which, in addition to whatever other harms may have occurred, is a *failure in moral relationship*. This suggests that forgiveness should restore, or return to a functioning state, the conditions of moral relationship. We need to remember that moral relations are those relations in which we reciprocally trust each other and ourselves to honor certain values and to avoid crossing certain boundaries out of a sense of responsibility. Forgiveness as a morally reparative process, then, must affirm values and standards (the boundaries) as shared among those with whom we deal, must stabilize trust in ourselves and others to be responsive to those standards, and must restore or instill a hopeful view of our moral values, ourselves, and each other. In this hopeful view we are moved to pursue and expect moral relations even in the face of all the evidence we have that this leaves us vulnerable to harm. Minor, even if hurtful, moral failure is an ordinary and everyday occurrence, while moral evil – on Claudia Card's definition, culpable wrongdoing that causes intolerable harm – is extraordinary in magnitude but also disturbingly common. Some people's everyday lives are filled with violence, torture, and abuse from parents, spouses, associates, neighbors, compatriots or political enemies, and people are unluckily randomly murdered, maimed, swindled, and seriously injured by the culpable acts of others every day, even in "well-ordered" societies.[18]

To realize how much reason we all have to be cynical about the actual power and grip of morality in human life, and yet to realize how much most of us rely in our daily lives on what protection and security it affords us, points to how resilient are our capacities to believe in the conditions of moral relationship. Most of us do believe in them, and not only in the very restricted circles in which we can keep track of people's trustworthiness and our exposure to mistreatment. In modern societies, especially, we are sustained in many anonymous transactions and encounters by a generalized trust, a moral "ground floor," although not all of us have

[18] Claudia Card, *The Atrocity Paradigm: A Theory of Evil.*

reason to trust all kinds of people in all kinds of settings. Often it is when we ourselves are wronged (or when serious wrongdoing comes too close) that we are shocked and shaken into fear, despair, or mistrust with respect to our ability to go on in a moral relationship with particular people, or to go on in a moral relationship with others generally, at least in respect to certain things. When we are the victims of wrongdoing, we are faced at least with the task of assessing any future relationship we might have with the one who has treated us wrongly; sometimes, if wrongdoing shocks us deeply enough, we may have to overcome a blow to our more general sense of trust in and hopefulness about others. That is in fact another thing for which we need to forgive the wrongdoer in serious cases: the shattering of some of the fixed points of our moral universe. This is the setting for forgiveness in the first case: when someone is a victim of wrong he or she decides at some point (or many different points) whether to remain in a position of grievance and demand with respect to the wrong-doer. This also shows that when there are secondary victims – those who are caused serious loss or suffering by a wrong done to someone else, as when family and friends cope with the murder of an individual – they, too, are confronted with that same question.[19]

When we are neither primary nor secondary victims, but wrongdoing to others unseats our own hopeful trust in the wrongdoer or in others generally, we may also face the question of whether what is done and the person who has done it is "forgivable." When serious harms to some have created fear, mistrust, and anger throughout some group or community, there is a role for forgiveness by that group or community. Forms of collective forgiveness can be embodied in informal gestures, such as the public embrace that signifies acceptance of a disgraced and spurned relation back into the good graces of a family. Collective forgiveness can also be conveyed by rituals for the purpose of reintegration, such as the "rehumanization" ceremonies in the traditions of some African societies that make someone who has been involved in bloodshed "a person again, not such a monster" in the words of development specialist Roberto Luis (speaking in Mozambique after an extraordinarily brutal civil war).[20] John Shay, in his profound explorations of the moral meaning of combat trauma, laments the absence in U.S. society of "a communal ritual with religious force" for returning veterans, something essential in his

---

[19] Govier distinguishes primary, secondary, and tertiary victims in *Forgiveness and Revenge*, 92–95.

[20] Quoted by Priscilla B. Hayner, *Unspeakable Truths: Confronting State Terror and Atrocity*, 193.

view for both the veterans and for their society.[21] Societies such as ours also have institutional versions of, or simulacra of, forgiveness, such as the exercise of judicial clemency or executive pardon, or the granting of parole or the restoration of civil rights to a convicted lawbreaker.

In any of these cases, of course, the gesture on behalf of a collective might not correspond exactly or even roughly to the sentiments against forgiving that continue to exist within individuals of the collective, and "representative" acts may fail to represent real attitudes prevalent in a group. On the other hand, forms of communal, collective, or institutional forgiveness allow secondary or tertiary victims to forgive an offender for what they have suffered when a primary victim refuses to forgive the primary injury. These situations are obviously fraught with unsavory possibilities of disrespect by indirect victims toward primary victims, or of "moral blackmail" of communities by unreasonably unforgiving victims. But they also remind us that moral injury is seldom a private matter, and all wrongdoing poses reparative tasks for smaller or larger communities. While the primary victim has a particular status, reintegration of those who have violated the security and trust of communities is not only permissible but indispensable. Here let's assume that we are dealing with primary and secondary victims, whose loss is distinctly personal. Which ways of relinquishing the position of grievance and demand can be seen as moral repair?

Forgiveness is reparative where it revives or stabilizes trust and hope in authoritative moral understandings, and in the viability of moral relations, for the one who forgives.[22] It must allow one to see these as secure, and to see oneself as secure and dignified by honoring them, for then it lets one decide to forgo insisting past a certain point on further demonstrations of their validity from the offender or others. Where possible, such a process reconnects wrongdoers and those wronged in relationship, but we have seen that this is not always *morally* possible, and we have seen why: doing so or even attempting to do so can damage the grip of standards, put resignation or self-deception where trust should be, or replace hope with cynicism or wishful thinking. Where it is not

---

[21] Jonathan Shay, *Odysseus in America: Combat Trauma and the Trials of Homecoming*, 245. See also John Braithwaite's classic work, *Crime, Shame, and Reintegration*, on the importance of a clear process of rejoining criminal offenders to their societies and, ideally, to their victims.

[22] For the broader view of moral understandings as the medium for mutual acknowledgment of our identities, relationships, and values, see my *Moral Understandings: A Feminist Study in Ethics*.

possible to reconnect the parties, what can still be restored is the injured party's confidence in the authority of moral standards in her community, trust in herself and trust in others (whether or not this includes the offender) as responsive and responsible actors, and hope that this trust is not simply misplaced. This means restoring for the injured party a sense of equilibrium in acting as a moral agent.

Equilibrium means freedom from a sense of threat to one's standards, to one's well-being, and to that control of the future that comes from being able to move through a world with reasonable confidence in others' meeting my normative expectations and my being capable of meeting theirs. I am not free from these threats if I need to stay in the position of demanding that the wrongdoer, or perhaps some community of moral judgment, confirm these things. This need can sometimes be relieved by a wrongdoer showing remorse and repentance, but this may not be sufficient. Nor should we see it as necessary, for that would hold the one injured hostage to the wrongdoer's willingness to take responsibility, admit wrongdoing or wrongful harm, and express contrition. Often those in the wrong are not inclined to admit the wrong, much less to repair it.

Wrongdoers' behavior and attitudes do sometimes hold the key to forgiveness. If a single person can shatter the sense of moral order on which we depend, that person can sometimes help to mend what is broken or rebuild something anew, and by doing so or even by indicating a willingness to do so, can make trust and hope seem attainable again. We are clearly vulnerable to individuals, especially trusted ones, who seem to be able to shake loose the fixed points of our moral universe, and who can sometimes help to render them stable again. Fortunately, however, the fixed points of our moral universe are not held in place by just one individual, lest we be held hostage to the very persons who have wronged us. When we are wronged, we often look beyond the offender for acknowledgment and redress; we also look, whether or not the offender is available and willing, to others to reassure us of our rightful claims against the offender and of their support for, or at least sympathy with, our grievance. A victim of wrong decides at some point whether to remain in a position of grievance and demand not only with respect to the wrongdoer but also many times with respect to others to whom the victim looks for assurance and support. The responsiveness of others to one's injury can affect not only the psychological possibilities of forgiveness of the offender but also the injured party's judgment of the viability of forgiveness as moral repair. Indeed, when we are *not* reassured or supported by others in ways that we feel do justice (a telling phrase) to the fact of our wrongful injury, there is potential for deepened anguish and despair, resentment, or outrage at those who now themselves wrong us with their lack of insistence on the violated standards or lack of concern for us as a victim of a violation.

Victims can be driven further into the position of self-defense, grievance, reproach, and demand when they sense there is no community of moral support where they expect it to be. For the same reason, though, a victim may be fortified in her confidence in the authority of moral standards and in the general trustworthiness of others by a real or imagined community of moral understanding with others. In some cases this sense of community may give her the equanimity to reaccept the offender, or to decide instead to let the offender be, even as someone who is not yet, or perhaps never will be, fully "reclaimable" within the community of moral understandings.[23] The offender may become an object of compassion or pity, someone seen as weaker than the one who forgives, someone lacking in the self-control, strength, or sensitivity that the one forgiving shows by releasing herself and the offender from further grievance and demand. The policy of no longer pressing claims against the wrongdoer is rooted in no longer having a need to do so. Some victims may draw on the reassurance of a divine authority and judgment in which they continue to believe. Others draw up the depth of their own conviction that morality is a greater power, or draw on unusual reserves of compassion, confidence, or optimism to reassert their moral equilibrium, whether or not they decide they can continue to include the wrongdoer within the sphere of the trusting and hopeful relations they continue with others. There are no doubt specific psychological conditions that enable or disable individual victims in satisfying or extinguishing the need to continue to protest, grieve, and demand. I am claiming, though, that the need itself is not, or not only, for some psychological state of ease or rest or strength. The need is for a reaffirmation of the conditions of moral relationship that make that state well-founded.[24]

To achieve the position of strength that is morally valuable forgiveness, one who is a victim of wrongdoing must cease to feel that denunciation of the offender is necessary to the defense of moral standards. Neither must one have fear of one's own defense, or concern that one's forgiving will be taken by a careless or malicious offender, or by an unresponsive

---

[23] See Lauritzen, "Forgiveness," for an illuminating discussion of how religious, and specifically Christian, belief suggests or compels views of forgiveness different from those of nonbelievers.

[24] Compare Hieronymi, "Articulating an Uncompromising Forgiveness," 553, on the conditions for forgiving unilaterally.

community, as condoning or conceding. One needs to be able to trust other people, and one needs to be able to trust oneself in making judgments about the conditions of moral relationship, about when standards are supported, and about when others, including the offender, are or are not trustworthy. It is a sad irony that capacities for self-trust are sometimes what is damaged, along with self-respect, when victims become, as many victims do, self-blaming or despondent. For these reasons the enormity of some offenses, the indifference or viciousness of some wrongdoers, or the shattered self-trust or terror of some victims, can place forgiving out of bounds, at least at a time and in a context. So too can the indifference of communities to certain forms of offense or to such offenses when visited on certain kinds of people place forgiving out of bounds. People are differently vulnerable to certain kinds of harms, and some people are forced to recognize that certain kinds of harms are often ignored or denied by others less likely to experience them. Think of women and assault or sexual violence by men; or nonwhites and racist violence and insult. Some face a different moral calculus than others in deciding whether to forgive these harms or to refuse to. Looking at forgiveness through the lens of moral repair reveals that possibilities of forgiveness depend on the magnitude or severity of offense, the meaning of the wrong act and of the act that would forgive it in their contexts, and the situation of those who have done wrong and of those who would forgive them. It reveals that victims and wrongdoers usually do not face each other alone in responding to the wrong they have done or have suffered. Communities of support can make a great difference in whether offenders offer what is needed for forgiveness, or whether victims feel in a position to forgive, with or without the offender's participation.

While forgiveness is often pictured as wiping a slate clean, or restoring the offending party to full faith and credit, it is possible for one injured to surrender certain grievances or claims against someone who is responsible for a particular wrong, while not surrendering all such claims for all wrongs. It is also possible for one to forgive while continuing to lack positive regard for the offender. Even if in some cases forgiving means extending to the wrongdoer a trusting and hopeful attitude, affirming the offender's eligibility for what J. Harvey calls "a life of moral endeavor" with fresh starts, not all cases need conform to the picture in which forgiveness involves restoring the positive standing of the wrongdoer in the eyes of the one forgiving.[25] In a comment on Simon Wiesenthal's *The Sunflower*,

[25] See Harvey, "Forgiving as an Obligation," especially 219–20.

Luise Rinser says about deciding not to hand over her denouncers in
Nazi Germany to the Americans in 1945: "What my two friends did to *me*
I have forgiven, in the sense that I abandoned any thought of revenge
and was ready to render them any sort of assistance had they asked
me for it. But I did *not* forgive them for declaring their solidarity with
the followers of a stupid and wicked ideology, which caused the deaths of
millions of people."[26] One finds also remarkable accounts of those who
forgive, and even assist, former tormentors out of a wish not to be what
their tormentors were, and perhaps still are, and to show their affirmation
of this above all to themselves.[27]

To forgive is, certainly, to recognize wrongdoers as human beings,
fallible and limited, capable of choice and worth, neither monstrous nor
beneath contempt; in forgiving one needs to humanize, rather than to
idealize or to demonize, the wrongdoer, because that puts the wrongdoer
back into a world of moral relations that morally valuable forgiveness
affirms. If forgiving necessarily requires an offender who is seen as a
human being, and not as "scum" or "animal," or "cockroach," and who
is relieved of further exposure to reproach and demand appropriate to a
human wrongdoer, this still does not preclude making a sober practical
judgment that the very human being forgiven is a flawed, unreliable, or
even a dangerous human being, one who is unlikely to do better, or one
who is unlikely to be capable of fully fresh starts. The bestowal of renewed
trust and hopefulness specifically on the person forgiven is part of certain
kinds of scenario. It has no place in others. Adopting a good opinion of
the offender's character and possibilities is not required for forgiveness,
and believing otherwise need not undermine it.[28]

[26] Luise Rinser, in Wiesenthal, *The Sunflower*, Book 2, 197.
[27] Other writers render the actual or notional reconnection as reaffirming the moral worth
of the offending person in terms of equality, respect, compassion, or the need to start
fresh on an improvable path of moral endeavor. For example, see Murphy and Hampton, *Forgiveness and Mercy*, on rejecting the view of the wrongdoer as morally "rotten";
Holmgren, "Forgiveness and the Intrinsic Value of Persons," for a modified Kantian
account of the need for respect and compassion; Lauritzen, "Forgiveness," on moral
equality; North, "Wrongdoing and Forgiveness," on trust and compassion; and Harvey,
"Forgiving as an Obligation," on ending the wrongdoer-to-victim relation so that the
doer of a wrong now past may try to do, and be, something better.
[28] Govier, *Forgiveness and Revenge*, ch. 7, "Monstrous Deeds, Not Monstrous People," defends
the claim that we should never give up on a human being, whatever wrong they have
done. Govier is convincing on the pitfalls of condemning too quickly or too globally,
and on the dangers of scapegoating, but at times seems to imply that either one sees the
offender as capable of moral transformation, or one sees the offender as "garbage" to
be tossed away. There is a lot of room here between selective disengagements and total
exclusion, and between hopeful trust and complete rejection.

Because conditions of moral relationship are multiple, are subject to degree, and can operate selectively, and because cases of wrongdoing threaten different aspects of us and of our moral worlds, and threaten them in different ways and to varying degrees for individuals in distinct contexts, there isn't a formula for when forgiving does exactly enough and the right kind of repair. Forgiving has moral value when the wronged individual can release the wrongdoer from further recrimination and demand, and can do so while keeping, or re-establishing, a steady hold on the conditions of moral relationship that have been shaken or damaged by wrongdoing, including a firm sense of moral value, of the individual's own and the offender's moral personality, and of the hopefulness that sustains us in relations of reciprocal trust. The victim can also decide, whether or not these conditions are threatened, or upon restoring them, not to forgive. Not to forgive is to hold the offender under threat of continuing recrimination, without relief. Usually victims have reasons to withhold forgiveness. Those reasons involve something – conviction, security, dignity, communal validation, repentance, amends – that victims need but know or fear they might not get if they decide to relieve the offender of future reproach and demand. It is not, then, the reconnection or the letting go that constitutes forgiveness, but the meaning of doing one or the other in the particular case.

Fixing a Wrong in the Past
The question of which relationships are restored in forgiveness, and what it means to restore them, turns out to be very complex. Perhaps the third candidate for a necessary feature of forgiveness is not so difficult to assess. The seemingly simplest factor in forgiveness is the idea that forgiving fixes a wrong in the past *as* a wrong, while releasing the future from its impact. Forgiveness as moral repair certainly does release both the injured person and the wrongdoer from a further need to protest, and grieve over, and make demands concerning the damage to moral relations that wrongdoing has done. In order to do so, must the wrongdoer's action be fixed securely in the past under an unambiguous description that identifies its wrongfulness?

This aspect of "settling" a wrong in the past is the least commonly emphasized in contemporary philosophical accounts, although it is central for some of them.[29] It might even seem strange to suggest that fixing a wrong in the past is an aspect of forgiveness. *That a wrong has been done*

---

[29] Accounts that do push this aspect forward are ones by Arendt, Tavuchis, Harvey, and Lang.

might seem the *occasion* for forgiving, what must be there in order that forgiveness is possible, rather than part of what forgiving is. While it is true that a wrong having occurred is the occasion of forgiveness, the forgiver's fixing a wrong in the past *as a wrong* involves more. The act or its results must not only constitute a wrong, but the one who forgives must be *aware* of the act or its results; and must be aware of them under some *description* that characterizes the act as *wrong*, and the injury as something that is *over*.

These sound like matters of definition: you can, logically, only forgive a wrong you know has been done (past tense) to you. Yet matters here are not merely ones of definition. Anguishing complications in settling *what was done* can trouble the process of forgiving both in cases where one does not reconnect to the offender and also in cases where one does. I may not be sure I know exactly what is the wrong done me, or I may find that my beliefs about this are unsettled or shift over time. Over time, what has happened may come to seem less significant or less bad to me, or it may come to seem much worse, as my understanding of it (and perhaps of the offender) deepens, and as the consequences of the act unfold over the longer run. Also, if the offender is a party to the process of forgiveness, his understanding of his offense may not match mine. Put pithily: we do not always know what we are doing, or later what someone has done; and even when we think we surely do know, we may find reasons to think differently later. Yet in forgiving people we necessarily forgive them *for* something; and at least part of what we are doing, whatever else happens with our feelings, or our past or future relations, forgiving involves setting *that particular offense*, the wrong thing done, to rest.

Identifying the wrong to be forgiven is straightforward and practically incontrovertible in many cases. Yet in others it can be elusive or uncertain. Ambiguities arise from common features of the descriptions we use to capture human actions. Act descriptions often incorporate assumptions about motivation or state of mind: Did you promise or merely state an intention? Did you want to spare my feelings or save your hide? Act descriptions take in some, but not all, of the consequences of a basic performance: Did you give her the wrong medication or did you kill her? Some act descriptions incorporate assumptions about what we think it is reasonable for a person to do. Were you merely careless or were you reckless? Did you despise me or were you indifferent?

My initial point here is that identifying the wrong to be forgiven is itself an act or a process of interpretation that is one *part* of the process of forgiving; it should not be confused with the bare fact of the occurrence of the wrong act. In many cases, we miss a great deal that is important in forgiving if we pass over this facet of the process lightly, although in fact it is the least dwelt upon in the philosophical discussions with which I am familiar. *Fixing* the nature of the offense is a real issue in many cases. Identification of a wrong precedes all questions of what practical and moral possibilities are open to repair it, whether by forgiveness or other means. Judgments of the likelihood, cost, and value of their success turn on it as well. In serious cases it can be a matter of urgency to settle on the right characterization, or at least a plausible or viable one, of what sort of harm has been done, although this may be difficult to do. Given that identifying the wrong sets a task, and sometimes a task shared among the injured party, the wrongdoer, or others, the process of identifying the wrong clearly, or in a way that is accepted by all, has positive and negative potential. Defining the wrong can be an awakening to deeper understanding, firmer judgment, or greater compassion for all involved. But it can also either continue or compound the original offense, or deepen confusion or bad feeling due to the offense or due to the (sometimes shared) attempt at definition.

In unilateral cases of forgiveness (ones that do not or cannot require a concrete reconnection through an acceptance of forgiveness), at least the forgiver must settle her mind on the offense. In interactive cases, forgiveness is played out interpersonally, either by the offender offering apologies, displaying contrition, or asking forgiveness, or by the injured person offering to forgive as a prelude to re-establishing an actual relationship or terminating the relationship in a morally saving way. It might seem that something is amiss if what the forgiver forgives is not the same as what the offender believes she has done. Surprisingly, this is not always true. Human motivations are not transparent, and the precise nature of an offense can be opaque or susceptible to rather different descriptions, even for actors themselves. Someone's hurtful remarks, for example, might have been careless chatter, a vindictive attack, an ill-considered flash of justified anger, or a deliberate act with an ulterior motive in which one was thoughtlessly made a pawn. Hence there could be different things, indeed different kinds of things with differing implications, to forgive here. And inasmuch as time and distance allow for the unfolding of both more extensive consequences and different interpretations of "what happened," one may be uncertain what one is trying to forgive, and whether one should or can forgive. One might not know whether it is fair to hold someone responsible for certain consequences of a wrong act that constitute additional harms. You failed to do what you promised, but are you responsible for the failure of my project, which was after all not completely dependent on your cooperation?

These examples are tame, but in the wake of large-scale wrongdoing, for example of oppressive and terroristic regimes that practiced torture, disappearance, massacre, and arbitrary detention, we have learned how profoundly the truth is wanted and needed, and how powerfully it can affect people's ability to set things in the past, even sometimes to forgive, horrific crimes, once they know "what was done." Truth commissions have now become an institution characteristic of political transitions in the late twentieth century, and South Africa's Truth and Reconciliation Commission transfixed a global audience with its largely public proceedings of taking testimony on murders and grave violations of human rights from both victims and perpetrators.[30] Some victims and survivors of such situations want to know why the wrongdoing occurred or why they or their loved ones were targeted. Crime victims, it is known, have deep needs to understand what has happened to them, and may see answers to certain questions, some of which can only be supplied by the one who hurt them, as part of what it means for them to "get justice."[31] Others, such as families of those disappeared, seem simply to need to know what happened, or to know it with specific detail and clarity. We surely do not know yet very much about how much official tribunals of truth can accomplish, beyond securing some desperately wanted and needed truths, and what they cannot hope to do. But they demonstrate how fundamental is the desire for the truth of what happened, and how often it is the threshold for the repair of selves and moral relations, including forgiveness. Sometimes a crucial bit of truth is enough. In other cases no amount of truth can ever allow the past to be fixed behind us; it bleeds into the present endlessly, swamping our abilities to let it go even if we want to.

[30] The most comprehensive and detailed account of truth commissions that have convened and the work they have done is Hayner, *Unspeakable Truths*. Henry J. Steiner, ed., *Truth Commissions: A Comparative Assessment*, is a searching roundtable discussion of truth commissions, and Robert I. Rotberg and Dennis Thompson, eds., *Truth v. Justice: The Morality of Truth Commissions*, examines many moral and political aspects of truth commissions.

[31] Howard Zehr, in *Changing Lenses: A New Focus for Crime and Justice*, begins the book with a discussion of victim needs. In a riveting example, Walter Dickey, "Forgiveness and Crime: The Possibilities of Restorative Justice," reproduces part of a victim-offender conference between a woman who was sexually assaulted and the man who raped her. The conference exemplifies both victims' needs to know more themselves and victims' needs to make offenders know what they have done. In many cases of wrongdoing, "articulating" the offense seems to play multiple and important roles.

Should we then conclude that forgiveness is only possible when a wrong can be fixed securely in the past under an unambiguous description? In some cases this will be true, yet I want to deny that forgiving is impossible unless a determinate wrong can be fixed as such in the past. Lingering indeterminacy in what was done, or persistent differences in interpretations between parties, or the clarifying or corrosive effects of time in which shifting narratives take up and reframe the events that constitute the past – these do not preclude forgiving. Two friends may rehash a painful rift to the point where it becomes clear that neither can honestly affirm precisely the other's version of what happened. But this need not prevent them from renewing mutual trust and continuing their relationship, in effect agreeing to split the interpretive difference in order to re-establish good will; this itself may show respect for each other's judgment and sensibilities. Victims of crime are sometimes able to achieve a morally reparative resolution of their attitude to their offenders without settling questions of offenders' motivations precisely. This can be good sense, for people do not themselves always know exactly why they do what they do, and there may be no honest reconstruction of this long after the fact. Or it can simply be generous, a decision to start with what a wrongdoer feels and understands and hopes for now, for example to make amends, to do better. Because one cannot foretell the future, yet forgiveness dares to lay down a grievance now without knowing how it might appear later, the act of forgiveness itself is an expression of hopefulness.

There is a crucial difference, though, when knowledge or acknowledgment of truth about past wrongs is withheld through silence, denial, or euphemism, as is so characteristic of cases of political violence or oppression, but which is also at work in personal betrayals and serious deceptions. This blocks the way to forgiving, as does the tormenting or infuriating sense that one's injury is belittled or condoned either by the offender or by one's community, so that one cannot rest on a stable shared judgment of how serious an injury one has sustained. In *some* cases, then, settling the fact of the matter or securing its acknowledgment releases the grip of bad feeling or estrangement, and of the need to keep up a protest and demand; yet in others the morally reparative effects of releasing offender and offended is what motivates one to relinquish the quest for a more settled or precise truth than is available.

Finally, there remains an instability in forgiveness that is due to the unavoidable nature of human understanding in narrative through time. We constantly revisit our individual and shared pasts, and we often bring with us new understandings from the present that make what has already happened look different from the later point of view. Some of this is interpretation, as when I decide, given your subsequent behavior, that your past deception of me really was cold-hearted and not just immature confusion, or that I really was more responsible than you for the ending of our relationship. More information, but also newly informed understanding, can make for different interpretations of something in the past. Some hindsight, however, is the product of original events still working their way out in time. Since many actions are accurately described only by incorporating their consequences (if I shoot you and you die of the wound, then I have killed you), and consequences can unfold over a great long time, the story that can be told about what someone did can be revised by later outcomes.

Most of the stories through which we retrieve and understand the past are mixtures of interpretation and more capacious redescriptions that capture later effects. Robert Sparrow writes: "It was undoubtedly the case that some of the government officials, representatives of churches, and foster parents who removed Aboriginal children from their homes and denied them knowledge of their origins and access to their culture did so in the sincere desire to do well by both individual children and the Aboriginal 'race' as a whole. But this does not alter the fact that, as we can now see, the theft of Aboriginal children from their homes was a great and terrible crime."[32] So too, was the crime done to American Indian peoples whose children were removed to boarding schools where they were forbidden to speak their languages or wear their own dress. Sparrow's broader point is that *what we will have done* may not be fully evident until, with the passage of time, historic events, both individual and collective, acquire their later interpretations and reveal the full extent of their impact: "The meaning of historical events and of what is required to do justice to them will change over time. This means that new claims for justice may arise. With new understandings of what justice requires comes a new sense of the injustices which were done and of what is required to undo or compensate for them. New aspects of old injustices may appear."[33] So, too, what is forgiven may not always be a case closed, if what one forgave at one time is not the same as what one comes to see later as the wrong done.

Only a falsely simplistic view of time and history could relieve us of this uncomfortable consequence. One lesson of it is that in the case of

---

[32] Robert Sparrow, "History and Collective Responsibility," 357.
[33] Sparrow, "History and Collective Responsibility," 358.

historical injustice, we need continuing practices of truth-telling and gestures of respect and reparation when the truths revealed are ugly ones of injustice, destruction, and humiliation. On the other hand, this consequence may be seen as an opportunity for moral growth, and not only something uncomfortable. Victoria McGeer argues that forgiveness can require "moral travel" that *correctly* transforms an oversimple sense of injury and victimization to a more complex understanding of the roles of both the forgiver and the one forgiven in what has happened between them. But McGeer also cautions that "entering into and feeling touched by the wrongdoer's view can lead the victim astray if she does not also maintain her sense of justice, or her vision of what is worth striving for in relationships of mutual respect."[34] But even when we do so with clear eyes and realistic understanding, *should* we always be open to forgiving?

The Unforgivable

It is staggering, sometimes scarcely credible, what individuals are capable of forgiving.

Lawrence Weschler describes Luis Perez Aguirre, a young Jesuit priest from a wealthy family who, during the severe repression under a military government that took power in 1973, was repeatedly imprisoned and tortured after founding a human rights organization in Montevideo, Uruguay, in 1981.[35] Still bearing the lines of scarred cigarette burns on his arms, he describes twice encountering on the street the man who tortured him: "He tried to avoid my gaze . . . But I took the initiative. I called him over. . . . He told me he is very depressed . . . I showed him in a practical way that I was not angry. I told him if he needed anything to come to me. And I told him I forgave him." Perez Aguirre attributes his ability to forgive to "profound Christian conviction" and "internal effort."[36]

Pumla Gobodo-Madikizela describes what she heard from Mrs. Pearl Faku, widow of a slain black policeman, to whom Eugene de Kock, notorious murderer in the South African security police, made an apology. Mrs. Faku's husband had been duped by the Pretoria police and blown up by remote control along with his colleagues under a plan fashioned by de Kock. Mrs. Faku said: "I was profoundly touched by him. . . . I couldn't

---

[34] McGeer, "Moral Travel and the Narrative Work of Forgiveness." An account of moral uses of reconstructing narrative self-understandings, especially for groups with stigmatized identities, is Hilde Lindemann Nelson, *Damaged Identities, Narrative Repair*.

[35] Lawrence Weschler, *A Miracle, A Universe: Settling Accounts with Torturers*, 154–55.

[36] Weschler, *A Miracle, A Universe*, 199.

control my tears. I could hear him, but I was overwhelmed by emotion, and I was just nodding, as a way of saying yes, I forgive you. I hope that when he sees our tears, he knows that they are not only tears for our husbands, but for him as well...I would like to hold him by the hand, and show him that there is a future, and that he can still change."[37]

Another post-apartheid South African story much more widely known is that of Amy Biehl's parents. Biehl, a white American and Fulbright scholar in South Africa, was driving home black friends who lived in a black township when she was murdered by a mob, who stoned and stabbed her to death. Two of the young men who murdered Amy Biehl served four years in jail before receiving amnesty from the Truth and Reconciliation Commission. The Biehls did not oppose the amnesty. They started a memorial trust to provide jobs and food to poor black South Africans, and they now employ two of the men who cornered, beat, and killed their daughter. Amy's father says: "I thought of them as young people used in a situation, in a horrible system." Amy's mother says "I feel very close to Amy when I'm with them." Many people find the Biehls' generosity beyond belief; some are awed by it, others see it as puzzling or as a bizarre form of denial of what, it is supposed, they surely must, or ought to, feel.[38]

Mr. Kassie Neou, who survived torture on the whim of guards to whom he recited Aesop's fables during the massive removals, mass killings, and systematic torture of the Khmer Rouge period in Cambodia, says "I told myself that when my time comes, I will take revenge five times worse than what they are doing to me." Yet after the Khmer Rouge government collapsed, Mr. Neou recognized one of his torturers in a refugee camp across the border in Thailand. "Because of his fear, and because his baby was dying, I completely changed my mind about taking revenge through anger." He took the man to a feeding center, gave him money for cigarettes, and arranged for care for the man's wife and child. When the former torturer trembled thankfully in tears, Mr. Neou decided that "At this point I realized that I had made my revenge."[39] This "revenge" sounds more like a triumph of forgiveness, and that is the phrase used in the article's title. Psychologist Gobodo-Madikizela explains that forgiveness can be seen as a kind of revenge in that it can represent a *triumph*

---

[37] Pumla Gobodo-Madikizela, *A Human Being Died That Night: A South African Story of Forgiveness*, 15.

[38] Linda Vergnani, "Parents of Slain Fulbright Scholar Embrace Her Cause in South Africa," accessed 18 January 2001.

[39] Seth Mydans, "Cambodian Aesop Tells a Fable of Forgiveness."

for the victim that "does not overlook the deed: it rises above it. 'This is what it means to be human,' it says. 'I cannot and will not return the evil you inflicted on me.'"[40]

For those with very demanding standards of humanity, even heroic compassion may seem inadequate to their ideal. The obituary of Ani Pachen describes her life as a warrior-nun who led her clan in Tibet in armed rebellion against the Chinese, and who spent twenty-one years as a prisoner, beaten and tortured, after being captured at age twenty-five. "I feel terrible for those who imprisoned me," she reportedly said. She also expressed sorrow for the captors who tortured her, attributing their cruelties to karma from their past lives. But in Ani Pachen's eyes she had not been able to do enough: "I have not reached enlightenment– the absence of negative feelings... I want to have full compassion, but I spent half my life in prison and I still have some anger."[41] Is it not then forgiveness that Pachen achieved?

At its farthest reaches the work of forgiveness seems well beyond what most of us expect human beings to be able to do, and it can be startling to see, as in Ani Pachen's case, what some human beings demand of themselves, rather than of others, when they have been the victims of terrible evils. Yet, human beings do forgive horrific wrongs they have suffered, and they sometimes make enormous demands on themselves to achieve this. Even if they are exceptions in the larger scheme, there are many exceptions. Many of us would no doubt be *unable* to forgive as some others have done; in that sense, we would find it psychologically impossible to achieve what they have achieved. Insofar as one can be at a time too angry, too shattered, or too frightened to let go of the protection or consolation of continuing to reproach and grieve, one can be unable to forgive *at a time*, and, if one never gets beyond these feelings, one might be *unable* to forgive at *any* time.

Can we, however, make sense of the idea that these astonishing acts of forgiveness, or any act of forgiveness, might be *wrong*, either at a time, or for all time? This would be to claim that some instances or some kinds of wrongdoing *ought not morally* to be forgiven, either at a time or at any time. Gobodo-Madikizela, who saw remarkable feats of forgiveness, as well as clear refusals of forgiveness, as a member of South Africa's Truth and Reconciliation Commission captures one view that some wrongs are unforgivable, even though it is apparently not a view she endorses: "There

---

[40] Gobodo-Madikizela, *A Human Being Died That Night,* 117.
[41] Douglas Martin, "Ani Pachen, Warrior Nun In Tibet Jail 21 Years, Dies."

is a desire to draw the line and say, 'Where you have been, I cannot follow you. Your actions can never be regarded as part of what it means to be human.'"[42] Following Hannah Arendt's idea that some kinds of evil can be neither punished nor forgiven, she notes that "no amount of punishment can balance what they have done.... no yardstick exists by which we can measure what it means to forgive them, and there is no mental disposition we can adopt toward them that would correct the sense of injustice that their actions have injected into our world."[43]

Let's first notice that there are actions that may be "unforgivable," not only psychologically but morally, *at a time* or *in a context*, which might yet be forgivable at another time or when the circumstances have changed. If morally valuable forgiveness requires regaining or consolidating self-trust, for example, someone might realize that it is "too soon" to forgive because she continues to doubt the accuracy of her assessment of the situation. Or if someone is prepared to forgive on condition that the offender acknowledge the full extent of the hurt, then it may not be possible to forgive until the offender comes to that recognition; to do so without that recognition might be to condone the wrongdoing. Forgiveness is often conditional on appropriate acknowledgment and truth-telling, on sincere repentance of the wrongdoer, or on amends having been made or punishment taken. Similarly, although forgiveness is often counterposed to retaliation or vengeance, it is perfectly possible to retaliate against someone for wrong, and *then* forgive them once they have paid *that* particular price, whatever else one might feel is owed. Where the reparative role of forgiveness is blocked or impossible due to some changeable feature of the situation, it may well be true that to forgive under those conditions would be wrong.

Let's also note that a wrong might be one that someone cannot forgive because that person is not the victim of that wrong. I believe it is correct

---

[42] Gobodo-Madikizela, *A Human Being Died That Night*, 103.

[43] Gobodo-Madikizela, *A Human Being Died That Night*, 123. The Arendt passage is in *The Human Condition*, 241, and it remains mysterious, because elliptical. Arendt says that "radical evil" can be neither punished nor forgiven, and that this is a "structural element" in human affairs, but the passage leaves unclear precisely what it is that makes these actions incapable of either punishment or forgiveness, although the passage implies that it is the same feature that makes them both so. Recent discussions of the unforgivable include: Cheyney Ryan, "Thinking About the Unforgivable"; Laurence Mordekhai Thomas, "Forgiving the Unforgivable?"; Nancy Potter, "Is Refusing to Forgive a Vice?"; Claudia Card, *The Atrocity Paradigm: A Theory of Evil*, ch. 8, "The Moral Powers of Victims"; Digeser, *Political Forgiveness*, ch. 2, "Political Forgiveness and Justice"; and Govier, *Forgiveness and Revenge*, ch. 6, "The Unforgivable."

that one can only forgive a wrong one has suffered. Matters become complex when there are secondary, and even tertiary victims, but the same rule applies: if there are primary, secondary, and tertiary victims, then the primary victim is in a position to forgive what was done to her, the secondary victims to forgive what they suffered because of what was done to the primary victim, and the tertiary victims to forgive the damage done to their community, or to the authority of its standards, or to the fabric of trust torn by the offense to the primary victim. Neither secondary nor tertiary victims, however, are in a position to forgive an offender what the offender did to the primary victim. Again, however, this can be complex in context. A child, for example, who has lived with malicious damage done by certain parties to a parent's reputation might rightly claim standing to forgive as an "heir" or "representative" of a deceased parent, as well as the standing to forgive or to withhold forgiveness for the losses and humiliation she suffered as a consequence of her parent's disgrace. Secondary and tertiary victims ought to be respectful and circumspect about exercising even their proper prerogatives to forgive when the primary victim does not forgive, lest they imply a lack of regard for the victim's loss and suffering, or a lack of support for the victim's task of repairing her own moral confidence, trust, and hopefulness. Respect and circumspection, however, do not prevent others who have suffered from a wrongdoing from deciding in some cases that the victim is being unreasonable or unyielding, and so to give their forgiveness for wrongs and harms done to them, even where the primary victim remains unmoved.

Even in a case like this, though, many of us are very reluctant to hold that victims are *obligated* to forgive, and *wrong* not to. The perspective on whether the conditions for moral relationship can be restored, or have been restored, will not necessarily be the same for all those affected by a wrong. A certain deference to the opinion of primary victims is both practical and moral. It is practical, in that others may not be in the best position to understand how well the primary victim feels she has restored the moral reference points and resources that enable her to go on with some equanimity. It is moral, because to coerce in any way a person already harmed or disrespected by a wrong into relinquishing her own need to grieve, reproach, and make demands may itself be harmful or disrespectful. In the opposite case, where primary victims forgive, but secondary and tertiary victims are reluctant to do so, or are opposed to doing so, those opposed are likely to argue that forgiveness is risky or destructive because it gives the wrong signal about standards, or lowers the bar for trustworthiness, or fails to demand enough of the wrongdoer in the way of remorse, retribution, or amends. Sometimes the unforgiving others respect the primary victim's decision to forgive, but take moral issue with it. They might say she is making a mistake, or that their judgment would be otherwise were they in her position. But it is also possible to recognize the entitlement of the victim to forgive the injury done to him, while reserving the right of others to deal unforgivingly with the implications of the wrongdoing for them.[44]

More delicate and fraught might be the situation of primary victims who suffered similar injuries, and who may feel that their prerogative to forgive is something shared, something that is common property. When some victims of a corporate or government negligence decide to forgive, and to accept private settlements and expressions of regret rather than pursue public redress, others may feel outraged and betrayed, and not only or primarily because they anticipate that this could lessen the compensation they might eventually win. They might object because they see the others' acceptance as sending a message that what they, too, suffered in fact can be compensated, or compensated too easily, or compensated without the full investigation and acknowledgment, or perhaps a legal finding of fault, for which they hold out. When people have suffered terrible injustice or cruelty because of their belonging (or because of the perception that they belonged) to a particular group, such as a persecuted ethnic, racial, religious, or political group, the fact that they were wronged *as* members of the group might cause some to feel that exercising an individual option to forgive either betrays the group, or shows a dangerous misunderstanding of their shared victimization as members of that group. They might see the forgiveness of some among them as signaling an acceptance or a lack of concern about the degree to which the group remains threatened, or is still looked down upon by other members of society. Unforgiving group members may feel certain that keeping alive their history of injustice and rightful grievance is necessary until a deeper understanding of the wrong that was done and of the still-threatened position of the group within a larger community is achieved; they may believe that keeping the grievance alive is a way to force that deeper understanding. Again, in this kind of case, it is claimed that some, in forgiving, are making a moral mistake. Victims' choices to forgive or not to forgive deserve to be respected but this does not mean that other

---

[44] A good discussion of prerogatives to forgive is Trudy Govier and Wilhelm Verwoerd, "Forgiveness: The Victim's Prerogative."

victims and the victims' community may not criticize those choices on moral grounds.

The conditions under which forgiveness is morally acceptable, then, are complex. Whether the conditions are fulfilled adequately, or at all, is a matter of judgment upon which observers and affected parties might differ. Claudia Card sees forgiveness as a "moral power" of victims and holds that there is no simple or general answer to the question whether some deeds are morally unforgivable, that is, whether it is morally wrong for the victim to exercise that power in particular cases. Forgiveness has multiple dimensions, so what might make it wrong to forgive one wrong might not be the same as what makes it wrong to forgive another.[45] Card's resistance to generalization about "unforgivability" is sound. Forgivability or unforgivability are best seen as conclusions reached at particular times by those whose option it is to forgive, and conclusions that are best based on an understanding that acknowledges the complexity of what forgiveness attempts, to release those wronged and their wrongdoers from grievance and reproach in a morally reparative way. As with other conclusions about what it is morally sound, necessary, or acceptable to do, decisions to forgive are open to the assessment and criticism of others on factual and moral grounds. Insofar as different conclusions about whether to forgive may depend on different assumptions and differing levels of optimism, there is not necessarily a uniquely right conclusion to draw, especially when the wrong is grave and many people are party to it.

There is nonetheless a dimension of wrongdoing that is deeply linked to the question of unforgivability in many contexts. It helps to explain the reticence many of us feel in criticizing the decisions of some victims to give or to withhold forgiveness, as well as our resistance to holding that forgiveness is obligatory for victims in some circumstances. This dimension of wrongdoing is *cost*. Pamela Hieronymi has captured this aspect of wrongdoing and its link to forgiveness well. She notes "when a wrong has been done *someone* will bear the cost of that wrong. In forgiveness, the one *wronged* absorbs the cost . . . Forgiveness is not *simply* a revision in judgment or a change in view or a wiping clean or a washing away or a making new. Someone will bear the cost in his or her own person. The wrong is less 'let go of' or washed away than it is digested and absorbed."[46]

---

[45] Card, *The Atrocity Paradigm*, 180–81.

[46] Hieronymi, "Articulating an Uncompromising Forgiveness," 551, n. 39. Hieronymi actually says the cost is absorbed "without retribution." But I have found the formulation that opposes forgiveness to any retaliation or retribution too neat. What is important here is

The issue of cost revives the core and oldest meaning of forgiveness, the meaning of a wronged person's excusing a debt, *giving up the demand that a cost be payed by one who in justice deserves to pay it.*

There is a very basic intuition that one who wrongs another should "pay." A simple embodiment of this intuition is the idea of "tit for tat," which can take the form of striking back at a wrongdoer, in kind or in proportion, or refusing to cooperate with an individual who does not behave cooperatively. Reprisal, or even its more dignified, impersonal, and socially expressive form, retributive punishment, however, is not the only intuitive form of demanding payment. John Braithwaite, in the opening to his recent book *Restorative Justice and Responsive Regulation*, provides examples from various historical and cultural settings of the social rituals and practices that address the human conviction that those who offend must "pay" for harms and losses they have wrongly inflicted on others. Traditions in many places involve reparations, material or symbolic payments or offerings, that follow some socially recognized script, such as the institution of Nanante of the Pashtun Afghanis, in which the offender makes food offerings as part of a ceremony, or the pattern of Scottish disputing that involved payments of compensation, religious offerings, or even giving kin in marriage between feuding families to settle serious wrongs.[47] When a wrong is serious, it is usually because someone has wrongfully caused someone else a loss or a suffering that is undeserved, and therefore has imposed a cost that the wronged party should not have to suffer or bear. The idea of making the wrongdoer (and in many societies, the wrongdoer's family or clan) cancel or compensate or assume the cost is at the root of many formal and informal reparative practices.

What exactly are the "costs" of wrongdoing? Generally, they include material losses and forms of pain and suffering, including exhausting and tormenting feelings that are hard to endure. Material losses and their consequent discomforts are sometimes easy to identify, as when

Hieronymi's identification of the placing of "cost." Psychologists who have developed a detailed psychological model of forgiveness also point out that forgiving involves "committing oneself *not* to pass on the pain of the injury to others, including the offender": see Robert D. Enright, Suzanne Freedman, and Julio Rique, "The Psychology of Interpersonal Forgiveness."

47 John Braithwaite, *Restorative Justice and Responsive Regulation*, ch. 1, "The Fall and Rise of Restorative Justice." Another restorative justice advocate, Zehr, also discusses the centrality of settlements in "community justice," in *Changing Lenses*, ch. 7, "Community Justice: The Historical Alternative."

someone destroys property and needs to replace the property or cover its replacement value. In legal contexts where compensation must be assessed for less easily measurable material losses, such as earning capacity over a period of many years, what is meaningful or proportionate in the way of money or other material compensation is not necessarily straightforward. Material losses are not always of money or replaceable goods. Loss of a limb or one's sight is a material loss, but clearly not only that. Whatever the material loss, it is probably the rare case when material compensation does not include a symbolic element, where the giving of compensation itself acknowledges responsibility, and the amount or kind of compensation sends a message about the seriousness of the wrong or the sincerity of responsible parties in trying to "make things right."

In the case of reparations paid to survivors of the forced removal and internment of Japanese-Americans by the U.S. government during the Second World War, the Civil Liberties Act of 1988 determined a one-time, tax-free, per capita compensation payment of $20,000 by the U.S. government to each survivor of the unjust internment. This obviously represented neither a reckoning of actual individual losses, nor exactly the amount of $25,000 sought by the Japanese American Citizens' League organized over a decade before.[48] Such awards attempt to offer enough to achieve the effect of sincere acknowledgment and concern and to avoid appearing trivial or insulting, but otherwise conform to no particular calculus, except perhaps the calculations of political viability in context. Importantly, the redress offered by the legislation included an apology from the President of the United States, presidential pardon for those convicted of violating statutes implementing the internment, restitution by government departments of status or entitlement lost due to wartime discrimination, and a foundation to sponsor research and education on the episode. The internment caused not only losses of income, investments, and property, but also humiliation, physical and emotional hardship, and complex histories of concealment and shame within families affecting several generations. For this reason, measures other than money were needed to restore dignity, reputation, accurate historical understanding, and clear acknowledgment of the blamelessness of the

[48] See Martha Minow's discussion in *Between Vengeance and Forgiveness: Facing History After Genocide and Mass Violence*, ch. 5, "Reparations"; Roy Brooks, ed., *When Sorry Isn't Enough: The Controversy Over Apologies and Reparations for Human Injustice*, collects original documents and analysis of the case, and Elazar Barkan, *The Guilt of Nations: Restitution and Negotiating Historical Injustices*, devotes a chapter to the episode.

victims. The costs were not only material in kind, and neither were the effective forms of redress.

Compare the case of the State of Florida's Rosewood Compensation Act of 1994, no doubt influenced by the reparations paid to Japanese-Americans a decade before. The Act responded to a white riot on New Year's Day, 1923, in the small town of Rosewood, Florida, in response to an allegation that a white woman was assaulted by a black man who had escaped from a road gang. Eight people were killed and dozens injured, hundreds were run out of their homes, and the town was destroyed, as law enforcement officers either participated or stood by. Seventy years later the State of Florida acknowledged the episode and accepted responsibility for its failure to intervene. In addition to requiring criminal investigation of the events and research and education about them, the state determined a payment of at least $20,000 per affected family for loss of property, as well as payment up to $150,000 for those who experienced the violence, and established a minority scholarship program with preference for descendants of the Rosewood families. The State of Florida, however, did not offer an apology to the residents of Rosewood, and the amounts actually paid were modest.[49] The State of Florida in effect acknowledged that the losses to Rosewood residents were wrongful and so the residents were deserving of material compensation for loss and suffering from the state, which did not fulfill its protective duties. In withholding apology, however, the State of Florida avoided taking on unilateral responsibility for what happened, and avoided putting the state as a whole, or the state government, in the position of the wrongdoer. Compensation programs, especially when they are largely material, can exploit the ambiguity between making amends for wrong done and relieving undeserved wrong and suffering independently of the exact nature and degree of responsibility that the compensating party bears for the wrongs that resulted in loss or suffering. The victims' judgment of whether to forgive is reasonably shaped by their sense of whether some responsible parties are unwilling to absorb enough of the moral, as well as the material, costs of a wrong.

Official cases of paying costs for wrongdoing reveal elements present in personal cases as well. Where wrongs harm, there might be material losses and the sufferings they entail. Some of these (such as lost property) can be literally "repaid" but others (lost opportunity, chronic pain from an assault, or debilitating persistent fear) can only be compensated. There

---

[49] Brooks, *When Sorry Isn't Enough*, 435–37.

are also no less real but essentially moral costs to be paid in the wake of wrongdoing. Social and psychic moral costs victims pay include sustaining protest and reproach in order to press their claims for acknowledgment and redress against wrongdoers, and perhaps upon others whose support they need. Those wronged may find themselves in the additionally humiliating and painful bind of having to insist on affirmation of their worth and dignity, thus conceding that these have been placed in question by ill treatment. Remaining in the state of grievance is demanding of time and energy, can severely tax social relationships, and can dominate a life that otherwise would have been devoted to other matters. Social and psychic moral costs also adhere to absorbing the rage, grief, resentment, fear, mistrust, and despondency that wrongdoing can visit on victims, and with which victims may struggle alone. Worse, the pursuit of payment may require victims to keep feelings of resentment, anger, insult or bitterness alive. These emotions take the form of reproach when aimed at wrongdoers but they can cause depression, shame, and humiliation when they are turned inward or when their expression is constantly, exhaustingly restrained. In forgiving, victims may be able to release themselves from the harrowing or grinding process of pursuing payment, in all its senses, as well as to release offenders from further grievance and demands that they pay.

Forgiveness is often, unsurprisingly, experienced by those who forgive, as much as by those forgiven, as being freed of a burden. Also unsurprising is the degree to which sincere efforts on the part of the wrongdoer to take responsibility, accept blame, reproach, and punishment, offer amends, and generally be responsive to what the injured person wants and needs in the way of repair count in favor of forgiveness in many cases.[50] These efforts at relieving, paying, or sharing costs are all the wrongdoer can do after the wrong is done, but they often matter greatly. They rarely relieve the victim of all unfair costs, but they can relieve some of them, and they show an understanding of what it is that the victim has been forced to bear.

This returns us to the question of whether there are cases in which releasing oneself and one's offender from the demand for payment is morally objectionable. One obvious answer will be that the demand for payment can be given up too easily, or can be considered paid at too cheap a rate; this is often what is meant by the charge that someone's forgiveness

---

[50] Thomas, "Forgiving the Unforgivable?," 30–31, points out the importance of allowing the victims to express justified moral outrage as a condition for proper forgiveness.

is really condoning a wrong by choosing to ignore it or downplay its seriousness. Yet morally reparative forgiveness is indeed, as Card says, a "moral power," and if the victim does not show other signs of lack of self-respect, or of fear of or domination by the offender, or of self-deception or denial about the reality and severity of the offense or the effects of the victims' absorbing the costs, why shouldn't we credit, even admire, the victim's impressive power to forgive? We have seen that people do forgive murderers and torturers and others who have caused terrible ruthless harms. In what sense might they be wrong, rather than exceptionally courageous and resourceful? Who decides the "acceptable" degree or type of repayment that opens the way to morally acceptable forgiveness? Who but the victim can decide what type or magnitude of cost she or he is prepared to absorb?

Peter Digeser suggests one answer to this question, although he intends it to apply to forgiveness in a political domain, where forgiveness is essentially a public performance. Digeser says that "the meaning of political forgiveness is parasitic on the notion of justice as receiving one's due," so that political forgiveness is dependent on "the demands of justice being addressed and at least minimally satisfied."[51] Where the limits of justice are reached, or where other important goods cannot be secured by seeking what is justly due, there political forgiveness has its role. Where minimal conditions of justice, especially establishing the truth about a wrong and about responsibility for it, have not been fulfilled, forgiveness is out of place, because demands of justice are urgent, and where they can be met they must not simply be put aside. On the other hand, where the wrong goes beyond anything that can be rectified, and so there is no measure of what is "due," Digeser suggests, there political forgiveness also has no place. Digeser clearly restricts his account to public contexts of politics and to cases where a relationship obtains between existing offender(s) and victim(s), and doubts that the same conditions delimit forgiveness in nonpublic cases. His framework is nonetheless useful, for it suggests that unconditional unilateral forgiveness may be morally questioned where nothing is required of offenders who are still in a position to assume some cost. It also implies that the magnitude of the offense is relevant: regardless of what offenders may do or offer in the way of repentance, compensation, and other repair, an offense that utterly outstrips all imaginable compensation is truly irreparable, and so there is no meaningful way to fill in the payment that is forgone.

---

[51] Digeser, *Political Forgiveness*, 5–10.

We seem now to have returned to a version of Arendt's dictum: we cannot forgive what we cannot punish, presumably because the offense exceeds any measure of what is "due" in justice either way. The intuitive examples would be those where wrongdoing is unfathomable in its motivation, at the extremes of cruelty or mindlessness, or unimaginable in its magnitude, affecting massive numbers of people or affecting people in ways that are massively, permanently devastating, or both. One can neither extract nor waive payment of an incalculable debt. Yet immeasurable loss and uncompensatable injury are, sadly, things that happen every day. These cases, including the murders of loved ones, are sometimes in fact found forgivable, and are forgiven in ways that are morally regenerative for those who forgive, and sometimes also for those who receive forgiveness; these appear to be admirable acts of moral courage and displays of moral integrity.

It might even be argued that the very fact that some wrongs could never be compensated is precisely what makes forgiveness valuable, as Arendt also said. Forgiveness might be the sole possibility of our actively releasing ourselves and those who wrong us from a debt that never *could* be made good. It is the one opportunity to retrieve something of moral worth and hopeful human possibility out of what otherwise remains devastating and hopeless, and to relieve those in grief of pursuing payment of a debt that can never possibly be paid. Marietta Jaeger's account of forgiving the murderer of her seven-year-old daughter, abducted on a family camping trip, illustrates a reaction like that of Mrs. Pearl Faku to her husband's murderer recounted earlier, and it is not uncommon in the stories of victims who forgive. Jaeger explains that by not forgiving she would violate the goodness of her daughter's life and of her own sense that "real justice is . . . restoration, not necessarily to how things used to be, but to how they really should be"; in her view, it should be the case that "all life is sacred and worthy of preservation."[52] Perhaps it is a mistake to think that any wrong, no matter how heinous, is beyond morally reparative forgiveness by at least some people.

It seems more productive at this point to go beyond asking how we justify the judgement that an act is or is not forgivable. Let's ask what it *means* for individuals, or for a group or society collectively, to declare an act unforgivable. What is the moral power of that declaration? To what moral position do we want to recruit each other, when we identify actions

[52] Marietta Jaeger, "The Power and Reality of Forgiveness: Forgiving the Murderer of One's Child."

as unforgivable? When Jaeger decided to forgive, she did so because she came to think it was just to act to "restore" the world to what it "really should be" instead of letting it remain shattered. This is clearly an act of hope, and fits Cheyney Ryan's description of forgiveness as an act that "requires hope and expresses hope," either in the person who has done wrong or in other things. I have explored the multiple dimensions of moral repair that are among the other things that have to be seen as possible to restore, at least to some extent, in order to undertake morally valuable forgiveness. These include renewed confidence in the authority of moral standards, trust in oneself as moral judge and moral agent, trust in others' senses of responsibility sufficient to sustain a moral community, and hopefulness about all of these things – that our standards are worth our allegiance, our trust not disastrously unfounded, our hopes not vain. Ryan says that "unforgivable acts are ones that *kill* hope."[53] Acts that defeat hope defeat the conditions of moral relationship that forgiveness exists to preserve or restore. Surely this describes many instances of wrong that people consider unforgivable.

Sometimes what the wrongdoer has done so blights the victims' senses of trust and so crushes important hopes that the victims live with a sense of wreckage and dislocation, so angry, fearful, mistrustful, despairing, cynical, that they keep alive a sense of grievance as a protection and a defense, a kind of vigilance for their own sakes and a warning to others of the vulnerability that trust and hope create in contexts where the risk is too high. Some victims of extreme violence and abuse experience themselves as "deadened" by the experience. Other victims have had to survive their own complicity in evil, a complicity in some cases forced upon them in armies, concentration camps, or abusive families, where they were, in Primo Levi's words, "deprived of even the solace of innocence."[54] The examples in which the judgment of unforgivability gets the clearest justification are atrocities and brutal and relentless terror and oppression. When victims of these say "never again," a phrase now linked both to memories of the Holocaust of the Nazi period and also to some of the famous early truth projects revealing the regimes of torture and murder in Latin America ("*nunca mas*"), they express the sense that particularly

---

53 Ryan, "Thinking About the Unforgivable." Emphasis in the original.
54 The phrase is from Primo Levi's harrowing account of "the gray zone" of complicity and brutality among inmates of concentration camps in his *The Drowned and the Saved*. Card discusses the creation of gray zones as diabolically evil in *The Atrocity Paradigm*. Lawrence Langer's *Holocaust Testimonies: The Ruins of Memory* contains discussions of deadening and doubling, and of "humiliated memory."

brutal or horrific wrongdoing should set permanent limits on the trust or hopefulness *in humanity* with which human beings may in conscience comfort themselves. "Never again" is a warning and an invitation. You must never again believe that such events as these do not happen. Join us in insisting that there is real evil in the world, and that not all human beings are willing to be, or capable of being, a part of anything recognizable as a human moral community based on reciprocal trust.

The lesson some victims and communities may take and urge on us is that outrage toward those who have demonstrated the reality of evil must never be weakened. They must be punished, but no punishment could pay their debt. So they and their capacity for evil must be decried without end. The perpetrators must be kept resolutely outside the community of morally decent, if fallible, and sometimes grievously fallible, folk. They and their deeds *must not*, on this view, be forgiven, and the thought that their surviving victims should in any way to any degree absorb the costs of what evildoers have wrought is indecent or grotesque. No one can absorb these unimaginable costs, and no one should ever try. Hence the association of the unforgivable with mass violence, massacre, atrocity, and genocide. These are paradigmatic cases revealing the truly dreadful human possibility that some human beings step outside any condition of moral relationship with whole classes of others. The response of calling these actions unforgivable is a way of saying that for those who have stepped outside any recognizable moral relationship to other human beings, their appropriate fate is to be left there, and kept there, unable ever to return. Victims also experience this reaction to wrongs on an individual scale that are shocking and tormenting in their brutality and destructiveness, such as murder or terrorizing physical and sexual abuse.

When victims and survivors see acts as unforgivable, they mark places where they no longer see the possibilities of trust or hope; where they themselves, or what they rely on to sustain trust and hope in human connections, are damaged in an irreparable way. These are places from which certain futures based on moral confidence and self-trust can no longer be reached, either with certain others, or with any others in a full and secure way. Alternatively, they see perpetrators who are capable of defying any humane thought or feeling, and so should be exiled permanently and without appeal from human moral communities to which they are assumed to be an outrageous insult and a standing peril. In many cases, both ideas apply. Holding wrongs "unforgivable" is a way to mark the enormity of injury and the malignancy of wrongdoing as exceeding anything that could be made to fit back into a reliable framework of moral relations. As Gobodo-Madikizela puts the view, they overwhelm or threaten a "clear distinction between what is depraved but conceivable and what is simply off the scale of human acceptability."[55]

The unforgivable is what is not only immoral, even gravely so, but what seems to throw the grip of morality on human beings in serious question, putting morality's effectiveness in doubt and its limits in the foreground. Some terrible wrongs make morality seem frighteningly flimsy, or dangerously wishful, a fragile bridge over a chasm of evil destructiveness that requires us to temper hope and trust, and never to relax our vigilance. Or, the enormity of some evils can make us feel that morality is indeed a powerful force, but its embodiment consists not only in our trusting and hopeful relations with others, but also in our resolute refusal to see some people as eligible, ever again, for that trust and hope. We define a moral community both by what and whom it comprehends and what it marks as beyond the pale. These are some of the meanings of "unforgivable." They have a lot on their side, especially when wrongs of obscene cruelty and shocking magnitude are in question. There are no obligations to forgive, and there are weighty reasons not to, in these cases. We might admire the moral optimism of some who are able to take a humane and hopeful view of some wrongdoers whom others of us would spurn. Even so, we may respectfully decline to share their judgment, and the implication of reciprocal moral fellowship with the offender that it implies. Hope is astonishingly resilient and powerful, but hope, too, has its limits. Like human beings, it is fragile; like them, it can be killed.[56]

---

55 Gobodo-Madikizela, *A Human Being Died That Night*, 103.

56 This chapter has roots in a short paper prepared for a conference on "Forgiveness: Traditions and Implications" at the Tanner Center for the Humanities, University of Utah, in 2000, which greatly influenced its current form. Versions of the first part of this chapter were presented at many places, and I found audiences able at every turn to introduce some new complication. Many questions they raised are still unanswered by, and for, me. I thank those present at: Georgetown University Law Center; Arizona State University's Lincoln Center for Applied Ethics Affiliates Luncheon; St. Olaf's College, 25th Annual Eunice Belgum Memorial Lecture, 2003; New York Society for Women in Philosophy; Florida Atlantic University; Hobart and William Smith Colleges; and University of San Francisco. Sara Ruddick and Victoria McGeer pressed me on the need for forgivers to avoid inflating and over-moralizing the wrong they may have suffered; I know I have not done justice to that point.

6

Making Amends

Accepting responsibility for one's actions and their consequences, and acknowledging that those actions or their consequences are wrong or harmful, is the minimal condition for those who have harmed or offended against others to "set things right" with them. "Amends" are intentionally reparative actions by parties who acknowledge responsibility for wrong, and whose reparative actions are intended to redress that wrong. Nothing anyone does to relieve a harmed person's pain or suffering, stress, anger, resentment, indignation or outrage will count as "making amends" without an acceptance of responsibility as the reason for the effort. Nothing anyone says or does to provide injured parties with compensation for losses, to restore a status quo prior to injury, to make a victim "whole," or to reaffirm or vindicate a victim's dignity can be a kind of "amends" without an acknowledgment of some kind of wrongdoing, wrongful complicity in harm, or wrongful profit from it. Without that acknowledgment, reparative actions are charitable, compassionate, or generous, even dutifully so, but they do not "make amends." Making amends involves taking reparative action, but only action that issues from an acceptance of responsibility for *wrong*, and that embodies the will to set right something for which amends are *owed*, counts as making amends. Yet it sometimes seems that the magnitude of injury and the disposition to take responsibility are inversely related.

I want to use this frustrating and disturbing fact to delve deeper into the nature and requirements of gestures and practices of amends. These requirements stem from the nature of moral repair, which involves our creating or restoring confidence in shared moral standards, trust in our responsiveness to them and responsibility under them, and hope that our confidence and trust are not misplaced. First I want to introduce some breathtaking examples of brazen denial by perpetrators of massive carnage and cruelty too evident to be sanely denied, and next I will turn to the sheer ordinariness of the occasions and assumptions of our familiar repertory of reparative gestures, and then to the inevitable strains that extreme and large-scale cases of wrongdoing place on what are after all our very everyday practices of repair. It is useful to remind ourselves of the intricate workings of those everyday practices as a way of better understanding several specific and predictable impediments to more challenging projects of moral repair, as in shattering interpersonal violence or betrayal or in cases of mass violence or historic injustice.

In concluding I want to consider the merits of *restorative justice* as an approach to crime, political violence, and historic injustice that makes amends central. I look at the unique, even if incomplete, resources of restorative justice to address not only the hard cases of violence, but what might be the hardest case for repair: historical injustice spanning centuries. I take as an illustrative example the continuing failure in the United States of America to make significant attempts to acknowledge and repair, either symbolically or materially, the history of violence towards and oppression of African-Americans and its contemporary consequences of gross disparities of wealth, education, and opportunity. The aim and means of pursuing restorative justice track the contours of moral repair more closely than do the purely compensatory approaches to "black redress" that have been often and eloquently urged, so far without notable effect. Restorative justice makes moral repair the dominant aim, rather than a hoped for effect, of "doing justice" in the wake of serious wrong.

The Pragmatics of Repair

Slobodan Milosevic, on trial at the International Criminal Tribunal for the former Yugoslavia, claimed the Serbian army was framed for the massacre of as many as 7,000 unarmed Muslim men and boys at Srebrenica in July 1995. Despite massive evidence that the Bosnian Serb army, the Serbian police, and paramilitary helpers were responsible, Milosevic blamed the massacre on French intelligence operatives and others who he claimed were trying to "make it seem" that Serbs had committed genocide.[1] In 2003, at the Hague where Milosevic was on trial, two senior Bosnian

[1] Marlise Simons, "Milosevic Says Srebrenica Was Plot to Frame Serbs."

Serb officers involved in the Srebrenica massacre testified, supported by credible evidence, that it was "a well planned and deliberate killing operation."[2] Milosevic died in 2006 while still on trial for genocide in this and other cases.

Another genocide, in Rwanda in 1994, was unprecedented in its grisly efficiency and its level of popular participation. Despite the fact that people were killed primarily by being hacked to death with machetes or beaten with clubs, as many as 800,000 people were killed in a period of three months. This was possible only because tens, perhaps hundreds, of thousands of ordinary Hutu people killed neighbors, family, even their own spouses in order to eliminate the Tutsi minority of Rwanda. This was done at the direct instigation of the Hutu government. And yet, reports from the area agree that relatively few people, including many of the 125,000 originally imprisoned for their participation, will admit that they took part in the killing, or that they knew about the killing, or that there had been a systematic, government-driven campaign aimed expressly at the extermination of a targeted group. Many prefer to view themselves as prisoners of a "war" that they simply had the misfortune to lose.[3]

General Augusto Pinochet took power in a bloody military coup and ruled Chile with a regime of repression, disappearance, and torture from 1973 to 1990. Pinochet was arrested in England in 1998 and held for 16 months pending extradition to Spain to answer charges of genocide, torture, kidnapping, and murder made by a Spanish judge. In 1987, Pinochet was quoted as saying "There is not a leaf in this country which I do not move."[4] In a 1999 report after his detention, Pinochet claimed of the brutal repression under his rule in Chile: "I didn't have time to control what others were doing," and "I am being humiliated. I am a general, 64 years service. I'm a gentleman who knows about honor."[5] Upon returning to

---

[2] Marlise Simons, "Officers Say Bosnian Massacre Was Deliberate."

[3] Mark Drumbl connects his own results interviewing prisoners after the Rwandan genocide with that of several other investigators of post-genocide perceptions in "Restorative Justice and Collective Responsibility: Lessons For and From the Rwandan Genocide." The best known of these other sources is Philip Gourevitch, *We Wish to Inform You That Tomorrow We Will Be Killed With Our Families: Stories from Rwanda*. As an international tribunal for the genocide handles a handful of cases, Rwanda has recently resorted to an adaptation of traditional community justice called "gacaca" to release over 50,000 prisoners willing to confess to lower levels of participation in the genocide back to their local communities for open-air hearings presided over by elected judges.

[4] Peter Stalker, "Visions of Freedom: A Journey through Pinochet's Chile."

[5] Warren Hoge, "With British Court Hearings Set, Pinochet Will Soon Know Fate," and Warren Hoge, "Trial Opens For Pinochet With Listing of 35 Crimes," respectively.

Chile after Britain refused to extradite him on grounds of poor health, Pinochet still faced over 100 criminal complaints based on his involvement in the disappearances of around 3,000 people. General Pinochet admits to nothing.

These examples remain startling even though they are hardly exceptional. They illustrate what is widely true in the wake of large-scale and heinous wrongdoing in the form of mass violence and state terror. Those involved typically *deny responsibility*. They say that it didn't happen, or that they knew nothing about it. Or they say that it happened, but that they were not involved or that they were involved but someone else was responsible for it. Or they explain that what happened was really something other than that of which they are accused. Or they say that they did what is claimed, but that it was justified, not wrong.[6]

Is persistent denial as commonplace in cases of ordinary wrongdoing or offense? That is, is denial as common in those breaches and injuries that occur between individuals in social and personal life? There is no way to answer this question precisely. There is research on the effectiveness of "restorative justice" practices in criminal contexts – such as face to face conferences between offenders and crime victims, often with support of other parties on both sides. Some of this research suggests that apologies, which necessarily imply some kind of admission of wrongdoing, are significantly more likely to happen in this kind of person-to-person context than in the highly ritualized context of the criminal court.[7] There is also empirical research on apology, some of which suggests that apologies and expressions of remorse – "responsibility-accepting accounts" – predominate over "responsibility-rejecting accounts," such as excuses and justifications, in how people respond to having caused harm or offense. This research also shows that excuses that diminish responsibility are accepted more often than not, perhaps because they are face-saving all around. They salve the hurt feelings of wronged parties and soften the culpability of those who have done harm.[8]

These studies do not deal with cases of gross violence – rape or murder – much less with sexual slavery or genocide or torture, however. It's

---

[6] Stanley Cohen, "Human Rights and Crimes of the State: The Culture of Denial," explores the psychology and sociology of denial in connection with state violence.

[7] For a broad view of the efficacy of practices and environments that aim to induce reparative and conciliatory responses from offenders, see John Braithwaite, *Restorative Justice and Responsive Regulation*, ch. 3, "Does Restorative Justice Work?"

[8] Ken-ichi Ohbuchi, "A Social Psychological Analysis of Accounts: Toward a Universal Model of Giving and Receiving Accounts."

hard to know if results based on missed appointments or small articles not promptly returned extend to such grave interpersonal injuries as extended deceptions, swindles, or infidelities, much less to violations of human rights. Common experience might suggest that in the middle ranges of serious offenses between involved individuals, including instances of physical harm, there is a lot of avoidance, denial, and strained excuses, but also in many instances a desire to mend fences, a desire that works its way out in apologies and attempts at amends. Whether it does so might depend on whether the relationship at peril is one the person in the wrong values enough that he or she is willing to suffer risk and discomfort to repair it, and if other circumstances, including social, family, or societal support, are favorable. Favorable circumstances for seeking to make amends are ones in which a path is visible to the wrongdoer that leads through amends to renewed good standing, and in which there is some incentive to take that path, especially the incentive of regaining a valued relationship or being released from the bad opinion or punitive responses of others.[9] Communities can informally support or even institutionalize such paths – as they do in restorative justice programs – or they can omit to do so.

Let's say then that three tendencies of wrongdoers are apparent: they tend to deny horrific wrongs, to apologize for slight ones, and to respond variably to serious interpersonal damage in between. Here's a simple but not negligible hypothesis that begins to explain these tendencies: reparative gestures, including admissions, apologies, and amends, but also excuses when apt and proportionate, are favored where they are most likely to "work." In cases of no great importance (slight tardiness), or ones unlikely to be repeated (stepping on a stranger's toes in a public conveyance), or ones in which an unpleasant or upsetting incident unsettles an otherwise tolerable or enjoyable situation that is ongoing (a friendship, an otherwise pleasant relation between neighbors or co-workers), there's a lot going on both sides for being accommodating and

---

[9] Heather Strang reports some remarkable results of a study of RISE (Reintegrative Shaming Experiment in juvenile justice, Canberra, Australia) where middle-range property and violence offences were randomly assigned to either standard court processing or to restorative justice conferencing, with offenders directly encountering victims. Ninety percent of all victims said they should receive apologies, but only 11% of the court-processed victims reported receiving apologies, while 82% of the conferenced victims did. Conferencing, including the opportunity to engage in the usual face-to-face patterns of repair, also reduced feelings of anger and fear in victims, and increased feelings of forgivingness. See Heather Strang, "Justice for Victims of Young Offenders: The Centrality of Emotional Harm and Restoration," 290–91.

gracious. Just saying "sorry" and having the other say "it's okay" and both being done with a small aggravation is not only an efficient way to clear the path ahead, but it's a way that allows for the contrite and the forgiving parties to feel good about themselves and each other. Being willing to apologize for offense and being willing to surrender disapproval or recrimination for the small price of simple apology shows good will and reasonableness of everyone involved. If excuses are often welcomed and usually accepted, it is likely to be for the same reason. Better for the wronged person to get a partial acceptance of responsibility and some acknowledgment of having deserved better, and for the injuring party to concede some fault and take a bit of responsibility, than for either to pursue things at great social and emotional expense. Excuses are the quick plea bargains of social life.

Ken-ichi Ohbuchi's research on excuse and apology finds that what seems to make excuses – which are after all responsibility-mitigating if not responsibility-rejecting accounts – acceptable is not so much that they seem to be true but that they are of standard types, ones that follow a culturally familiar script for excuses.[10] This strongly suggests that it is the little ceremony of showing you know something is owed, and showing that you know your partner in the ceremony is expecting something of a particular sort to be offered that settles accounts on the spot. In excuses one proffers a bit of remedial explanation that shows you know something appears offensive in another's eyes and needs to be rendered fairly innocent by a different or more elaborate description, and this seems to do the trick. If the excuse is not the worse for being formulaic ("So sorry not to have called back, I've been buried at the office"), this seems to show that the content of the excuse is not as important as the fact that the excuse is offered: someone shows that she knows she stands in need of an account of herself in someone else's eyes. This seems to be acknowledgment enough to take care of many gaffes and ordinary breaches.

Yet many of us have experienced the dismal quagmire of trying to make excuses for offenses that run deeper, where attempts to excuse oneself only make the problem worse, and sometimes very much worse. There are questions of timing as well. Even very contrite apology can be angering if it comes "too soon," as if one needed to wait until the wronged party is able and willing to complete the transaction that the

[10] Ohbuchi, "A Social Psychological Analysis of Accounts," 28–29.

apology instigates. If they are not at all ready for it, one's apology may itself seem bullying or presumptuous. It is a common limitation of the philosophical study of excuses (and justifications) that the focus tends to be entirely on the *content* of excuses, on the question of what particular circumstances *should* get someone off the hook. The performative aspect of excuses – that they occur and how they are carried off – should not be slighted; the performative dimension needs to be examined in all cases of reparative gestures.

When we draw together cases where wrongdoing is horrific yet obstinately denied, cases where wrongdoing is slight but dutifully acknowledged, and all the variety of cases in between, some facts about making amends come forward. The first fact is the sheer *ordinariness of a familiar stock of reparative gestures and practices.* This ordinariness is easily overlooked when we focus on extremely difficult or very disturbing cases that call for redress. Once we put this ordinariness back in the foreground, we should find it unsurprising. Of course we need a common repertory of easily conveyed and readily recognized gestures that are at hand for occasions of offense. These are standard offerings, verbal and otherwise, that count as attempts at amends. We all learn the very simplest – "Say you're sorry" – at mothers' knees. Other standard offers of amends include those of service, repayment, replacement, or other compensation; often these turn out to be unnecessary precisely because they have been offered.[11] The second fact is the degree to which our established reparative practices are fitted to the large run of *ordinary cases of small or moderate offense* where we are smoothing out little or medium-sized injuries in ongoing relations within a relatively peaceable shared social existence. The third and specially important fact is the *ordinary response of acceptance* that we anticipate, with good reason and correctly for the most part, when we, as wrongdoers, make these offerings, at least in cases of modest or moderate offense. The lesson "Don't be mad anymore – see, he's sorry" teaches offender and offended how to complete the transaction. This tells us that gestures of amends, in their most common occurrence and forms, are duets of call and response which assume the probability of a *successful return to*

---

[11] It also seems that institutions can save money by unhesitating and prompt disclosure and apologies. An Associated Press story reports that hospitals in the University of Michigan Health System since 2002 have encouraged doctors to apologize for mistakes, with dramatic reductions in both attorney's fees and law suits. "Doctors Encouraged to Tell Patients, 'I'm Sorry,'" *Arizona Republic*, 12 November 2004. A similar effect was found several years earlier in a Veteran's Affairs hospital in Kentucky.

the status quo. The promise of success at low cost is motivating; even high cost might be accepted if return to the status quo is valued enough.[12]

These facts about the ordinariness of our reparative gestures, the wrongs they address, and the outcomes they anticipate predict how arduous, uncertain, puzzling, and ineffective reparative gestures are likely to be in extreme cases, cases that are shatteringly disruptive or massive and violent, for example. Remembering the ordinariness of our reparative gestures magnifies the gap between our everyday practices and the extreme situations in which we nonetheless must resort to them, shedding light on why the inclination to reparative responses may be stymied almost before it begins. Finally, these facts predict something profoundly sad, and socially and politically discouraging. We most need to attempt and succeed at repair where avoidable harm is severe, the suffering caused by wrongdoing is great, and the actions that cause harm are inexcusable. Repair is also most unquestionably deserved as well as needed by those who are victims of blatant injustice, extreme mistreatment, or life-altering harms. Yet it is often in the most egregious cases of harm that significant reparative actions are resisted and seem shallow, meager, and incomplete where attempted. These difficulties in no way relieve responsible parties of the obligation to make amends. Instead, these facts form part of the pragmatics of moral repair; they need to be anticipated, understood, and addressed in attempts at repair, including the design of reparative programs and official gestures needed in large-scale cases, as well as the assessment of their "success." Both the performance and the content of reparative gestures must be open for assessment and reconsideration by and between injured parties and those who wish to make amends.[13]

Ordinary Measures, Extraordinary Cases

A view of moral repair needs to root itself in an understanding of how moral relations in the everyday are stabilized and renewed *routinely*, for it

---

[12] Primatologist Frans de Waal's studies of the moral interactions and conciliatory practices of our primate relatives help us think about how fundamental these practices of order and peacemaking are. See Frans de Waal, *Good Natured: The Origins of Right and Wrong in Humans and Other Animals.*

[13] Mari J. Matsuda, "Looking to the Bottom: Critical Legal Studies and Reparations," makes an extended argument for giving privilege to the perspective of victims of historical injustice in defining the groups who injured and the responsible parties, the nature of damages in need of reparation, and the nature of satisfactory remedies. See especially 368ff.

is in the routine and reliable workings of repair that we can see the basic elements of repair and their conditions of success. This in turn is precisely what we need to understand to see what makes hard cases hard – especially what makes them *morally hard*, and not just conceptually or practically challenging. Our stylized and scripted reparative maneuvers have well-marked places and reasonably anticipated results in most cases where they are called into play. Admissions, apologies, amends, and forgiveness, and the interplay among them, have ritualized features, but these are the rituals of everyday social existence, such as taking turns in a conversation; they are not sacramental acts with mysterious powers. Or rather, if the power of conventional reparative acts, saying "I'm sorry," or extending a hand, seems mysterious – for example, all out of proportion to the performances themselves – it may appear so because we are not thinking about the deep background of confidence, trust, and hope that in average cases (and sometimes in serious cases) of wrongdoing remains there to be activated. It is not then the few words of apology, or even the bowed head or the tears of remorse, that magically mend a torn fabric of relationship but what deep reservoirs of trust and still flowing springs of hope can be tapped.[14] It is these everyday and normal conditions for successful repair that need to be identified clearly. A pragmatics of repair, by identifying these elements and conditions, enables us to sort out distinct kinds of impediments and resistances to repair, and so helps us to identify accessible means and visible paths to repair. While the success of reparative attempts in hard cases is always uncertain and often at best incomplete, the accountability of responsible parties is the gateway to repair, and the elements of accountability are fairly clear.

"Accountability" means, literally, to be required to give an account of yourself and to have to settle accounts with others through admission, elaboration, explanation, justification, excuse, amends, and assurances concerning what you have done.[15] When someone who has done wrong or done harm is ready to take responsibility and try to settle accounts,

---

[14] Nicholas Tavuchis, *Mea Culpa: A Sociology of Apology and Reconciliation*, is a rich full-length study of apology. Tavuchis, however, early on in his account invites the view that there is something "mysterious" – even "paradoxical and talismanic" – about the power of apology (5). While I think this is colorful rather than literal language, it is not entirely innocent.

[15] See Anita Allen, *Why Privacy Isn't Everything: Feminist Reflections on Personal Accountability*, for a succinct and useful discussion of accountability followed by extensive illustrations. My own work features the notion of "practices of responsibility" that are continually renewed or shifted as accountabilities are reconfigured. See *Moral Understandings: A Feminist Study in Ethics*, chs. 4 and 5.

he or she must be prepared to acknowledge, accept, and undertake a great deal. One taking responsibility in its full sense must acknowledge the authority of shared norms that define what they have done as unacceptable (or worse); accept the indignation, hostility, or alienation of wronged parties; and accept the liability to demands for satisfaction from those wronged and from the community that embodies and enforces the violated norms. The wrongdoer has put his or her judgment and character in question before that community, and he or she is now justly exposed to the community's appraisal. A wrongdoer's repentance is insincere or shallow without the recognition that she or he has not only broken rules but has caused or contributed to injury and suffering of particular human beings who are the victims of the wrongdoing, carelessness, or complicity. Those responsible for wrong or harm must recognize that wronged or wrongfully harmed parties now have a claim against them for redress. A wrongdoer must desire to retrieve good standing in the eyes of those he or she has injured, the larger community, and himself or herself. He or she must see that this depends on taking reparative action that will be meaningful in the eyes of both those offended and the community whose order is violated.

The process initiated by taking responsibility is likely to be difficult and painful for those who have done serious wrong or are responsible for harm. It requires accepting the power and the right of others, especially victims of wrong but also the morally authoritative community, to give their own accounts of the damage and insult done and to express their anger, despair, fear, and grief in response to it. This entails that wrongdoers relinquish a good deal of control over accounts of what has happened, especially reckonings of what harm they have done to others and what they have revealed about themselves in so acting. No wrongdoer is required to be a scapegoat for falsely or unfairly attributed harm. Yet if he or she is indeed implicated in serious wrong, too legalistic a defense (at least outside of a courtroom, and even sometimes in one) is likely to appear as denial or evasion and to add the proverbial insult to injury. Finally, one in the wrong must acknowledge the necessity of offering something as amends that will be recognized as well-intentioned and proportionate, even if it is symbolic, in the eyes of those wronged and their shared community. In this final dimension – the business end of making amends, but one that presupposes all the foregoing if it is truly amends that are to be made – the full brunt of relinquishing primary authority over the definition of the offense, the features of one's character that it exposes, and the measure of satisfactory response come home to those in the wrong. When we do wrong or take responsibility for harm, we become participants in a process that we do not control, and that in its nature requires a vulnerability to others that is risky. We open a transaction in which we have by our admission yielded certain prerogatives to others, to judge us and to place demands upon us. In the flagrant cases of denial I introduced earlier, what we see is not only a refusal to admit responsibility for wrong and harm. We also see an insistence on controlling a version of events that does not expose the wrongdoer to judgments and demands from wronged parties and a judging community. Typically in such cases what is repudiated is the very right of certain others to judge.[16]

Our inclination to engage in repair is also trained up in ordinary circumstances to seek a characteristic response. It is fortified by an expectation, or at least a hope, that our responsibility-accepting and responsibility-settling accounts will be *rewarded*. There are normative expectations that responsible individuals owe others an accounting when there is injury or offense, and that acceptance of responsibility for injury or offense should prompt reparative gestures or actions. There are also corresponding normative expectations that reparative behavior will be taken into account by those injured and will be at least weighed, if not welcomed, in favor of accepting a transaction of repair. This thick tissue of normative expectation is what holds us together in relations that are recognizably moral ones, and it is the tissue itself that is part of what we are repairing in repairing wrongs.

In ordinary contexts in the lower and middle ranges of offenses, many of the requirements of accountability are not so difficult to meet. In the case of serious wrongdoing the requirements do not change. But where wrongdoing is very serious, the stakes in meeting the requirements, the likelihood of failure or rebuff, and the degree of exposure, discomfort, and cost may be steep. These factors are disincentives to undertaking repair, or to putting oneself in the position of being expected to do so by taking responsibility. They stand in the way of attempts at repair that will seem sincere and proportionate to both wrongdoers and those who are wronged. Impediments to repair do not in any way erase or reduce responsibility, although they can undercut the motivation to take responsibility and fortify the inclination not to take it. It is no surprise that admitting wrong and making right is bothersome and painful, and

---

[16] Tavuchis, *Mea Culpa*, 7–9, discusses the issue of "membership in a designated moral community" that is at stake in known wrongdoing and the attempt to get others to recertify our claim to membership.

often we will avoid it if we can, but it is helpful to understand this in a more fine-grained way. A more detailed understanding can be especially useful in the larger scale political and historical cases that today so tax our imagination and responsibility.

Wrongdoers sometimes fail to share the norms that define their responsibility, or to recognize the right of particular victims and communities of moral judgment to hold them accountable. Wrongdoers may refuse to allow their own judgment or character to be put in question. They can be indifferent to, or hold in contempt, those they have injured and others who presume to judge them, seeing their victims and judges as incompetent, arrogant, worthless or evil. Hate crimes, race-based crimes, and sex crimes all partake of this pattern. These circumstances also often obtain in political violence organized and perpetuated by or within states. The very contempt and indifference of those with the power to arm and order 10-year-old boys to kill, maim, and terrorize a population, to hold women in sexual slavery for mass rape and impregnation, or to torture and murder people who are politically inconvenient is both a source of the crime and what ensures that those responsible are likely to disdain judgments of wrong or shrug off responsibility. The problem of contempt for, or indifference or hostility to, those harmed also plagues cases of historical injustice.

With historical injustices – long-running and still-running eras of unjust treatment – there is the question of what is owed now by contemporary societies to groups, peoples, or other societies who continue to suffer the life-diminishing effects of prior conquest, slavery, cultural destruction, and expropriation of land and resources. For the white settler societies of the United States, Canada, and Australia, for example, the continuing and often ravaging effects on indigenous people of forced removal from ancestral lands, genocidal and ethnocidal political and social policies, impoverishment in health, income, and education may be somewhat less denied or disputed than they used to be. Yet the telling of these histories often still prompts impatience or resentment in those who do not belong to the historically subjected and violated population. Similarly the continuing legacies in the United States of the 400-year history of the forced removal and enslavement of Africans, decades of legal segregation and accepted racist violence, continuing individual and institutional racism against African-Americans, and the enormous cumulative effects of white privilege persist without decisive attempts at official recognition and targeted repair. Suggestions that the U.S. government, from its birth till the mid-twentieth century the official guarantor of slavery and then of something worse than second-class citizenship, might apologize to African-American descendants of slaves are repudiated by an overwhelming majority of white Americans.

Individuals are apt to resist the suggestion that something they want to think of as "long ago" could in any way be their responsibility now, or that their decency could be called into question by strangers toward whom they might have compassion but whose suffering is not their fault and not really their business. Many express skepticism about whether members of those groups who inherit the legacies of historical injustice and who experience its continuing effects today are their proper judges; the heirs to injustice are said to be oversensitive or paranoid, "professional victims," looking for a free ride, or trying to bully blameless people into giving them special treatment. To address all these forms of resistance, to sort out those that are founded from the many that are not, and to find the key to getting acknowledgment in those cases where it is blocked by denial and evasion, is the ground floor of moral repair in these cases.

Finally, the normal expectation of responsiveness to reparative efforts – and in many cases the expectation of success – is put in doubt in any case of severe injury or affront, especially if it appears intentional, callous, or malignant. And these expectations might not seem well founded for the large-scale, and especially the historical, context of wrongdoing and harm. In these hard cases attempts at repair will likely be uncertain, their progress halting, their "success" hard to define as well as to achieve. To so much as attempt repair may invite immediate, fresh outpourings of resentment, mistrust, outrage, and grief. Efforts might stall or break down due to mutual mistrust, the defensiveness of responsible parties, or the outrage or despair of injured parties. The pitfalls can be matters of tact and timing, but also matters of moral judgment, and it is not always easy to distinguish them.

An apology that arrives too soon, one that precedes a full examination of the nature and magnitude of wrongdoing and appears to head off a full expression of the grief and anger of victims, becomes an insult.[17] It may signify a self-serving interest of those burdened with responsibility who want to cut their costs and protect their sense of decency from being challenged. The suggestion that amends can be made may infuriate those who have suffered loss or injury they find irreparable. An offer of reparation in a currency that does not carry the needed message – words

---

[17] For clear discussion of the constituents and the success conditions for apologies, see Aaron Lazare, *On Apology*.

alone where there needs to be material compensation, or material compensation without the needed words – can tear open unhealed wounds. Women kidnapped and coerced into sexual slavery in wartime brothels by the Japanese army have differed in their reactions to reparations payments raised by a private organization. Some will not accept money that does not come from the nation of Japan along with an admission of responsibility and official apology; others think it is at least a recognition of the wrong they were done and an offer of something tangible they can point to as proof that they were wronged and that something is owed to them.[18] American Indians pursuing repatriation of human remains that cannot any longer be traced to particular Indian nations or tribes, or Native peoples pursuing official U.S. government tribal recognition that will open up possibilities of economic and political self-determination are faced with opportunities that still incorporate, for many, an indignity: the entitlements being recognized rest on definitions of membership and descent that are controlled by the conquering power. Here the transaction that should shift power to the injured parties repeats their domination instead.[19]

Repair for wrongdoing depends on several interconnected types of acknowledgment and acceptance that are difficult even for sincerely remorseful wrongdoers to accept or achieve. Repair also needs to draw upon or replenish some reservoir of trust and hopefulness available to victims that gives reparative efforts a chance of succeeding. It may be difficult or impossible to get wrongdoers to fulfill the requirements. Those who have suffered serious harm or grave injustice may struggle to summon the

---

[18] Maria Rosa Henson, *Comfort Woman: A Filipina's Story of Prostitution and Slavery under the Japanese Military*, is a first person account of one woman who accepted a reparation payment from a private fund organized by the Japanese government. On this story, see also Seth Mydans, "Inside a Wartime Brothel: The Avenger's Story." Roy Brooks, ed., *When Sorry Isn't Enough: The Controversy Over Apologies and Reparations for Human Injustice*, collects excerpts of discussion and some official documents from the earlier portion of the reparations movement and debate. A detailed overview of the unsuccessful attempts, legal and political, to get the Japanese government to take the kind of responsibility sought by advocacy organizations and the international community is given by Keisuke Iida, "Human Rights and Sexual Abuse: The Impact of International Human Rights Law on Japan."

[19] Elazar Barkan, *The Guilt of Nations: Restitution and Negotiating Historical Injustices*, ch. 8, provides an overview of some Native American reparations claims. On repatriation of remains and artifacts, see Rebecca Tsosie, "The Native American Graves Protection and Repatriation Act," accessed 26 May 2005, and "Privileging Claims to the Past: Ancient Human Remains and Contemporary Cultural Values." See also Elazar Barkan, "Amending Historical Injustices: The Restitution of Cultural Property – An Overview."

trust and renew the hope that repair requires, and they may yet have good reasons to withhold these. So the conditions for repair may be shaky or absent, especially in the hard cases. This is what makes them hard *morally*. When one really looks at the complex conditions of acknowledgment, and the multiple concrete tasks of creating or restoring confidence in shared moral standards, initiating or replenishing trust among responsible actors, and nourishing or igniting hope in both the standards and in ourselves, it is not surprising that moral repair is discouraging work exactly where it is most profoundly needed and required. The worse the wrong, one might say, the more arduous is the work and uncertain the possibility of repair. It is easy, then, to give up too soon, or to simply shirk the attempt.

If there are obligations of repair, however, to give up on the task of repair or to turn away from broaching it is not only *not* to do something, it is *to do wrong once again*. Failures to repair wrongs are additional wrongs that create additional obligations to repair the failures. Where wrongs persist unrepaired repeatedly, in an extended series of refusals or failures to repair, the lack of reparative effort on the part of those responsible for repair accrues layers of disregard, indifference, disrespect, contempt, belittlement, or intended or careless humiliation. In addition to the original injury and the failure to repair, the added insult is the attitude of "That's their problem," or "That all happened so long ago," or "Get over it." Unrepaired wrongs on a large scale, which determine life experiences and life chances for generations, do not go away; even when they are silenced, they have a way of coming back. They tend to get worse as new generations not only inherit the continuing patterns of disadvantage and injustice that stem from grave wrongs in the past, but also experience outrage, mistrust, and despair at the continuing denial, indifference, or self-justification of those who have profited or continue to profit not only from the original wrong but also from its continuing effects.

Worse than inaction or refusals to act, as time passes there is also in historical cases typically a history of concerted and institutionally supported denial. The maintenance of this history is itself a collective work in which some construct and shore up falsehoods while others are incurious, complacent, or actively resist opportunities to know the truth. Failure to acknowledge the facts of a wrong, much less the wrongness of a wrong, is no less angering and alienating to those affected in large-scale or historical cases than it is in any others. The effect of a collective work of avoiding or preventing the emergence of the truth is a collective indignity to those whose histories of injustice are diminished or disappeared. Those continuing a history of denial refuse to see victims rightfully putting claims, and instead see losers who are whining, lying, exaggerating, or begging for special favors; in some cases they refuse to see the victims at all.[20] Victims of many types of violence now choose to refer to them-selves as "survivors" rather than victims; the emphasis on endurance and agency, rather than passivity and vulnerability, is important for them in how they identify themselves. It is good nonetheless to remember that the movement from being seen (and repetitively socially imaged) by others as a loser to being seen by others as someone who was wronged, a victim, is a promotion. It makes all the difference morally.

When individuals or societies or social groups evade the task of repair, the deeper damage may be that possibilities of moral relationship rooted in trust and nourished by hopefulness are crushed or poisoned between individuals or between groups within society. People can live together this way; unfortunately, in the current state of things they often do live together this way. But it is not a way of going on together in a relation-ship morally adequate to the burdens and benefits of shared life. It is a way that is fragile and that allows mistrust and resentment to fester; it breeds cynicism if not despair; and it is poised to degenerate into hostil-ity. If repair cannot in hard cases be simple, quick, steady, and without cost, that is not an argument that it is not needed and is not morally owed. It is an argument that those of us who stand responsible – indi-vidually and communally – for repairing moral relations should expect that task in some cases to be complicated, lengthy, faltering, painful, and disturbing, entailing sacrifices of control, comfort, complacency, pride, power, and material and social resources. In the hard cases, moral repair is apt to be chancy; it will probably need to be ongoing and might remain unstable, frustrating, and ultimately less than complete on all sides. One may even question whether "repair" can possibly be meaningful in any case of severe mistreatment, violence, or death, the harms we often call with good reason "irreparable," whether they occur in individual or in large-scale contexts.

When we remember once again, however, how ordinary and perva-sive are our everyday means of getting past wrong and hurt, and how human beings and their societies do successfully rely on these practices

---

[20] On the importance of clarifying the historical record, see Roy L. Brooks, *Atonement and Forgiveness: A New Model for Black Reparations,* 148–51. Jean Harvey explores the distor-tions of relationship that result from persistent moral neglect or contempt in *Civilized Oppression.*

to sustain and renew common life, we can see the cup of repair as at least half full. Taking a morally reparative approach to terrible violations of individuals, to mass violence, or to historical injustice is hardly pointless; it signals acknowledgment and concern to victims. With due care and effort, attempts at repair might lessen some loss, misery, resentment, and despair, or rekindle some trust and hope, within or between people or groups. Restorative justice, a way of thinking about conflict, harm, and violence that has grown up in theory and practice over recent decades, advances this view. All serious wrongs are violations of actual individuals by others who then are obligated to attempt to make amends and to try to restore relationships; those harmed and others responsible must use the familiar means – explanation, apology, amends, and reassurance – to render offending parties accountable, to give victims voice and validation, and to begin restoration of the moral fabric of relationships. Restorative justice addresses both common crime and political repression and violence. Restorative justice as an approach to hard cases of serious harm and violence has special virtues and features uniquely suited to addressing historical injustice, perhaps the hardest case for moral repair.

Restorative Justice and Hard Cases

Is making amends simply put to the side in cases of "irreparable" harm such as severe violence and mistreatment, whether among individuals or on a massive scale? Perhaps retribution is both necessary and sufficient in responding to serious crimes and severe harms. Is making amends largely out of reach in cases of historical injustice? Where many crimes or abuses lie in the distant past some think they should be interred there along with their supposedly long-departed perpetrators and victims. Restorative justice offers a different perspective: all crime and wrong creates obligations on those responsible and able to repair harm and restore relationships, whatever else is done.

Restorative justice is a relatively new concept. Many people discovered restorative justice through the proceedings of South Africa's Truth and Reconciliation Commission, which drew international attention. The TRC was the principal and very public instrument the newly democratic South Africa in the late 1990s used to deal with gross violations of human rights during the struggle over the white supremacist apartheid state between 1960 and 1995. The TRC expressly adopted the banner of restorative justice, emphasizing in its final report (1998) the "healing and restoration of victims," as well as offenders, families, and communities, and the "accountability" of offenders, with full participation by all directly affected parties.[21] The TRC's practice embodied a set of core ideals that had been developed in the previous twenty years of restorative theory and practice in ordinary criminal justice and some civil contexts.[22] Restorative justice values can be captured in these six ideals:

1. Restorative justice aims above all to repair the harm caused by wrong, crime, and violence.

2. Restorative justice makes central the experiences and needs (material, emotional, and moral) of victims.

3. Restorative justice insists on genuine accountability and responsibility taking from those who are responsible for harm, ideally directly to those who have suffered the harm.

4. Restorative justice seeks to return ownership of the resolution of wrong, crime, and harm to those primarily affected and those who can in turn effect meaningful repair: to those who have done wrong or are responsible for harm, to victims, to the immediate communities of care of victims and offenders, and to larger affected or interested communities.

[21] The TRC Report said restorative justice: seeks to redefine crime from offence against the state to an injury to and violation of particular human beings; is based on reparation as the healing and the restoration of victims, but also of offenders, their families, and the larger community; encourages victims, offenders, and the community to be directly involved in resolving conflict, with the state and legal profession in facilitating roles; and aims at offender accountability, and full participation of both the victims and offenders and making good or putting right what is wrong. See Truth and Reconciliation Commission, *Truth and Reconciliation Commission of South Africa Report.*

[22] On the domestic criminal justice side, sources include Howard Zehr, *Changing Lenses: A New Focus for Crime and Justice*; Dennis Sullivan and Larry Tifft, *Restorative Justice: Healing the Foundations of Our Everyday Lives*; Gordon Bazemore and Mara F. Schiff, eds., *Restorative Community Justice: Repairing Harm and Transforming Communities*; and Heather Strang and John Braithwaite, *Restorative Justice and Civil Society*. John Braithwaite, *Restorative Justice and Responsive Regulation*, is most comprehensive in its theoretical scope and review of empirical studies. A recent Google search for "restorative justice" turned up over 700,000 items, mostly concerned with restorative justice programs in criminal justice systems around the world. A useful site for research is "Restorative Justice Online," edited by Daniel Van Ness, a major contributor to the literature, at www.restorativejustice.org. The TRC itself gave impetus to a burgeoning literature on using restorative justice to address mass violence and political wrongdoing, including a significant literature on the TRC itself. See Martha Minow, *Beyond Vengeance and Forgiveness: Facing History After Genocide and Mass Violence*; Charles Villa-Vicencio and Wilhelm Verwoerd, *Looking Back Reaching Forward: Reflections on the Truth and Reconciliation Commission of South Africa*; Ruti Teitel, *Transitional Justice*; Robert I. Rotberg and Dennis Thompson, eds., *Truth v. Justice: The Morality of Truth Commissions*; Trudy Govier, *Forgiveness and Revenge*; and Carol A. L. Prager and Trudy Govier, *Dilemmas of Reconciliation: Cases and Concepts.*

5. Restorative justice aims at offering those responsible for wrong and harm the opportunity through accountability and repair to earn self-respect and to be reintegrated without stigma into their communities.
6. Restorative justice seeks to build and strengthen individuals' and communities' capacities to do justice actively, and not to surrender justice to experts, professionals, or "the state," which should play facilitating roles.[23]

These core values serve the ultimate aim and guiding norm of restorative justice, "restoring relationships." In restorative justice what demands repair is not only material loss or damage, but a state of relationship that has been *shaken, broken, distorted, or fouled,* and so one that might be an ongoing source of threat, insult, anger, fear, and grief. It is not always possible, nor is it always desirable, to restore any relationship between those who have done harm and those who have suffered at their will or from their carelessness. In some cases where restoration between victims and offending persons is possible it can mean only a civil or wary coexistence. In any case, however, it is necessary to attempt to restore morally habitable conditions for those wronged within their supporting network of relationships and in their communities. At a minimum, others must acknowledge the wrong and harm done to them and accept the legitimacy of their demands for validation and vindication. Normative abandonment, including victim blaming or indifference to a victim's violation and suffering, is the antithesis of restoration: it tells the victim that the wrong is denied or that the victim does not matter.

The terminology of "restoration" is sometimes criticized because it seems to imply the need to *return* relationships and communities to a prior state. In cases of oppression, mass violence, and historic injustice, there may not be a morally acceptable status quo ante. In many instances of common crime, there is no antecedent relationship in the usual sense. Serious harm to individuals, however, creates a relationship charged with powerful negative feelings and burdened with losses that can continue to mar a victim's life. Therefore, we can understand "restoration" in all contexts as normative. "Restoration" refers to repairs that move relationships in the direction of *becoming morally adequate,* whether or not they have been adequate before. The central issue for restorative justice thus

---

[23] Gerry Johnstone, ed., *A Restorative Justice Reader: Texts, Sources, Context,* provides a detailed overview of the field.

comes very close to the theme of this book, the *repair of moral relations*, and we have seen that even those zones of "default trust" in which we depend implicitly on the restraint or responsibility of strangers around us are part of the tissue of relationships that constitute our moral world. It is not always possible or desirable to restore relations between victims and those who have hurt them, but it is always necessary to assist and support victims in repairing the moral fabric of their world.[24]

Morally adequate relations, as explored in this book, are ones in which three conditions obtain. In them, people are *confident* that they share some basic standards for the treatment of each other. People are able to *trust* each other to abide by those standards or at least to acknowledge fault if they (or others) do not abide by them. And so, finally, people are entitled to be *hopeful* that unacceptable treatment will not prevail, that unacceptable behavior will not be defended or ignored where it occurs, and that victims will not be abandoned in their reliance on our shared commitment to our standards and to each other. Hopefulness, we have seen, is not the icing on the cake, but is the pan in which the cake is baked. In relations characterized by violation, violence, and complacent and profound contempt, any attempt to regain or stabilize the trust that holds us together in moral relations will have to find a foundation of hope – an energizing belief in and desire for something of value that might seem at times to be nothing more than possible. Restorative justice captures this need for renewed confidence and trust that will "restore" us to a working moral order. Hopefulness is the opposite of the bitterness or despair that comes from victims feeling isolated and abandoned within or by their communities.

The aim of restorative justice clearly distinguishes it from both retributive and compensatory justice. Retribution in theory and practice centers on offenders and what they "deserve," without central attention to victims. Compensatory justice is directed primarily at victims and at "making good" the victim's wrongful loss. But compensatory justice focuses on material restitution or compensation in order to "make the victim whole," or restore the status quo ante. Restorative justice, too, typically seeks reparation for victims. In restorative justice, though, material amends play instrumental and symbolic roles in the attempt to set things right

[24] Harvey M. Weinstein and Eric Stover propose "reclamation" as a more fitting term for retrieving a social and moral situation from barbarity or disorder. See their "Introduction: Conflict, Justice, and Reclamation," in their *My Neighbor, My Enemy: Justice and Community in the Aftermath of Mass Atrocity,* 15.

between people. Reparation often includes restitution or compensation to make repair concrete and in some cases to give weight to other interpersonal gestures, such as apologies and expressions of sorrow, shame, guilt, or the wish to make amends. Some studies of restorative justice practice find that victims value symbolic reparation more than its material tokens.[25]

Neither compensatory justice nor retributive justice directly addresses the *moral quality of future relations* between those who have done or benefited from harm and those who have suffered it. While this makes restorative justice distinct in its aims and practice from these other familiar varieties of justice, it is not opposed to them. Restorative practices may be coupled with retributive measures and usually involves an emphasis on compensation. Practices in the realm of ordinary crime include victim-offender mediation, a direct dialogue that allows victims to confront the person who harmed them, to express directly to the offender what their violation has meant to them and the pain it has caused, and to seek information that puts facts in the place of vague images, fears, and stereotypes. Offenders, too, have opportunities to "humanize" themselves and the people they hurt, and to express regret, offer apology, and even seek forgiveness if their situation permits. Other restorative justice formats involve larger networks surrounding victims and offenders, such as the model of "family group conferencing" pioneered in New Zealand and Australia that brings families, community representatives, and other interested parties to participate in determining the terms of reparation. Indigenous traditions in Canada and the USA have been adapted as well into forms of conference or sentencing (or healing) circle formats that can involve significant portions of small local communities as well as legal professionals.[26] In the case of violent crimes where the offender is incarcerated, mediation can still occur at the offenders' place of detention if all parties are willing. For many victims, needs to confront offenders, to seek explanations, and to seek resolution do not end when punishment

[25] See Strang, "Justice for Victims of Young Offenders," 287–90. See also the previous discussion of the failure to secure adequate acknowledgment from the government of Japan for its role in sexual slavery in the Second World War.

[26] A brief overview of current restorative justice practices is provided by Gordon Bazemore and Mark Umbreit, two leaders in the field, in "A Comparison of Four Restorative Conferencing Models," in Johnstone, *A Restorative Justice Reader*, See also Bazemore and Schiff, *Restorative Community Justice*. On peacemaking circles, see Kay Pranis, Barry Stuart, and Mark Wedge, *Peacemaking Circles: From Crime to Community*. On Arizona's Navajo Peacemaker Courts, see Robert Yazzie, "'Life Comes From It': Navajo Justice Concepts," and Barbara E. Wall, "Navajo Conceptions of Justice in the Peacemaker Court."

is assured.[27] Restorative justice practices are also sometimes used for juvenile offenders or for nonviolent crimes to replace prosecution or detention and to focus directly on repair and reintegration.

Restorative justice also increasingly frames ways of coming to terms with political repression and violent conflict. Whether or not criminal prosecutions are possible and productive in the wake of large-scale violations, restorative justice practices – truth commissions, public apologies, commemorations, and some kinds of reparations programs (especially those embedded in a process of public acknowledgment and apology) – are increasingly used.[28] While the proceedings of a truth commission or the issuance of a public apology lacks the direct and personal element of smaller scale restorative practices, they are directed to the same ends: addressing the human costs of violence and conflict, seeking validation and vindication for victims, inviting accountability from (or placing it on) those responsible for harm, pursuing a historical record that will minimize future denial and evasion, and offering victims material and symbolic reparation for their suffering and losses.

The ideal of restorative justice is that its values should be expressed both in the structure of processes of dealing with violence and injustice and in the outcomes of doing so. Yet the very nature of restorative justice practices tends to blur a sharp process/outcome distinction, for such practices as victim-offender dialogue, group conferences, truth commissions, or public apologies not only aim at more adequate forms of relationships but typically begin to *act out* the more morally adequate relationships at which they aim. The practices involve responsive and respectful forms of encounter, interaction, and expression, such as offenders directly facing and hearing victims; victims being able to confront offenders and to seek information directly from offenders about what happened and why they were targeted, information that is often critical to the victims' own understanding, peace of mind, and sense of blamelessness. Offenders, too, are able to represent themselves, and in doing so may be able to represent their own human vulnerabilities, their regret or shame, and their willingness to offer apologies or amends. In some formats other participants encourage more honest, responsive, and responsible interaction, and they can exert pressure as well as provide

---

[27] Walter J. Dickey, "Forgiveness and Crime: The Possibilities of Restorative Justice," provides a transcript of one meeting between a woman sexually assaulted in her own home and the man who assaulted her.

[28] Minow, *Between Vengeance and Forgiveness*, and Teitel, *Transitional Justice*, explore the spectrum of approaches.

support for plans of restitution, compensation, or service that aim at repair.

Restorative justice, then, takes the view that making amends as a way to restore relationships is an *obligation* to be taken up ideally by offending or responsible parties, and also, or by default, by larger communities. And it takes the position that the goal of repair – restoring relations – should already be implemented in the very structure of restorative practices and what people are asked to do and are able to do within them. Is the commitment to restoring relations through making amends an idealistic pipe dream? With the growth of restorative justice practice in the criminal and political realm, there is a mounting body of evidence that suggests it is not. Restorative justice practices do not necessarily remove the need for retributive measures or for legally secured compensation. Yet there is a basis for using restorative justice alongside these others, and a need for restorative justice where these others are ill-advised or impracticable, as is the case with excessive incarceration in contemporary U.S. society or in the wake of large-scale violence that can leave behind tens of thousands of victims and perpetrators of political crime. In his comprehensive overview of recent research on restorative justice practices, John Braithwaite summarizes the results of a large number of studies that show fairly consistently that restorative justice satisfies victims, offenders, and communities better than does existing (retributively based) criminal justice practices. In particular, many studies confirm that restorative justice practices such as mediations and conferences get high marks for procedural fairness and respect for participants, tend to lead to higher rates of completion of restitution agreements, tend to elicit apologies from offenders much more frequently, and tend to reduce fear, anger, and vengeful feelings among victims.[29] While most studies track restorative justice practice with juveniles or with nonviolent or less violent crimes, those who work more directly with post-incarceration mediation for violent offenses also find it can offer significant benefits for victims and offenders.[30]

---

[29] See Braithwaite, *Restorative Justice and Responsive Regulation*, ch. 3. On the Reintegrative Shaming Experiment (RISE), in addition to Strang, "Justice for Victims of Young Offenders," see Kathleen Daly, "Restorative Justice: The Real Story," in Johnstone, *A Restorative Justice Reader*, for results from the South Australian Juvenile Justice study. Information on the RISE and SAJJ Australian studies can be found at www.aic.gov.au/rjustice, accessed 1 June 2005.

[30] Howard Zehr collects remarkable stories of victims or families of victims meeting offenders in *Transcending: Reflections of Crime Victims*.

In the political arena, South Africa's TRC modeled the restorative justice idea in many aspects of its practice. Victims were validated with transcribed officially recognized testimonies, some of them made publicly with overtly sympathetic support from the Commission. Perpetrators of murder and torture pursuing individual amnesties in return for full disclosure of violent deeds often provided survivors with details that otherwise would not have been available, and sometimes went beyond admitting their involvement by expressing remorse and offering apologies (although they were not required to do so, and many did not). The Commission produced both an absorbing international spectacle and a five-volume report that attempted to strip the mask of nobility and decency from many operations of the South African apartheid government and state "security" apparatus, while also confirming gross human rights violations and civilian deaths caused by the African National Congress and other anti-apartheid forces. The TRC also secured modest reparations payments for those who were officially certified as victims through their own or others' testimony.[31] The Commission was from its inception contested, criticized, and challenged, most so for its adoption of the unique policy of trading individual amnesty from both criminal and civil prosecution for truth about violent crimes. The most bitter accusation was that the TRC traded "justice for truth." Did the TRC do any kind of justice? And did it move closer to its aim of "reconciliation"– a broad and vague term, but one that encompassed the idea of restoring relationships in a society riven by relentless and official racial segregation and profound oppression of the black majority?[32]

Some research is beginning to appear that addresses these questions. It bears on the issue of whether amends can be made, or whether when made can make a difference to victims of political violence. James Gibson conducted a detailed survey study of 3,700 South Africans in 2001, selected to represent the four principal racial groups that apartheid classification made an entrenched reality in South Africa. Gibson's central question was: did the acceptance of the truth (as represented by the TRC's Report) lead to reconciliation among South Africans? Gibson's data explored a variety of facets of post-TRC reconciliation through

---

[31] An analysis of this "construction" of victims and perpetrators in the South African context is Tristan Anne Borer, "A Taxonomy of Victims and Perpetrators: Human Rights and Reconciliation in South Africa."

[32] Rotberg and Thompson, *Truth v. Justice,* exposes the controversy about amnesty for truth surrounding the TRC. See also Charles Villa-Vicencio and Erik Doxtader, eds., *The Provocations of Amnesty: Memory, Justice and Impunity.*

questions relating to interracial acceptance (improved overall), political tolerance (in short supply), respect for human rights culture (mixed and weak), and belief in the legitimacy of the new democracy's political institutions (minimal).[33] While the results and analysis are too rich to be reprised here, two findings might be important not only for South Africa. First, in examining the truth-reconciliation link, Gibson found that for black South Africans truth-acceptance had no significant impact on attitudes toward whites, but that "among whites in particular, the relationship is remarkably strong."[34] Gibson hypothesized that the different experiences among blacks under apartheid, some faring better and some worse than others, created differences in their attitudes toward whites that canceled each other out in their reactions to the TRC's truth-telling. On the side of whites, however, while truth-acceptance and reconciled racial attitudes seemed reciprocally to influence each other, Gibson found evidence that coming to know the truth – "that the defense of the apartheid state involved numerous indefensible actions" – had affected their racial attitudes.

The importance of truth-telling in cases of extended and systemic oppression is of the greatest importance for other cases, to which I return shortly. Here we see one more feature of restorative justice practices that appears also in the criminal context. Restorative justice practices often create the conditions to *leverage responsibility*, that is, to move people from a minimal or peripheral sense of connection and responsibility for a wrong or harm to a richer and more demanding perception of what is wrong and how they might be related to it. In victim-offender mediation, group conferences, or peacemaking circles, once victims, offenders, and other concerned parties are willing to engage in restorative justice practice, it is not uncommon for this movement to greater responsibility to occur. Those who have already assumed responsibility for a harm come to a deepened sense of the full reality and consequences of what they have done to those harmed. Others who are concerned may begin to see themselves as implicated, either by connections they have not before examined or admitted (a violent domestic atmosphere or ignoring an alcohol problem), or by a realization that they can make a difference by contributing to or assisting with some form of repair. Victims, too,

---

[33] James L. Gibson, *Overcoming Apartheid: Can Truth Reconcile a Divided Nation?* A summary view of main conclusions of the research is given in James L. Gibson, "Overcoming Apartheid: Can Truth Reconcile a Divided Nation?"

[34] Gibson, *Overcoming Apartheid*, 132 and 150. See also 334 on the strength of the truth-reconciliation link for different groups.

can want to exercise influence on the outcome of a restorative process and its impact on the offender. In this way, restorative practice is *dynamic with respect to responsibility*. Retributive and compensatory justice establish a prior fact of responsibility in order to determine who will "pay" for wrong, and justice is exacted in the form of punishment or compensation. With restorative justice, it is somewhat different. One might say: you don't establish responsibility once and for all in order to do restorative justice; rather, you do restorative justice in order to induce, deepen, extend, and clarify responsibilities that may seem limited, shallow, or nonexistent at the outset.[35]

A second set of suggestive findings comes from an embedded study Gibson calls the "Justice and Amnesty Experiment." The Experiment gathered reactions to a vignette in which a combatant named "Philip," identified as belonging to whatever group a particular respondent most dislikes, receives amnesty for setting off a bomb that kills several innocent people. The vignette is varied to include or exclude aspects associated by Gibson with different kinds of justice: whether Philip's family says they are ashamed (retributive), whether victims get to tell how the crime affected their lives (procedural), whether Philip's apology is accepted by the families (restorative), and whether families of the victims are given compensation by the government (distributive). Respondents rate the vignettes for fairness, and it emerges, perhaps unsurprisingly, that amnesty instead of prosecution is overall judged not to be very fair (only 24.3% of participants found the outcome fair, while 51.2% judged the outcome as quite unfair, and 22.9% as somewhat unfair).

Nonetheless there is considerable variability in how *unfair* the outcome is seen to be, and these variations are revealing: the single strongest predictor of perceived fairness is that the victims receive compensation. In addition, receiving an apology and having a chance to tell one's story were the other fairness-enhancing features (while the "retributive" – shaming – factor has no effect). Gibson comments, "the effects of procedural and restorative justice together are roughly two-thirds the size of the effect of distributive justice."[36] That is, voice and apology vie with compensation to enhance significantly the perceived fairness of an otherwise unfair response to an "irreparable" harm. Gibson cautions that this experiment

[35] On the "transformational" momentum of restorative justice, see Marc Forget, "Crime as Interpersonal Conflict: Reconciliation Between Victim and Offender," in Prager and Govier, *Dilemmas of Reconciliation*.

[36] Gibson, *Overcoming Apartheid*, 278.

does not assess reactions of actual victims, and he emphasizes that amnesty for deadly crimes is not perceived as fair by most South Africans. Yet, he says, "Whether people are willing to tolerate amnesty depends in part on whether other forms of justice are present."[37] This outcome is encouraging for restorative justice, which typically incorporates all of the measures – voice, apology, and compensation – that Gibson sorts into distinct "procedural," "restorative," and "distributive" categories, and so aims to address even those irreparable harms, whether or not retributive justice is available.[38]

Restorative justice correctly situates "making amends" within the broader task of repairing the moral fabric of relationship that serious wrongdoing weakens, tears, or destroys. Restorative practices begin from the outset in their structure to enact more connected, respectful, attentive, and responsive forms of relation among participants, thus building the desired outcome into the process as much as possible. Restorative justice leverages responsibility, opening a path to a broader, deeper, and more nuanced understanding of where responsibilities, retrospective and prospective, fall. Restorative justice keeps the victim's plight central, orienting the process and outcomes toward genuine repair of harm victims have suffered, a multifaceted repair that typically includes information, validation, compensation, and apology. Restorative justice stands against the abandonment of the victim and offers the offending and other responsible parties an active role in doing justice in the wake of wrong. Those with reason to feel shame or regret have an opportunity to demonstrate respect for victims and to affirm their self-respect and moral competence by participating in setting right a wrong, including by offering the moral satisfaction of apology. While forgiveness is never obligatory, and no victim should feel pressured to forgive, restorative justice creates a space where the familiar transaction of apology and forgiveness may be attempted and is sometimes completed, even in cases where wrongs are deeply serious.

---

[37] The Justice and Amnesty Experiment is reported in Gibson, *Overcoming Apartheid*, 268–88. The quoted comment appears on 284.

[38] A comparison to Gibson's South Africa study is a study of reparation in the Czech Republic, which found satisfaction with financial compensation to be the most powerful predictor of positive outcomes of reparation. Unsatisfied desire for retribution was not found to inhibit reparation, and public truth-telling – not an officially orchestrated event in the Czech Republic as it was in South Africa – stood in a more complicated relationship to sociopolitical redress and inner healing of victims. Roman David and Susanne Choi Yuk-Ping, "Victims on Transitional Justice: Lessons from the Reparation of Human Rights Abuses in the Czech Republic."

Finally, restorative justice invites "communities," of varying sizes and descriptions, to participate both as actors in repair and as guarantors of repair, whether in the form of community boards involving citizens in settling disputes and minor crimes, or as participants within conferences who help design restitution agreements, or as citizens who participate in public projects of truth-telling, education, or commemoration. When responsible individuals are unrepentant or contemptuous, repair devolves to communities or networks of support within communities. Restorative justice, finally, captures the idea that moral repair is more than doing good; it is doing what we are *obliged* to do, and that is why it is *justice*. But what of the hardest cases, where responsibility seems elusive and the status of "victim," "offender," or "responsible party" is unclear or hotly contested? How does one make amends for historical injustice, and upon whom does this responsibility fall?

Historical Injustice and Black Redress

Historical injustices include large-scale wrongs that are distant in time and ones that involve an extended, usually continuing history of ill-treatment, domination, and disrespect (or worse) between groups. The wrongs at issue in historical injustice are usually group-based massacre and ethnic, religious, or political persecution; dispossession of ancestral lands; forced removals; broken or fraudulent treaties and agreements; policies of deliberate cultural destruction and assimilation visited on indigenous people or national minorities; colonization and the exploitation of labor and resources; and histories of slavery, apartheid, legal segregation, second-class citizenship, and continuing racial discrimination, exclusion, and violence. Often cases are a mix of various of these wrongs. Historical injustices raise problems of individual, collective, and shared responsibility, as well as questions of whether obligations to repair and rights to repair are a legacy that can be handed down through generations.

Despite apparent obstacles – conceptual, practical, and political – to understanding and righting historical wrongs, discussion of how to do it, and why it is required, has accelerated.[39] From the 1990s, there

---

[39] Contemporary discussions of reparative measures, their rationales, and their varying effects include Howard McGary, "Justice and Reparations"; Matsuda, "Looking to the Bottom"; Minow, *Between Vengeance and Forgiveness*; Teitel, *Transitional Justice*; Barkan, *The Guilt of Nations*; Randall Robinson, *The Debt: What America Owes to Blacks*; Brooks, *When Sorry Isn't Enough*; Peter Digeser, *Political Forgiveness*; Brooks, *Atonement and Forgiveness*; Rodney C. Roberts, ed., *Injustice and Rectification*; Trudy Govier and Wilhelm Verwoerd,

seemed to be momentum for recognition of historic wrongs, and interest in methods of redress, including material and moral satisfaction to
unjustly treated groups or to their individual members through restitution, compensation, apology, official documentation of wrongs and
histories of injustice, commemorations and memorials, and preventive
legislation and education. Some have dubbed the end of the twentieth
century an "age of apology" due to an unprecedented stream of official
expressions of regret, remorse, guilt, responsibility, and repentance by
religious leaders, heads of state, corporate entities, and social groups.[40]
Japanese-Americans unjustly interned in camps during the Second World
War have received official acknowledgment of the racism and hysteria
behind internment policies, a symbolic payment of monetary compensation, and an official apology from the U.S. government. While the Prime
Minister of Australia refused to apologize to Aboriginal peoples for the
kidnapping and forcible removal of children from Aboriginal communities by the Australian government, a government report, *Bringing Them
Home*, documented the cruel policies and their disastrous results, and
recommended reparations for displaced individuals, families, and communities. The nation of Canada began an accounting of its destructive
treatment of Aboriginal peoples in a five-volume report in 1996, and has
since confronted the dark histories of abuse of Aboriginal children in
Canada's residential schools.[41] These are only a few of many examples.

"The Promise and Pitfalls of Apology"; Max du Plessis, "Historical Injustice and International Law: An Exploratory Discussion of Reparation for Slavery"; Prager and Govier,
Dilemmas of Reconciliation; Janna Thompson, *Taking Responsibility for the Past: Reparation
and Historical Injustice*; John Torpey, *Politics and the Past: On Repairing Historical Injustices*;
Chris Cunneen, "Reparations and Restorative Justice: Responding to Gross Violations
of Human Rights"; and Pablo de Greiff, *The Handbook of Reparations*.

[40] Emily Mitchell, "The Decade of Atonement," gives a list of public apologies from 1988
to 1998. Another list and a clear discussion of representative apologies is Richard Joyce,
"Apologizing." Aaron Lazare, *On Apology*, contains a wealth of examples and analysis.
Official expressions of regret and institutional apologies are discussed in Jean Harvey's
Civilized Oppression, ch. 7.

[41] See Minow, *Between Vengeance and Forgiveness*, on the Japanese-American reparations
movement. On the removal of mixed race Aboriginal children in Australia, see Human
Rights and Equal Opportunity Commission of Australia, *Bringing Them Home, The Report
of the National Inquiry into the Separation of Aboriginal and Torres Strait Islander Children from
Their Families*. Testimonies from the report are excerpted in Carmel Bird, ed., *The Stolen
Children: Their Stories*. A moving and critical assessment of Canadian attempts to address
the mistreatment of Aboriginal people is Roger Epp's "We Are All Treaty People: History, Reconciliation, and the 'Settler Problem.'" Brooks, *When Sorry Isn't Enough*, provides
documentation and debate on a variety of cases of historical injustice, and Barkan, *The
Guilt of Nations*, overviews a number of reparations movements since World War II.

Retributive and compensatory justice concerns are certainly fitting and may be necessary in dealing with historical injustice. The attempt to prosecute those responsible for killings and other grave crimes now decades old is a clear rejection of impunity; it shows that grave wrongs of the past cannot simply be buried along with their victims. Movements or legal actions seeking recognition of wrong through compensation similarly insist that an unrepaired wrong still requires redress decades – and possibly centuries – later. I would like, however, to examine some ways that a restorative justice approach addresses issues differently, and addresses different issues, than either a retributive or compensatory approach, but may also in fact pave the way for them. Because "historical injustice" is a broad idea and can encompass cases that differ greatly from each other, I will focus on a particular instance that has eluded serious reparative efforts and has profound significance in the United States context. I take as my example the problem of "black redress," to use Roy Brooks's term for the still unredressed history of slavery, legal segregation, and institutionally implemented or tolerated racial discrimination, starting, in Brooks's description, in 1638 with the beginning of customary institutionalized slavery of Africans in New England, and ending juridically "only thirty years ago with the passage of a federal law, the Equal Employment Opportunity Act of 1972."[42] I believe that the case of black redress illustrates a morally ravaging kind of historical injustice in which the problems of deformed and destructive attitudes, lack of trust, misplaced resentment of wrongdoers and beneficiaries, and the dangers of despair or cynicism are written large. As a result, the ideal of "restoring relationships" takes on a particular poignancy and urgency.

A distinguishing feature of the absence of black redress is its continuing, pervasive, and negative impact on the self-understanding and relationships within a whole society. Current relationships among individuals and groups are grossly distorted by the persistent and accumulating impact of profoundly violent, transgenerationally destructive, and unrepaired racial injustices that continue to be felt today. The wrongs at issue in black redress are not only those that happened "long ago." Those long-ago wrongs (slavery, Jim Crow, de facto segregation and exclusion), some of them experienced by individuals who are still alive today are enfolded within a continuing history of unrepaired wrongs and fresh insults that are a fact of present daily relationships as human beings and as citizens in the USA. Responsibility for the past in the present in this

---

[42] Brooks, *Atonement and Forgiveness*, 2, 21.

case – like those of massacre, theft of land, and the cultural destruction of indigenous peoples in white settler societies – is responsibility for the *past as the living present.*[43] Melissa Williams has talked about citizenship as involving "shared fate," a situation of interdependence not controlled by choices and elective commitments. In the case of the intertwined history of African-Americans and other Americans, a fate all Americans share as citizens is this brutal and polarizing history, even now not fully acknowledged and even now sometimes minimized or denied, with which all Americans still live.[44] Its results are all around us; as important, they are within us, in distorted patterns of perception, understanding, and feeling that continue to shape the raced relationships of contemporary U.S. society. Others have made strong arguments for reparation to African-Americans and for the primary responsibility of the U.S. government (and, one might add, state governments) as the persisting institution that both enforced and permitted gross racial injustice, and failed to make amends, for over more than two centuries.[45] I find these arguments compelling, but I look instead at the task of repair and the question of responsibility as seen through a restorative justice lens. How and where does a restorative justice approach distinctively find responsibility in this kind of case, and what is the particular nature of the repairs to be attempted?

Characteristically, restorative justice puts communities, and not only individual offenders, into the field of responsibility. In ordinary criminal justice contexts, restorative justice sees "communities" as central in two ways. Communities may be harmed by crimes, and so may figure as primary or secondary victims with a right to repair from responsible parties. Even when they are not harmed, however, communities bear responsibility for taking effective measures to address and redress wrongs in their midst, to aid victims, and to place demands on offending parties for proper response. In restorative justice, communities are seen as

---

[43] On this past that lives in the present, see Robert Sparrow's "History and Collective Responsibility."

[44] Melissa Williams, "Citizenship as Identity, Citizenship as Shared Fate, and the Functions of Multicultural Education." See also Sheldon Wolin, *The Presence of the Past: Essays on the State and the Constitution*, on "birthright."

[45] On the U.S. government's obligation to make reparation, see Robert Fullinwider, "The Case For Reparations," accessed 12 August 2005; Brooks, *Atonement and Forgiveness*; and Rahul Kumar, "Responsibility and Rectification for Past Injustice: The Case of American Chattel Slavery." See Brooks, *When Sorry Isn't Enough*, on the reparation measures taken by the State of Florida in response to a white race riot that destroyed the black town of Rosewood.

responsible at a minimum for clearly reiterating baselines of acceptable conduct, and acceptable conduct includes reparative efforts from those who have done wrong or caused harm. The community has the role of reiterating standards and demanding a reparative response whether or not those who wrongfully harm are present, able, responsive, or responsible. When they are not – when those who are most clearly responsible for harm are absent, unavailable, or unresponsive – then communities must by default take up some of the efforts to provide, at the least, acknowledgement, validation, and reassurance to victims of wrong. This bears on the case of black redress, where the wrongs at issue involve extreme forms of violation and dereliction in the past that form a continuous history persisting in the present with society's acquiescence in serious inequalities of freedom, civic respect, and life prospects for African-Americans. Injustices have historically been inflicted through laws, and institutions, and now involve de facto practices and failures to take decisive reparative and remedial action; the injustices at issue, and the neglect or refusal of repair, have occurred with the explicit or tacit support of large segments of a majority white population.

The idea of "community" is used flexibly to the point of vagueness in restorative justice, but there is a practical basis for allowing the identification of community relevant to repair to vary in context. The harmed community and the community that can effectively respond to support repair need not be the same collectivity. It can happen that neither community possesses an organizational structure and executive function to seek or undertake reparative actions corporately and representatively. Relevant collectivities might be relatively unstructured or informal – a locality or neighborhood – and it might be that a community with potential to respond effectively need not do so, or cannot do so, corporately. Instead, its members or some groups of members might act from within it on its behalf or in its name. Communities able to respond might also be multiple, some institutionally embodied and represented, and others not. The key point is that for restorative criminal justice, "communities" bearing responsibilities of repair can be multiple and differently situated with respect to a crime.

As important, communities capable of responding are not always well-defined or given in advance, but may be *formed* in response to the demands of repair. They may be formed out of a recognition of some shared fault that contributed to harm, or out of a sense of forward-looking task responsibility, or out of a sense of necessity to participate in the repair the community itself needs. In other words, a community may see itself as having contributed to or failed to prevent or forestall harm; it can recognize a need and see within itself the resources and capability to meet the needs created by a wrong, or it can take charge or take a role in mending within itself what a wrong has damaged. It is, of course, individual members of communities who in cooperative and shared ways make these assessments and undertake these tasks. But they can do so with a sense that they are acting "for" – out of, on behalf of – a group and they are doing so together with others. The collectivity in question can be a very diffuse or unclearly bounded group, such as "our neighborhood" or "the parents concerned about this problem," or it can be a highly articulated and organized collectivity, such as a team, an organization, or an institution. Writing in the context of ordinary crime, Paul McCold and Benjamin Wachtel speak of "micro-communities created by the incident of a crime" as the "means through which healing and reintegration is possible."[46]

In the case of black redress, "the wrong" is not a discrete event. There is a continuous history of legally protected, enforced, and legitimated oppression implemented by deprivation, humiliation, violence, and neglect, and a repeated failure or refusal to make reparation, with continuing contemporary effects on wealth, health, and achievement that are alarming.[47] There are many events that might be the focus of repair, and there are many sites for efforts of citizens, groups, and institutions to conduct, support, and demand repair. Even if the U.S. or state or local governments are principal persisting entities with responsibilities of repair for institutionalized racial injustice against African-Americans, some aspects of repair at issue in black redress can only be effectively pursued by widely diffused projects and activities carried out by citizens in varied ways through groups and institutions. There is no zero-sum relationship between the federal and state governments, groups of citizens, or local governmental or nongovernmental institutional actors taking initiatives to address and redress historical injustice. Diverse groups and institutions can express a nation's or a community's responsibility

---

[46] Paul McCold and Benjamin Wachtel, "Community Is Not a Place: A New Look at Community Justice Initiatives," 298, 300.

[47] Melvin L. Oliver and Thomas M. Shapiro, *Black Wealth/White Wealth*, analyzes the wealth gap and the historical circumstances that produced it. Brooks, *Atonement and Forgiveness*, devotes a lengthy chapter to "Harms to Descendants" in power, wealth, and education. Amartya Sen reports the startling conclusion based on official government statistics that "African-Americans as a group have no higher – indeed have a lower – chance of reaching advanced ages than do people born in the immensely poorer economies of China or the Indian State of Kerala (or in Sri Lanka, Jamaica or Costa a Rica)," in *Development as Freedom*, 21–24.

to repair unredressed wrongs. At the same time, the actions of diverse publics and institutions can create a climate of disapproval of governmental negligence with respect to racial repair. They can educate a broader public, mobilizing interest, conscience, and imagination in the service of repair. This is crucial, because from a restorative justice perspective the most fundamental meaning of repair is the *restoration of relationships* among segments of the U.S. population whose very understanding of themselves as segments, and whose alienation as citizens, has been produced by the history of raced relationships legitimized and enforced by political institutions. These raced divisions continue to be reinforced by de facto patterns of segregation, exclusion, and exposure to disproportionate risk.

I began to think about restorative justice and black redress when I heard of two local institutional initiatives to address difficult histories and episodes in America's history of race. One of these, the Brown University Steering Committee on Slavery and Justice, was formed in 2003 at the behest of Brown's President Ruth Simmons to investigate the University's and Rhode Island's connections to the slave trade. The Committee has sponsored academic and community events, and will report its recommendations for contemporary actions to President Simmons. The other initiative is the first self-denominated U.S. truth commission. The "Truth and Community Reconciliation Project" in Greensboro, North Carolina, was created in 2003 by citizens to revisit and document the murders of five antiracist community activists in 1979, and to make recommendations concerning reconciliation in the Greensboro community. Despite videotapes of the murders, no one has been convicted in state and federal trials, although a civil court did find several participants liable for one death. Like South Africa's famous truth commission, the Greensboro commission seeks some resolution through public truth-telling; unlike the TRC, Greensboro's commission is not governmentally sponsored. It is the product of hopeful citizen action. These initiatives illustrate how restorative justice as community justice can be attempted in historical cases.[48]

---

[48] On the Committee, see Brown University's website http://www.brown.edu/Research/ Slavery_Justice/, accessed 6/8/2005. On Greensboro, see Ellis Cose, *Bone to Pick: Of Forgiveness, Reconciliation, Reparation, and Revenge*, 119–25. Cose also discusses attempts to get reparation for survivors and descendants of victims of the Tulsa Race Riot of 1921 that resulted in many deaths and wholesale destruction of a prosperous black community of Greenwood (148–55). Neither a formal state commission of inquiry nor legal proceedings has achieved any redress for black victims.

What responses are needed under the heading of black redress? From a retributive justice standpoint, there are outstanding crimes of the Jim Crow and civil rights periods that can still be prosecuted, and a continuing need to document and prosecute racially motivated illegal discrimination and violence. Several high profile murder cases of the civil rights era – the murders of Medgar Evers, of four African-American girls in an Alabama church bombing, and of three civil rights workers in Mississippi – have been reopened and prosecuted successfully in the past decade in what are sometimes meaningfully called "atonement trials."[49] From the standpoint of compensatory justice, legal efforts to wrest compensation from major corporations for their involvement in slavery has been attempted but has not yet met with success. Roy Brooks, supporting an "atonement model" rooted in part in restorative justice, argues that the "tort model" – for example, legally pursuing compensation for forced labor based on World War II precedents concerning Germany or Japan – has been ineffective in securing compensation for slavery, and is in any case "too confrontational" to contribute to racial reconciliation.[50]

I believe neither the retributive or compensatory paths should be abandoned. Race-based violence continues, and the prosecution of old cases, where feasible, sends a strong message that crimes of racial violence and terrorism have never been anything other than an outrage, then as much as now. Dramatic differentials in wealth that are a continuing legacy of slavery, racial hierarchy, educational disadvantage, job and residential segregation, and violence need to be addressed materially. It might be, however, that the "restoration of relationships" sought within a restorative justice approach could create better conditions for legal retributive or compensatory justice for African-Americans in individual legal cases, and for a politically viable movement for black reparations. In a climate in which a large majority of white Americans oppose so much as an official apology from the U.S. government for slavery (although in 1993 the U.S. Congress passed a resolution formally apologizing to Native Hawaiians for the overthrow of the Kingdom of Hawaii in 1893), it would seem the time for more robustly material measures is not yet ripe.[51] Glaring inequalities between white

---

49 Shaila Dewan, "Revisiting '64 Civil Rights Deaths, This Time in a Murder Trial."
50 Brooks, *Atonement and Forgiveness*, ch. 4, 98.
51 Joe R. Feagin and Eileen O'Brien, "The Growing Movement for Reparations," cites a 1997 ABC News poll that reports two-thirds of white Americans resist the idea of an apology from the federal government for slavery, and 88% rejected reparations. Ellis Cose reports a more recent (September 2003), poll finding 30% of whites (compared

Americans and African-Americans in income, wealth, health, longevity, educational access and achievement, and incarceration, are continually studied and reported. Many white Americans appear to see these gross disparities as undisturbing, and even as unremarkable. White incuriosity, complacency, or resistance to seeking the truth about slavery, Jim Crow, continuing racism and their persistent effects in the present day looks like a disconnection, the absence of a relationship. It is actually itself the expression of a very definite kind of relationship. It is a relationship of *normative contempt*, which restorative justice would aim to change.

Contempt is an attitude of disdain that comes in two linked kinds. Contempt can be aggressive disrespect, hostility, and rejection to the point of violent and degrading treatment. Yet there is also a contempt that is complacency, lack of concern, and a lack of felt connection to what doesn't feel important or deserve attention. Contempt is "normative" for one group's attitudes to another when the attitude of hostility or indifference is scarcely noted, when it is the attitude taken within that group to be normal and unremarkable, if not actually required, toward something or someone. The contempt of indifference and the contempt of hostility are linked: what we are comfortable complacently ignoring often becomes the focus of active hostility when it makes itself uncomfortably difficult to ignore, when it insists on our attention and connection. When we have blandly indifferent contempt for other people in their unjustly disadvantaged situations, we can become defensive, irritated, hostile, or aggressive when these people seek to involve us in something that we are unwilling to see as our problem. We can become exceptionally resistant to exploring any connection to their disadvantage that might imply our responsibility for it, or for its repair.

Normative contempt captures both the indifference and the easily tapped hostility of many white Americans toward African-Americans, and especially toward the suggestion that African-Americans are *owed* something – really, are owed *anything*, if only an apology. It is the absence of a sense of connection that might suggest responsibility, yet it is also a charged and brittle complacency that quickly turns to anger and rejection when disturbed. It is the attitude that allows whites not to experience – literally, not to *feel* – themselves as a part of an urgent present problem

to 79% of blacks) believe blacks are due an apology for slavery, and 4% of whites are in favor of compensation for slavery, compared to 67% of blacks. See Cose, *Bone to Pick*, 171. In a surprising move in 2005, the United States Senate passed by voice vote an apology for failing to enact federal legislation against lynching decades ago. See Sheryl Gay Stolberg, "Senate Issues Apology Over Failure on Lynching Law."

concerning "the color line" that DuBois spoke of, nor to view themselves as sharing responsibility for its resolution. It allows whites to think of the history of African-Americans as what happened to *them* (ideally "long ago") – and not what happened to white Americans, indelibly stamping our self-understandings. These understandings are reproduced every day, and a part of them is not to know, and when prodded to evade knowing, and when made to know to be angry at knowing what whiteness means in terms of differential privilege and advantage that it took a couple of centuries to embed very deeply in our shared lives.[52] It allows many whites to disavow the ugly contempt of overt racism from within the safe contempt of indifference.

"Restoration" in restorative justice means to reconstruct relations in some minimally morally adequate form in which they can hopefully embody a reasonable degree of mutual trust and some confidence that shared standards of basically respectful conduct and mutual concern prevail. The achievement of a state of minimal trust among white and black Americans is yet a remote possibility.[53] To see interracial trust as possible we need to understand and effectively confront what stands in its way. Applied to black redress, restorative justice insists that we focus on the distortion of relationship that is involved in American histories of race, and confront the normative contempt of a white majority that is largely complacent or hostile. The ideal of restoring relations moves us toward exploring the tangled skein of belief and feeling of whites and blacks that is a specific legacy of a continuous and continuing history. This legacy cannot be undone by single gestures or policies, but particular gestures or policies are the medium for that exploration, and projects of repair can come from diverse organizations, communities, and governmental institutions. There are in fact a variety of ways to make amends and pursue repair in the case of historical injustice. It is not a hopeless case of "too many people, too irreparable the harm, too long ago." Restorative measures include attempts to uncover and preserve the truth, to enunciate wrongs and the obligations they create, to educate about the past and its role in our present and future, to acknowledge the terrible suffering, humiliation, and grinding loss of an enslaved and then subjected minority, to affirm the dignity, creativity, and resiliency of people under

---

[52] A generation of critical race theory has repeatedly made this point about the privilege and the importance to privilege of "not knowing." See, for example, Charles Mills, *The Racial Contract*, on the "epistemology of ignorance."

[53] Danielle Allen, *Talking To Strangers: Anxieties of Citizenship Since Brown v. Board of Education*, explores race relations in terms of trust and its role in democracy.

severe and unjust conditions, to apologize where apology is due, to celebrate our moral growth as individuals and citizens who are competent at the business of justice. Reparation policies of monetary compensation or collective investment by the U.S. government might be an ultimate objective of black redress; but without the extended work of restoration, compensation is unlikely, and without restoration, the meaning of compensation, were some compensation achieved, might not be a respectful and reparative one.[54]

Where to begin? The adoption of John Conyers' HR 40 resolution, introduced every year since 1989, for a commission to study reparations for African-Americans has a feature welcome to restorative justice. It proposes a process – a kind of truth commission, a communal restorative process with both concrete objectives and symbolic meanings – that might precipitate new recognitions of responsibility and spur other processes in turn. But the work of restoration almost certainly needs to be done in many different kinds of communities, groups, and institutions. Locally responsive actors can prime larger communities for a truer appreciation of their responsibilities and consequent tasks. Many initiatives at different levels might contribute to a progressively wider vision of our communities and our responsibilities. Practicing restorative justice in the domain of black redress would not only commit us to the aim of restoring relationships, creating a basis for trust and hope, but would already reject the going terms of black/white relationships, breaking decisively with complacency, disconnection, and denial on the one side, and inviting trust and offering hope on the other. Truth-telling and apology without significant amends might not be enough to signal firm repudiation of a long history of racial oppression and disadvantage. Material reparations might be welcome but would not magically instill interracial trust. It will take transgenerational efforts and changes to create stable conditions of moral relations where the devastation of racial hierarchy and violence is itself transgenerational. Yet restorative measures might ignite hope – the attitude that attunes us to, and tends to move us toward, a possible future that holds a desired good. Hope is, after all, the most fundamental element that sustains moral relationship, and it is the only force powerful enough to revive it.

---

54 Andrew Valls, "Racial Justice as Transitional Justice," argues that the category of transitional justice, usually applied to cases where a human rights-abusing regime is succeeded by one with a commitment to respecting human rights, is the appropriate category under which to see the unfinished business of racial justice in the USA.

Restorative justice exemplifies moral repair at individual and collective levels in the context of crime, political violence, and systemic and historical injustice. It captures the truth at the center of moral repair: morality as a practice of human life is embodied in relationships that require confidence, trust, and hope, and in interactions that in turn renew these morally sustaining attitudes. When serious wrongs occur, our morally sustaining attitudes are not renewed and they are sometimes terribly damaged. When that happens, reiterating our moral standards is necessary but is not enough. We must also secure or replenish the trust among us and the hopefulness that each of us needs to live with others within a sturdy and resilient web of normative expectations. The practices that aim to reinvite trust and ignite hope can be as simple as saying "I'm sorry" or as complex as designing a program of reparations for victims of political violence. We must learn to do in the hard cases what we know how to do in the more ordinary instances of human inattention, callousness, anger, or bad judgment. Putting on a patch might be enough for simple cases, but reweaving a moral fabric is essential if we are counting on a livable shared future.[55]

[55] Versions of parts of this chapter were presented at St. Olaf's College as one of the 25th Annual Eunice Belgum Lectures; at the Columbia University Seminar on Moral Education; to Brown University's Committee on Slavery and Justice, and at the Conference, "Historical Injustices: Restitution and Reconciliation in International Perspectives," March 18–20, 2005; and at Princeton University's Center for Human Values. I thank those present for very useful criticisms. Special thanks to Alice Crary and Hilde Lindemann for comments, and to Neta Crawford for the invitation to participate in Brown's extraordinary study of its own institutional historical involvement in the slave trade.

Bibliography

Achilles, Mary, and Howard Zehr. "Restorative Justice for Crime Victims." In *Restorative Community Justice: Repairing Harm and Transforming Communities*, edited by Gordon Bazemore and Mara F. Schiff. Cincinnati: Anderson Publishing, 2001.

Adams, David Wallace. *Education for Extinction: American Indians and the Boarding School Experience*. Lawrence: University Press of Kansas, 1995.

Addis, Adeno. "Economic Sanctions and the Problem of Evil." *Human Rights Quarterly* 25 (2003): 573–623.

Allen, Anita. *Why Privacy Isn't Everything: Feminist Reflections on Personal Accountability*. Lanham, MD: Rowman & Littlefield, 2003.

Allen, Danielle. *Talking To Strangers: Anxieties of Citizenship Since Brown v. Board of Education*. Chicago: University of Chicago Press, 2004.

Améry, Jean. *At the Mind's Limits: Contemplations by a Survivor on Auschwitz and Its Realities* [1966]. Translated by Sidney Rosenfeld and Stella P. Rosenfeld. Bloomington: Indiana University Press, 1980.

Amnesty International. "Transition at the Crossroads: Human Rights Violations Under Pinochet Rules Remain the Crux." In Amnesty International website. 6 March 1996. <http://web.amnesty.org/library/index/ENGAMR22001199>.

Anderson, Benedict. *Imagined Communities: Reflections on the Origin and Spread of Nationalism*. London: Verso, 1983.

Arendt, Hannah. *The Human Condition*. Chicago: University of Chicago Press, 1958.

Aristotle. *Nicomachean Ethics*. Translated by Sir David Ross. Oxford: Oxford University Press, 1980.

Baier, Annette. *Commons of the Mind*. Chicago and LaSalle, Il: Open Court, 1997.

Baier, Annette. *Moral Prejudices: Essays on Ethics*. Cambridge: Harvard University Press, 1994.

Baker, Judith. "Trust and Rationality." *Pacific Philosophical Quarterly* 68 (1987): 1–13.

Barkan, Elazar. "Amending Historical Injustices: The Restitution of Cultural Property – An Overview." In *Claiming the Stones, Naming the Bones: Cultural Property and the Negotiation of National and Ethnic Identity*, edited by Elazar Barkan and Ronald Bush. Los Angeles: Getty Research Institute, 2002.

Barkan, Elazar. *The Guilt of Nations: Restitution and Negotiating Historical Injustices.* Baltimore: Johns Hopkins University Press, 2000.

Barnett, Randy E. "Restitution: A New Paradigm of Criminal Justice." *Ethics* 87 (1977): 279–301.

Barnett, Victoria J. *Bystanders: Conscience and Complicity During the Holocaust.* Westport: Praeger Paperbacks, 1999.

Bass, Gary Jonathan. *Stay the Hand of Vengeance: The Politics of Wartime Tribunals.* Princeton: Princeton University Press, 2000.

Bazemore, Gordon, and Mara F. Schiff, eds. *Restorative Community Justice: Repairing Harm and Transforming Communities.* Cincinnati: Anderson Publishing, 2001.

Benn, Piers. "Forgiveness and Loyalty." *Philosophy* 71 (1996): 369–83.

Bennett, Jonathan. "Accountability." In *Philosophical Subjects: Essays Presented to P. F. Strawson*, edited by Zak Van Straaten. New York: Oxford University Press, 1980.

Bird, Carmel, ed. *The Stolen Children: Their Stories.* Sydney: Random House, 1998.

Borer, Tristan Anne. "A Taxonomy of Victims and Perpetrators: Human Rights and Reconciliation in South Africa." *Human Rights Quarterly* 25 (2003): 1088–116.

Bovens, Luc. "The Value of Hope." *Philosophy and Phenomenological Research* 59 (1999): 667–81.

Braithwaite, John. *Crime, Shame, and Reintegration.* Cambridge: Cambridge University Press, 1989.

Braithwaite, John. *Restorative Justice and Responsive Regulation.* New York: Oxford University Press, 2002.

Brison, Susan. *Aftermath: Violence and the Remaking of a Self.* Princeton: Princeton University Press, 2002.

Brison, Susan. "Letter to the Editor." *Boston Review* February/March 2003. In *Boston Review* website. <http://bostonreview.net/BR28.1/letters.html>.

Brooks, Roy L., *Atonement and Forgiveness: A New Model for Black Reparations.* Berkeley and Los Angeles: University of California Press, 2004.

Brooks, Roy L., ed. *When Sorry Isn't Enough: The Controversy Over Apologies and Reparations for Human Injustice.* New York: New York University Press, 1999.

Brown, Bertram Wyatt. *Southern Honor: Ethics and Behavior in the Old South.* New York: Oxford University Press, 1982.

Brown University. Brown University Steering Committee on Slavery and Justice website. <http://www.brown.edu/Research/Slavery_Justice/>.

Brudholm, Thomas. "'An Ugly Intrusion': Resentment in the Truth and Reconciliation Commission of South Africa." Manuscript, 2004.

Buss, Sarah. "Appearing Respectful: The Moral Significance of Manners." *Ethics* 109 (1999): 795–826.

Butler, Joseph. *Butler's Fifteen Sermons Preached at the Rolls Chapel and A Dissertation of the Nature of Virtue* [1726]. Edited and with an introduction and additional notes by T. A. Roberts. London: Society For Promoting Christian Knowledge, 1970.

Calhoun, Cheshire. "Changing One's Heart." *Ethics* 103 (1992): 76–96.

Campbell, Sue. *Interpreting the Personal: Expression and the Formation of Feelings.* Ithaca: Cornell University Press, 1997.

Card, Claudia. *The Atrocity Paradigm: A Theory of Evil.* New York: Oxford University Press, 2002.

Carnegie Commission on Preventing Deadly Conflict. "Preventing Deadly Conflict: Final Report." In Carnegie Corporation of New York Carnegie Commission on Preventing Deadly Conflict website. <http://wwics.si.edu/subsites/ccpdc/pubs/rept97/finfr.htm>.

Cohen, Stanley. "Human Rights and Crimes of the State: The Culture of Denial." *Australian and New Zealand Journal of Criminology* 26 (1993): 97–115.

Conroy, John. *Unspeakable Acts, Ordinary People: The Dynamics of Torture.* Berkeley and Los Angeles: University of California Press, 2001.

Cose, Ellis. *Bone to Pick: Of Forgiveness, Reconciliation, Reparation, and Revenge.* New York: Atria Books, 2004.

Creedon, Jeremiah. "To Hell and Back: To Break the Cycle of Revenge Countries Must Look Beyond the Law." *Utne Reader* 99 (March–April): 56.

Cunneen, Chris. "Reparations and Restorative Justice: Responding to Gross Violations of Human Rights." In *Restorative Justice and Civil Society*, edited by Heather Strang and John Braithwaite. Cambridge: Cambridge University Press, 2001.

Daley, Kathleen. "Restorative Justice: The Real Story." In *A Restorative Justice Reader: Texts, Sources, Contexts*, edited by Gerry Johnstone. Portland: Willan Publishing, 2003.

Dallaire, Romeo. *Shake Hands With the Devil.* New York: Random House, 2003.

Damasio, Antonio. *Descartes' Error: Emotion, Reason, and the Human Brain.* New York: Avon Books, 1994.

Danieli, Yael, ed. *International Handbook of Multigenerational Legacies of Trauma.* New York: Plenum Press, 1998.

Danieli, Yael. "Introduction." In *International Handbook of Multigenerational Legacies of Trauma*, edited by Yael Danieli. New York: Plenum Press, 1998.

Dauenhauer, Bernard. "Hope and Its Ramifications for Politics." *Man and World* 17 (1984): 453–76.

David, Roman, and Susanne Choi Yuk-Ping. "Victims on Transitional Justice: Lessons from the Reparation of Human Rights Abuses in the Czech Republic." *Human Rights Quarterly* 27 (2005): 392–435.

Day, J. P. "Hope." *American Philosophical Quarterly* 6 (1969): 89–102.

de Greiff, Pablo, ed. *The Handbook of Reparations.* New York: Oxford University Press, 2006.

de Waal, Frans. *Good Natured: The Origins of Right and Wrong in Human and Other Animals.* Cambridge: Harvard University Press, 1996.

Delbo, Charlotte. *Auschwitz and After.* Translated by Rosette C. Lamont. New Haven: Yale University Press, 1995.

Dewan, Shaila. "Revisiting '64 Civil Rights Deaths, This Time in a Murder Trial." *New York Times* 12 June 2005.

Dickey, Walter J. "Forgiveness and Crime: The Possibilities of Restorative Justice." In *Exploring Forgiveness*, edited by Robert D. Enright and Joanna North. Madison: University of Wisconsin Press, 1998.

Digeser, Peter. *Political Forgiveness*. Ithaca: Cornell University Press, 2001.

"Doctors Encouraged to Tell Patients, 'I'm Sorry.'" *Arizona Republic* 12 November 2004.

Dorfman, Ariel. "Ariel Dorfman on Memory and Truth." Interview by Carlos Reyes and Maggie Patterson. *Amnesty International Journal* July 1997. In Amnesty International website. <http://www.amnesty.org.uk/journal_july97/carlos.html>.

Dorfman, Ariel. *Death and the Maiden*. New York: Penguin Books, 1991.

Douglass, Frederick. "Narrative of the Life of Frederick Douglass" [1845]. In *The Classic Slave Narratives*, edited by Henry Louis Gates. New York: Penguin Books, 1987.

Downie, R. S. "Forgiveness." *Philosophical Quarterly* 15 (1965): 128–34.

Drumbl, Mark. "Restorative Justice and Collective Responsibility: Lessons For and From the Rwandan Genocide." *Contemporary Justice Review* 5 (2002): 5–22.

du Plessis, Max. "Historical Injustice and International Law: An Exploratory Discussion of Reparation for Slavery." *Human Rights Quarterly* 25 (2003): 624–59.

Duggan, Colleen, and Adita Abusharaf. "Reparation of Sexual Violence and Democratic Transition: In Search of Gender Justice." In *The Handbook of Reparations*, edited by Pablo de Greiff. New York: Oxford University Press, 2006.

Edkins, Jenny. *Trauma and the Memory of Politics*. Cambridge: Cambridge University Press, 2003.

Elster, Jon. *Closing the Books: Transitional Justice in Historical Perspective*. Cambridge: Cambridge University Press, 2004.

Enright, Robert D., Suzanne Freedman, and Julio Rique. "The Psychology of Interpersonal Forgiveness." In *Exploring Forgiveness*, edited by Robert D. Enright and Joanna North. Madison: University of Wisconsin Press, 1998.

Enright, Robert D., and Joanna North, eds. *Exploring Forgiveness*. Madison: University of Wisconsin Press, 1998.

Epp, Roger. "We Are All Treaty People: History, Reconciliation, and the 'Settler Problem.'" In *Dilemmas of Reconciliation: Cases and Concepts*, edited by Carol A. L. Prager and Trudy Govier. Waterloo, Ontario: Wilfrid Laurier University Press, 2004.

Epstein, Helen. "Enough to Make You Sick?" *New York Times Magazine* 12 October 1989.

Erskine, Toni. "Assigning Responsibilities to Institutional Moral Agents: The Case of States and 'Quasi-States.'" In *Can Institutions Have Responsibilities? Collective Moral Agency and International Relations*. Houndmills and New York: Palgrave Macmillan, 2003.

Feagin, Joe R., and Eileen O'Brien. "The Growing Movement for Reparations." In *When Sorry Isn't Enough: The Controversy Over Apologies and Reparations for Human Injustice*, edited by Roy Brooks. New York: New York University Press, 1999.

Fiske, Susan T. *Social Beings: A Core Motives Approach to Social Psychology*. Hoboken, NJ: John Wiley & Sons, 2004.

Flanigan, Beverly. "Forgivers and the Unforgivable." In *Exploring Forgiveness*, edited by Robert D. Enright and Joanna North. Madison: University of Wisconsin Press, 1998.

Flanigan, Beverly. *Forgiving the Unforgivable: Overcoming the Bitter Legacy of Intimate Wounds*. New York: Hungry Minds, Inc., 1992.

Fletcher, Laurel E., and Harvey M. Weinstein. "Violence and Social Repair: Rethinking the Contribution of Justice to Reconciliation." *Human Rights Quarterly* 24 (2002): 573–639.

Forget, Marc. "Crime as Interpersonal Conflict: Reconciliation Between Victim and Offender." In *Dilemmas of Reconciliation*, edited by Carol A. L. Prager and Trudy Govier. Waterloo, Ontario: Wilfrid Laurier University Press, 1997.

Foster, Andrea L. "Brown University Panel Will Explore Institution's Ties to Slavery and Consider Reparations." In *The Chronicle of Higher Education* website. <http://chronicle.com/daily/2004/03/2004031503n.htm>.

French, Peter A. *Collective and Corporate Responsibility.* New York: Columbia University Press, 1984.

French, Peter A. *The Virtues of Vengeance.* Lawrence: University Press of Kansas, 2001.

Frye, Marilyn. *The Politics of Reality.* New York: Crossing Press, 1983.

Fullinwider, Robert. "The Case For Reparations." *Report of the Institute for Philosophy and Public Policy* 20 (2000). In the University of Maryland Institute for Philosophy and Public Policy website. <http://www.puaf.umd.edu/IPPP/reports/vol20sum00/case.html>.

Gibbard, Alan. *Wise Choices, Apt Feelings: A Theory of Normative Judgment.* Cambridge: Harvard University Press, 1990.

Gibson, James L. *Overcoming Apartheid: Can Truth Reconcile a Divided Nation?* New York: Russell Sage Foundation, 2004.

Gibson, James L. "Overcoming Apartheid: Can Truth Reconcile a Divided Nation?" *Politikon* 31 (2004): 129–55.

Giles, Wenona Mary, and Jennifer Hyndman, eds. *Sites of Violence: Gender and Conflict Zones.* Berkeley and Los Angeles: University of California Press, 2004.

Glover, Jonathan. *Humanity: A Moral History of the Twentieth Century.* New Haven: Yale University Press, 2000.

Gobodo-Madikizela, Pumla. *A Human Being Died That Night: A South African Story of Forgiveness.* Boston: Houghton Mifflin, 2003.

Goldie, Peter. *The Emotions: A Philosophical Exploration.* New York: Oxford University Press, 2000.

Golding, Martin P. "Forgiveness and Regret." *Philosophical Forum* 16 (1984–85): 121–37.

Gourevitch, Philip. *We Wish to Inform You That Tomorrow We Will be Killed With Our Families: Stories From Rwanda.* New York: Picador USA, 1998.

Govier, Trudy. *Forgiveness and Revenge.* New York: Routledge, 2002.

Govier, Trudy. *Social Trust and Human Communities.* Montreal and Kingston: McGill-Queen's University Press, 1997.

Govier, Trudy. "What Is Acknowledgment and Why Is It Important?" In *Dilemmas of Reconciliation*, edited by Carol A. L. Prager and Trudy Govier. Waterloo, Ontario: Wilfrid Laurier University Press, 2003.

Govier, Trudy, and Wilhelm Verwoerd. "Forgiveness: The Victim's Prerogative." *South African Journal of Philosophy* 21 (2002): 97–111.

Govier, Trudy, and Wilhelm Verwoerd. "The Promise and Pitfalls of Apology." *Journal of Social Philosophy* 33 (2002): 67–82.

Gowans, Christopher. *Innocence Lost: An Examination of Inescapable Moral Wrongdoing*. New York: Oxford University Press, 1994.

Greensboro Truth and Reconciliation Commission. Greensboro Truth and Reconciliation website. <http://www.greensborotrc.org>.

Groopman, Jerome. *The Anatomy of Hope: How People Prevail in the Face of Illness*. New York: Random House, 2004.

Halligan, Marion. "Hope." In *The Eleven Saving Virtues*, edited by Ross Fitzgerald. Port Melbourne: Minerva, 1995.

Halperin, Jodi, and Harvey M. Weinstein. "Empathy and Rehumanization After Mass Violence." In *My Neighbor, My Enemy: Justice and Community in the Aftermath of Mass Atrocity*, edited by Eric Stover and Harvey M. Weinstein. Cambridge: Cambridge University Press, 2004.

Hamber, Brandon. "Reparations as Symbol: Narratives of Resistance, Reticence and Possibility in South Africa." In *Reparations*, edited by Jon Miller and Rahul Kumar. New York: Oxford University Press, 2006.

Hardin, Russell. "The Street-Level Epistemology of Trust." *Politics & Society* 21 (1993): 505–29.

Hartfield, Bernadette W. "A Story of Anger Compounded." In *Overcoming Racism and Sexism*, edited by Linda A. Bell and David Blumenfeld. Lanham, MD: Rowman & Littlefield, 1995.

Harvey, Jean. *Civilized Oppression*. Lanham, MD: Rowman & Littlefield, 1999.

Harvey, Jean. "Forgiving as an Obligation of the Moral Life." *International Journal of Moral and Social Studies* 8 (1993): 211–22.

Hatzfeld, Jean. *The Machete Season: The Killers in Rwanda Speak*. Translated by Linda Coverdale. New York: Farrar, Straus and Giroux, 2002.

Hayner, Priscilla B. *Unspeakable Truths: Confronting State Terror and Atrocity*. London: Routledge, 2001.

Hedges, Chris. *War Is a Force That Gives Us Meaning*. New York: Anchor Books, 2002.

Henson, Maria Rosa. *Comfort Woman: A Filipina's Story of Prostitution and Slavery under the Japanese Military*. Lanham, MD: Rowman & Littlefield, 1999.

Herman, Judith. *Trauma and Recovery: The Aftermath of Violence – From Domestic Abuse to Political Terror*. New York: Basic Books, 1997.

Hesse, Carla, and Robert Post, eds. *Human Rights in Political Transitions: Gettysburg to Bosnia*. New York: Zone Books, 1999.

Hieronymi, Pamela. "Articulating an Uncompromising Forgiveness." *Philosophy and Phenomenological Research* 62 (2001): 529–56.

Hoffman, Eva. *After Such Knowledge: Memory, History, and the Legacy of the Holocaust*. London: Seeker and Warburg, 2004.

Hoge, Warren. "Trial Opens For Pinochet With Listing of 35 Crimes." *New York Times* 28 September 1999.

Hoge, Warren. "With British Court Hearings Set, Pinochet Will Soon Know Fate." *New York Times* 27 September 1999.

Hollis, Martin. *Trust Within Reason*. Cambridge: Cambridge University Press, 1998.

Holmgren, Margaret R. "Forgiveness and the Intrinsic Value of Persons." *American Philosophical Quarterly* 30 (1993): 341–52.

Holton, Richard. "Deciding to Trust, Coming to Believe." *Australian Journal of Philosophy* 72 (1994): 63–76.

Houston, Barbara. "In Praise of Blame." *Hypatia* 7 (1992): 128–47.

Hughes, Paul M. "Moral Anger, Forgiving, and Condoning." *Journal of Social Philosophy* 25 (1995): 103–18.

Human Rights and Equal Opportunity Commission of Australia. *Bringing Them Home, The Report of the National Inquiry into the Separation of Aboriginal and Torres Strait Islander Children from Their Families.* 1997. At www.austlii.edu.au/special/rsjproject/rsjlibrary/hreoc/stolen/, accessed 23 March 2006.

Hursthouse, Rosalind. "A rational Actions." *Journal of Philosophy* 88 (1991): 57–68.

Iida, Keisuke. "Human Rights and Sexual Abuse: The Impact of International Human Rights Law on Japan." *Human Rights Quarterly* 26 (2004): 428–53.

Immarigeon, Russ, and Kathleen Daly. "Restorative Justice: Origins, Practices, Contexts, and Challenges." *ICCA Journal on Community Corrections* 8 (1997): 13–18.

Jacoby, Susan. *Wild Justice.* New York: Harper and Row, 1983.

Jaeger, Marietta. "The Power and Reality of Forgiveness: Forgiving the Murderer of One's Child." In *Exploring Forgiveness,* edited by Robert D. Enright and Joanna North. Madison: University of Wisconsin Press, 1998.

Jaggar, Alison M. "Love and Knowledge: Emotion in Feminist Epistemology." In *Gender/Body/Knowledge: Feminist Reconstructions of Being and Knowing,* edited by Alison M. Jaggar and Susan R. Bordo. New Brunswick, NJ: Rutgers University Press, 1989.

Janoff-Bulman, Ronnie. *Shattered Assumptions: Towards a New Psychology of Trauma.* New York: Free Press, 1992.

Johnstone, Gerry, ed. *A Restorative Justice Reader: Texts, Sources, Context.* Portland: Willan Publishing, 2003.

Jones, Karen. "Trust and Terror." In *Moral Psychology: Feminist Ethics and Social Theory,* edited by Peggy DesAutels and Margaret Urban Walker. Lanham, MD: Rowman & Littlefield, 2004.

Jones, Karen. "Trust as an Affective Attitude." *Ethics* 107 (1996): 4–25.

Jones, Karen. "Trust (Philosophical Aspects)." In *International Encyclopedia of the Social and Behavioral Sciences,* edited by Neil Smelser and Paul Bates. Amsterdam: Elsevier Science, 2001.

Joyce, Richard. "Apologizing." *Public Affairs Quarterly* 13 (1999) 159–73.

Kant, Immanuel. *Grounding for the Metaphysics of Morals* [1785]. Translated by James W. Ellington. Indianapolis: Hackett Publishing Company, 1981.

Kant, Immanuel. "An Old Question Raised Again: Is the Human Race Constantly Progressing?" In *On History.* New York: Library of Liberal Arts, 1963.

Khan, Mahvish. "To Keep Peace, Study Peace." *New York Times* 27 July 2002.

Kilgannon, Corey. "Something in Common: Horror: Survivors Describe Evils of Genocide." *New York Times* 14 January 2004.

Kiss, Elizabeth. "Saying We're Sorry: Liberal Democracy and the Rhetoric of Collective Identity." *Constellations* 4 (1998): 387–398.

Kolnai, Aurel. "Forgiveness." In *Ethics, Value, and Reality: Selected Papers of Aurel Kolnai.* Indianapolis: Hackett Publishing Co., 1978.

Korsgaard, Christine. *Sources of Normativity*. Cambridge: Cambridge University Press, 1996.

Kritz, Neil, ed. *Transitional Justice: How Emerging Democracies Reckon With Former Regimes: Laws, Rulings, and Reports*. Washington, DC: United States Institute of Peace Press, 1995.

Krog, Antje. *Country of My Skull: Guilt, Sorrow, and the Limits of Forgiveness in the New South Africa*. New York: Random House, 1998.

Kumar, Rahul. "Responsibility and Rectification for Past Injustice: The Case of American Chattel Slavery." Manuscript. Lecture delivered at Princeton University Center for Human Values, February 27, 2004.

Kutz, Christopher. *Complicity: Ethics and Law for a Collective Age*. Cambridge: Cambridge University Press, 2000.

Kymlicka, Will. *Politics in the Vernacular: Nationalism, Multiculturalism, and Citizenship*. New York: Oxford University Press, 2001.

Lang, Berel. "Forgiveness." *American Philosophical Quarterly* 31 (1994): 105–17.

Langer, Lawrence. *Holocaust Testimonies: The Ruins of Memory*. New Haven: Yale University Press, 1991.

Lauritzen, Paul. "Forgiveness: Moral Prerogative or Religious Duty?" *Journal of Religious Ethics* 15 (1987): 141–54.

Lazare, Aaron. *On Apology*. New York: Oxford University Press, 2004.

Lazarus, Richard S. "Hope: An Emotion and a Vital Coping Resource Against Despair." *Social Research* 66 (1999): 653–78.

Lean, Sharon F. "Is Truth Enough? Reparations and Reconciliation in Latin America." In *Politics and the Past: On Repairing Historical Injustices*, edited by John Torpey. Lanham, MD: Rowman & Littlefield, 2003.

Lesch, Johanna. "Hope, Agency, and Self: An Understanding of Its Human Position." Manuscript, 2001.

Lesch, Johanna. "The Necessity of Hope in Human Life." Manuscript, 2002.

Levi, Primo. *The Drowned and the Saved*. New York: Vintage International, 1989.

Levison, Sanford. *Written in Stone: Public Monuments in Changing Societies*. Durham, NC: Duke University Press, 1998.

Linenthal, Edward T. *The Unfinished Bombing: Oklahoma City in American Memory*. New York: Oxford University Press, 2001.

Lomax, Eric. *The Railway Man: A POW's Searing Account of War, Brutality, and Forgiveness*. New York: W.W. Norton, 1995.

Lugones, María. "Hard-to-Handle Anger." In *Overcoming Racism and Sexism*, edited by Linda A. Bell and David Blumenfeld. Lanham, MD: Rowman & Littlefield, 1995.

Margalit, Avishai. *The Ethics of Memory*. Cambridge: Harvard University Press, 2002.

Martin, Douglas. "Ani Pachen, Warrior Nun in Tibet Jail 21 Years, Dies." *New York Times* 18 February 2002.

Matsuda, Mari J. "Looking to the Bottom: Critical Legal Studies and Reparations." *Harvard Civil Rights-Civil Liberties Law Review* 22 (1987): 323–99.

May, Larry. *Sharing Responsibility*. Chicago: University of Chicago Press, 1992.

McCold, Paul, and Benjamin Wachtel. "Community Is Not a Place: A New Look at Community Justice Initiatives." In *A Restorative Justice Reader: Texts, Sources, Context*, edited by Gerry Johnstone. Portland: Willan Publishing, 2003.

McFall, Lynne. "What's Wrong With Bitterness?" In *Feminist Ethics*, edited by Claudia Card. Lawrence: University Press of Kansas, 1991.

McGary, Howard. "Forgiveness." *American Philosophical Quarterly* 26 (1989): 343–51.

McGary, Howard. "Justice and Reparations." *Philosophical Forum* 15 (1978): 250–63.

McGeer, Victoria. "The Art of Good Hope." *Annals of the American Academy of Political and Social Science* 592 (2004): 100–27.

McGeer, Victoria. "Moral Travel and the Narrative Work of Forgiveness." Manuscript, 2004.

McGeer, Victoria. "Trust, Hope, and Empowerment." Manuscript. Delivered at Conference on Trust, University of California at Riverside, February 28, 2004.

Meyers, Diana. "Emotion and Heterodox Moral Perception: An Essay in Moral Social Psychology." In *Feminists Rethink the Self*, edited by Diana T. Meyers. Boulder: Westview Press, 1997.

Miller, William Ian. *The Anatomy of Disgust*. Cambridge and London: Harvard University Press, 1997.

Mills, Charles. *The Racial Contract*. Ithaca: Cornell University Press, 1997.

Minow, Martha. *Between Vengeance and Forgiveness: Facing History After Genocide and Mass Violence*. Boston: Beacon Press, 1998.

Mitchell, Emily. "The Decade of Atonement." *Utne Reader* 1999 (March/April): 58–59.

Murphy, Jeffrie. *Getting Even: Forgiveness and Its Limits*. Oxford: Oxford University Press, 2003.

Murphy, Jeffrie G., and Jean Hampton. *Forgiveness and Mercy*. Cambridge: Cambridge University Press, 1988.

Mydans, Seth. "Cambodian Aesop Tells a Fable of Forgiveness." *New York Times* 28 June 1997.

Mydans, Seth. "Cambodian Leader Resists Punishing Top Khmer Rouge." *New York Times* 29 December 1998.

Mydans, Seth. "Inside a Wartime Brothel: The Avenger's Story." *New York Times* 12 November 1996.

Mydans, Seth. "Under Prodding, 2 Apologize for Cambodian Anguish." *New York Times* 30 December 1998.

Narayan, Uma. "Forgiveness, Moral Reassessment, and Reconciliation." In *Explorations of Value*, edited by Thomas Magnell. Amsterdam and Atlanta: Rodopi Press, 1998.

Neier, Aryeh. *War Crimes: Brutality, Genocide, Terror, and the Struggle for Justice*. New York: Random House, 1998.

Nelson, Hilde Lindemann. *Damaged Identities, Narrative Repair*. Ithaca: Cornell University Press, 2001.

Nietzsche, Friedrich. *The Genealogy of Morals*. Translated by Francis Golffing. New York: Doubleday/Anchor Books, 1956.

Nino, Carlos Santiago. *Radical Evil on Trial*. New Haven: Yale University, 1996.

North, Joanna. "Wrongdoing and Forgiveness." *Philosophy* 62 (1987): 499–508.

Novitz, David. "Forgiveness and Self-Respect." *Philosophy and Phenomenological Research* 58 (1998): 299–315.

Nussbaum, Martha. *Women and Human Development: The Capabilities Approach.* Cambridge: Cambridge University Press, 2000.

Ohbuchi, Ken-ichi. "A Social Psychological Analysis of Accounts: Toward a Universal Model of Giving and Receiving Accounts." In *Japanese Apology Across Disciplines,* edited by Naomi Sugimoto. Commack, NY: Nova Science Publishers, Inc., 1999.

Oliver, Melvin L., and Thomas M. Shapiro. *Black Wealth/White Wealth.* New York: Routledge, 1997.

Partnoy, Alicia. *The Little School: Tales of Disappearance and Survival.* San Francisco: Midnight Editions, 1998.

Pettit, Philip. "The Cunning of Trust." *Philosophy and Public Affairs* 24 (1995): 202–25.

Phelps, Teresa Godwin. *Shattered Voices: Language, Violence, and the Work of Truth Commissions.* Philadelphia: University of Pennsylvania Press, 2004.

Potter, Nancy. "Is Refusing to Forgive a Vice?" In *Feminists Doing Ethics,* edited by Peggy DesAutels and Joanne Waugh. Lanham, MD: Rowman & Littlefield, 2001.

Prager, Carol A. L., and Trudy Govier, eds. *Dilemmas of Reconciliation: Cases and Concepts.* Waterloo, Ontario: Wilfrid Laurier University Press, 2004.

Pranis, Kay, Barry Stuart, and Mark Wedge. *Peacemaking Circles: From Crime to Community.* St. Paul, MN: Living Justice Press, 2003.

Ramsey, Nancy. "Filming Rwandans' Efforts to Heal Wounds." *New York Times* 24 April 2003.

Report of the Chilean National Commission on Truth and Reconciliation. Translated by Phillip E. Berryman. Notre Dame, IN: Notre Dame University Press, 1993.

Richards, Norvin. "Forgiveness." *Ethics* 99 (1988): 77–97.

Roberts, Rodney C., ed. *Injustice and Rectification.* New York: Peter Lang, 2002.

Robinson, Randall. *The Debt: What America Owes to Blacks.* New York: Plume, 2000.

Roca, Ana. "Madness or Divine Sense? Revisiting Ariel Dorfman's *Death and the Maiden.*" *Hemisphere* 12 (2003): 7–9.

Roht-Arriaza, Naomi. "The Need for Moral Reconstruction in the Wake of Past Human Rights Violations: Interview with Jose Zalaquett." In *Human Rights in Political Transitions: Gettysburg to Bosnia,* edited by Carla Hesse and Robert Post. New York: Zone Books, 1999.

Roht-Arriaza, Naomi. "Reparations in the Aftermath of Repression and Mass Violence." In *My Neighbor, My Enemy: Justice and Community in the Aftermath of Mass Atrocity,* edited by Eric Stover and Harvey M. Weinstein. Cambridge: Cambridge University Press, 2004.

Rohter, Larry. "A Struggle With Memories of Torture Down the Street." *New York Times* 8 March 2005.

Rohter, Larry. "A Torture Report Compels Chile to Reassess Its Past." *New York Times* 24 April 2003.

Rohter, Larry. "Uruguay Tackles Old Rights Cases, Charging Ex-President." *New York Times* 31 July 2005.

Rotberg, Robert I., and Dennis Thompson, eds. *Truth v. Justice: The Morality of Truth Commissions.* Princeton: Princeton University Press, 2000.

Ryan, Cheyney. "Thinking About the Unforgivable." Manuscript. Presented at conference on "Forgiveness: Traditions and Implications," Tanner Center for the Humanities, University of Utah, April 12–15, 2000.

Sayre-McCord, Geoffrey. "Criminal Justice and Legal Reparations as an Alternative to Punishment." *Philosophical Issues* 11 (2001): 502–29.

Scheman, Naomi. "Anger and the Politics of Naming." In *Women and Language in Literature and Society*, edited by Sally McConnell Ginet, Ruth Borker, and Nelly Forman. New York: Prager, 1993.

Schwarcz, Vera. "The Pane of Sorrow: Public Uses of Personal Grief in Modern China." In *Social Suffering*, edited by Arthur Kleinman, Veena Das, and Margaret Lock. Berkeley and Los Angeles: University of California Press, 1997.

Seligman, Martin E. P. *Learned Helplessness: A Theory for the Age of Personal Control.* New York: Oxford University Press, 1993.

Sen, Amartya. *Development as Freedom.* New York: Anchor Books, 1999.

Sevenhuijsen, Selma. "Too Good to Be True? Feminist Thoughts About Trust and Social Cohesion." *Focaal* 34 (1999): 207–22.

Shay, Jonathan. *Odysseus in America: Combat Trauma and the Trials of Homecoming.* New York: Scribner, 2002.

Simons, Marlise. "Milosevic Says Srebrenica Was Plot to Frame Serbs." *New York Times* 28 September 2002.

Simons, Marlise. "Officers Say Bosnian Massacre Was Deliberate." *New York Times* 12 October 2003.

Smith, Adam. *The Theory of Moral Sentiments* [1759]. Washington, DC: Regnery Publishing, 1997.

Solomon, Robert. *A Passion for Justice.* Lanham, MD: Rowman & Littlefield, 1995.

Sparrow, Robert. "History and Collective Responsibility." *Australasian Journal of Philosophy* 78 (2000): 346–59.

Spelman, Elizabeth V. "Anger and Insubordination." In *Women, Knowledge, and Reality*, edited by Ann Garry and Marilyn Pearsall. Boston: Unwin Hyman, 1989.

Spelman, Elizabeth V. *Repair: The Impulse to Restore in a Fragile World.* Boston: Beacon Press, 2002.

Stalker, Peter. "Visions of Freedom: A Journey through Pinochet's Chile," *New Internationalist* 174 (1987): 6.

Steiner, Henry J., ed. *Truth Commissions: A Comparative Assessment.* Cambridge: World Peace Foundation, 1997.

Stolberg, Sheryl Gay. "Senate Issues Apology Over Failure on Lynching Law." *New York Times* 14 June 2005.

Stover, Eric, and Rachel Shigekane. "Exhumation of Mass Graves: Balancing Legal and Humanitarian Needs." In *My Neighbor, My Enemy: Justice and Community in the Aftermath of Mass Atrocity*, edited by Eric Stover and Harvey M. Weinstein. Cambridge: Cambridge University Press, 2004.

Stover, Eric, and Harvey M. Weinstein, eds. *My Neighbor, My Enemy: Justice and Community in the Aftermath of Mass Atrocity.* Cambridge: Cambridge University Press, 2004.

Strang, Heather. "The Crime Victim Movement as a Force in Civil Society." In *Restorative Justice and Civil Society*, edited by Heather Strang and John Braithwaite. Cambridge: Cambridge University Press, 2001.

Strang, Heather. "Justice for Victims of Young Offenders: The Centrality of Emotional Harm and Restoration." In *A Restorative Justice Reader: Texts, Sources, Context*, edited by Gerry Johnstone. Portland: Willan Publishing, 2003.

Strang, Heather, and John Braithwaite, eds. *Restorative Justice and Civil Society*. Cambridge: Cambridge University Press, 2001.

Strawson, Peter F. "Freedom and Resentment." In *Studies in The Philosophy of Thought and Action*, edited by P. F. Strawson. New York: Oxford University Press, 1968.

Sullivan, Dennis, and Larry Tifft. *Restorative Justice: Healing the Foundations of Our Everyday Lives*. Monsey, NY: Willow Tree Press, 2001.

Tavuchis, Nicholas. *Mea Culpa: A Sociology of Apology and Reconciliation*. Stanford: Stanford University Press, 1991.

Teitel, Ruti. *Transitional Justice*. New York: Oxford University Press, 2000.

Thomas, Laurence Mordekhai. "Forgiving the Unforgivable?" In *Moral Philosophy and the Holocaust*, edited by Eve Garrard and Geoffrey Scarre. London: Ashgate Press, 2003.

Thomas, Laurence Mordekhai. "Power, Trust, and Evil." In *Overcoming Racism and Sexism*, edited by Linda A. Bell and David Blumenfeld. Lanham, MD: Rowman & Littlefield, 1995.

Thompson, Janna. *Taking Responsibility for the Past: Reparation and Historical Injustice*. Oxford: Polity Press, 2002.

Tobar, Hector. "Argentina Justices Overturn Amnesty for Soldiers Linked to Rights Abuses." *Los Angeles Times* 14 June 2005.

Todorov, Tzvetan. *Facing the Extreme: Moral Life in the Concentration Camps*. New York: Henry Holt and Company, 1996.

Torpey, John. *Politics and the Past: On Repairing Historical Injustices*. Lanham, MD: Rowman & Littlefield, 2003.

Truth and Reconciliation Commission. *Truth and Reconciliation Commission of South Africa Report*. London: Palgrave Macmillan, 1999.

Tsosie, Rebecca. "The Native American Graves Protection and Repatriation Act." Congressional Testimony, July 25, 2000. In U.S. Senate Committee on Indian Affairs website. <http://indian.senate.gov/2000hrgs/nagpra_0725/tsosie.pdf>.

Tsosie, Rebecca. "Privileging Claims to the Past: Ancient Human Remains and Contemporary Cultural Values." *Arizona State Law Journal* 31 (1999): 583–677.

Tutu, Archbishop Desmond. Interview with Bill Moyers. Public Broadcasting Service, WNEW, 27 April 1999.

Tutu, Archbishop Desmond. *No Future Without Forgiveness*. New York: Doubleday, 1999.

Umbreit, Mark S., Robert Coates, and Ann Warner Roberts. "Cross-National Impact of Restorative Justice Through Mediation and Dialogue." *ICCA Journal on Community Corrections* 8 (1997): 46–50.

United Nations. "The Administration of Justice and the Human Rights of Detainees: Revised Set of Basic Principles and Guidelines on the Right to Reparation for Victims of Gross Violations of Human Rights and Humanitarian Law Prepared by Mr. Theor van Boven Pursuant to Sub-Commission Decision 1995/117." United Nations Document E/CN.4/Sub.2/1996/17. In

Trial Watch/Trial-ch.org website. <http://trial-ch.org/doc/tunisie/Van_Boven_ English.pdf>.

United States Institute of Peace. "Truth Commissions Digital Collection." In United States Institute of Peace website. <http://www.usip.org/library/ truth.html#tc>.

Valls, Andrew. "Racial Justice as Transitional Justice." *Polity* 36 (2003): 53–71.

Van Ness, Daniel W., ed. "Restorative Justice Online." In Restorative Justice website. <www.restorativejustice.org>.

Van Ness, Daniel W., and Mara F. Schiff. "Satisfaction Guaranteed? The Meaning of Satisfaction in Restorative Justice." In *Restorative Community Justice: Repairing Harm and Transforming Communities*, edited by Gordon Bazemore and Mara F. Schiff. Cincinnati: Anderson Publishing, 2001.

Varshney, Ashutosh. *Ethnic Conflict & Civic Life: Hindus & Muslims in India.* Second edition. New Haven: Yale University Press, 2003.

Vergnani, Linda. "Parents of Slain Fulbright Scholar Embrace Her Cause in South Africa." *The Chronicle of Higher Education*, 19 January 2001. In *The Chronicle of Higher Education* website. <http://chronicle.com/cgi2-bin/printable.cgi>.

Villa-Vicencio, Charles, and Erik Doxtader, eds. *The Provocations of Amnesty: Memory, Justice and Impunity.* Claremont, South Africa: Africa World Press, 2003.

Villa-Vicencio, Charles, and Wilhelm Verwoerd. *Looking Back Reaching Forward: Reflections on the Truth and Reconciliation Commission of South Africa.* London: Zed Books, 2000.

Wadler, Joyce. "Years After Torture, a Cry Against Pinochet," *New York Times* 3 February 1999.

Walker, Margaret Urban. "'The Cycle of Violence.'" *Journal of Human Rights* 5 (2006): 81–105.

Walker, Margaret Urban. *Moral Contexts.* Lanham, MD: Rowman & Littlefield, 2003.

Walker, Margaret Urban. "Moral Psychology." In *The Blackwell Guide to Feminist Philosophy.* Oxford: Blackwell Publishers, 2006.

Walker, Margaret Urban. *Moral Understandings: A Feminist Study in Ethics.* New York: Routledge, 1998.

Wall, Barbara E. "Navajo Conceptions of Justice in the Peacemaker Court," *Journal of Social Philosophy* 32 (2001): 532–46.

Wallace, R. Jay. *Responsibility and the Moral Sentiments.* Cambridge: Harvard University Press, 1996.

Waller, Signe. "Creation of First Truth and Reconciliation Commission in USA Begins." In Zmag.org website. February 17, 2004. <http://www.zmag.org/ content/showarticle.cfm?SectionID = 1&ItemID = 5001>.

Watson, Gary. "Responsibility and the Limits of Evil." In *Responsibility, Character, and the Emotions*, edited by Ferdinand Schoeman. Cambridge: Cambridge University Press, 1987.

Weinstein, Harvey M., and Eric Stover. "Introduction: Conflict, Justice, and Reclamation." In *My Neighbor, My Enemy: Justice and Community in the Aftermath of Mass Atrocity*, edited by Eric Stover and Harvey M. Weinstein. Cambridge: Cambridge University Press, 2004.

Wendell, Susan. *The Rejected Body.* New York: Routledge, 1996.

Weschler, Lawrence. *A Miracle, A Universe: Settling Accounts with Torturers.* Chicago: University of Chicago Press, 1998.

Wheatley, J. M. O. "Wishing and Hoping." *Analysis* 18 (1958): 121–31.

Wiesenthal, Simon. *The Sunflower: On the Possibilities and Limits of Forgiveness, with a Symposium,* edited by Harry James Cargas and Bonny V. Fetterman. Revised and expanded edition. New York: Shocken Books, 1997.

Williams, Melissa. "Citizenship as Identity, Citizenship as Shared Fate, and the Functions of Multicultural Education." In *Education and Citizenship in Liberal-Democratic Societies: Teaching For Cosmopolitan Values and Collective Identities,* edited by Kevin McDonough and Walter Feinberg. New York: Oxford University Press, 2003.

Wilson, J. "Why Forgiveness Requires Repentance." *Philosophy* 63 (1988): 534–35.

Wittgenstein, Ludwig. *Philosophical Investigations.* Translated by G. E. M. Anscombe. New York: Macmillan Company, 1958.

Wittgenstein, Ludwig. *Zettel.* Translated by G. E. M. Anscombe. Berkeley and Los Angeles: University of California Press, 1970.

Wolin. Sheldon. *The Presence of the Past: Essays on the State and the Constitution.* Baltimore: Johns Hopkins University Press, 1989.

Woozley, Anthony D. "Injustice." In *Injustice and Rectification,* edited by Robert C. Roberts. New York: Peter Lang, 2002. First published in *American Philosophical Quarterly Monograph Series,* no. 7, edited by Nicholas Rescher, Oxford: Blackwell, 1975, 109–23.

Yazzie, Robert. "'Life Comes From It': Navajo Justice Concepts," *New Mexico Law Review* 24 (1994): 175–90.

Young, Iris M. *Justice and the Politics of Difference.* Princeton: Princeton University Press, 1990.

Young, William E. "Resentment and Impartiality." *The Southern Journal of Philosophy* 36 (1998): 103–30.

Zehr, Howard. *Changing Lenses: A New Focus for Crime and Justice.* Scottsdale, PA: Herald Press, 1995.

Zehr, Howard. *Transcending: Reflections of Crime Victims.* Intercourse, PA: Good Books, 2001.

Index

abandonment. *See* normative abandonment
Aboriginal children, Australia's removal of, 174, 219
Bringing Them Home, report on, 219
accountability, 199, 201, 208, 209, 212
adaptive preferences, 102
African Americans, 13, 192, 221–28
apology from U. S. government to, 225
compensation for, 228
and Jim Crow, 220, 225, 226
and reparations, U. S. government responsibility for, 202, 221. *See also* black redress
slavery and segregation of, 12, 37, 63, 202–3, 220, 225, 226
and U. S. Senate apology regarding lynching, 14
and white Americans, 226–27
See also civil rights era
African National Congress, 214
"age of apology," 219. *See also* apology
Aguirre, Luis Perez, 175
alienation. *See* normative alienation
amends, 7, 10, 25, 27–28, 34, 38, 95, 156, 191–207, 212, 213, 217
definition of, 191

American Indians, 174, 204
Améry, Jean, 140–44
amnesty, 145, 214, 216–17
apology, 8, 10, 25, 34, 59, 139, 145, 194, 195–97, 199, 203, 212, 213, 216, 217
Arendt, Hannah, 151, 178, 187
Argentina, 4, 13
At the Mind's Limits (Jean Améry), 140
"atonement model," 225
atonement trials, 13, 225
Auschwitz, 43, 56
Auschwitz and After (Charlotte Delbo), 43
Aylwin, Patricio, 59

Baier, Annette, 76–77, 78
Balkans, 14, 21
Goražde, 41
Srebrenica, 192, 193
Bessie K., 60, 61
Biehl, Amy, 176
black redress, 220–28
and restorative justice, 221–28
Bovens, Luc, 50–55
Braithwaite, John, 182, 213
Brison, Susan, 16, 93
Brooks, Roy, 220, 225
Brown, Bertram Wyatt, 100

Brown University Steering Committee on Slavery and Justice, 224
Buchenwald, 60, 61
Butler, Joseph, 112–13, 115–16, 117, 120, 128, 133, 134, 136, 137, 149

Card, Claudia, 162, 181, 186
Chile's National Commission on Truth and Reconciliation, 2, 16. *See also* Pinochet
Chile's Reconciliation and Reparation Corporation, 2
Civil Liberties Act of 1988, 183
civil rights era, 225
communal responsibility, 7–8, 29–34, 138–39, 144, 218, 221–22
three tasks of, 30–33
to reassert norms, 30–32
community, 30, 84, 167
restorative justice and, 222–23
compensation, significance of, 216, 217
concentration camps, 43, 56, 60, 61
confidence in moral standards, 24, 29, 33, 44, 66–67, 135, 165, 166, 179, 188, 191, 199, 205, 227, 229
confirmation. *See* normative confirmation
contempt, 226
normative, 226–27
Conyers, John, 228
Creedon, Jeremiah, 3

Damasio, Antonio, 61
case of "Elliott," 61–62
case of Phineas Gage, 61–62
Dauenhauer, Bernard, 56
Day, J. P., 47, 48
Death and the Maiden (Ariel Dorfman), 1–5
Delbo, Charlotte, 43–44, 56, 59, 64
Descartes' Error (Antonio Damasio), 61
Digeser, Peter, 186
Dorfman, Ariel, 1, 2, 3–4, 5, 18
DuBois, W. E. B., 227
Douglass, Frederick, 103

East Timor's National Commission for Reception, Truth, and Reconciliation, 14–15
Equal Employment Opportunity Act of 1972, 220
Evers, Medgar, 225
excuses, role of, 195–97
expectation. *See* normative expectation

Faku, Pearl, 175–76, 187
Fejzić, Fadil, 41
Flanigan, Beverly, 90, 92, 152
forgiveness, 8, 27, 38, 151–90, 199, 217
act descriptions and, 170, 174
collective, 163–64
conditional, 157, 159, 178
of the dead, 159–60
interactive, 171
moral content of, 162, 169
moral relations and, 162, 163, 166
moral repair and, 153, 162, 164–65, 167
overcoming resentment in, 153, 154–58
as practical policy, 157
primary, secondary, and tertiary victims and, 179–81
political, 186
restoring relationship in, 153, 154, 158–69
settling a wrong in the past in, 153, 154, 169–74
unilateral, 171
Forgiveness and Mercy (Jean Hampton and Jeffrie Murphy), 113, 121

genocide, 11, 12, 14, 35, 94, 104, 107, 189, 192, 193, 194. *See also* Rwandan genocide
Gewirtzman, David, 107
Gibson, James, 21, 214–17
Gobodo-Madikizela, Pumla, 175, 176, 177, 190
Goffman, Erving, 124
Goldie, Peter, 49

Govier, Trudy, 77–79
Greensboro Truth and Reconciliation
    Commission, 13–14, 224

Hague, the, 192
Halligan, Marion, 40
Hampton, Jean, 113, 117, 118–23, 133
Hartfield, Bernadette W., 143, 144
Harvey, J., 167
Hedges, Chris, 41
Hieronymi, Pamela, 181
historical injustice, 34, 36, 144, 192,
    202–3, 207, 209, 218–20
Hollis, Martin, 73
Holocaust, the, 9, 11, 42, 107, 141, 188
    German Federal Republic,
        reparations for, 11
Holton, Richard, 79
hope, 27, 44–71, 188
    death of, 27, 41–42, 44, 60–65, 188,
        190
    elements of, 44–47, 60
    as emotion, 44–49
    expressive gestures and, 58–59
    false, 52, 57, 59
    magical thinking and, 54–56
    in moral relations, 24, 66–71, 210,
        228
    moral repair and, 28, 165, 191, 199
    value of, 49–59
    wishful thinking and, 53–54
House of Games (David Mamet), 72–73
House Resolution 40, 228
human rights violations, 11, 92. *See also*
    genocide; mass rape; sexual
    slavery; torture

indignation, 8, 67. *See also* resentment
injustice. *See* historical injustice
International Criminal Tribunal for
    the former Yugoslavia, 192
isolation. *See* normative isolation

Jaeger, Marietta, 187–88
Japanese-American internment
    Japanese-American Citizens'
        League response, 183

Presidential apology for, 183
    reparations for, 183–84, 219
Johnson, Samuel, 40
Jones, Karen, 75–76, 78–79
justice, 4, 5, 6, 7, 15, 19, 21–22, 94,
    186, 187
    compensatory, 210, 211, 216, 220,
        225
    restorative, 14–15, 22, 28, 91, 139,
        192, 194, 195, 207–18, 224, 229;
        black redress and, 220–28; six
        core values of, 208–9;
        communities in, 222–23
    retributive, 13, 139, 210–11, 216,
        220, 225. *See also* retribution
    transitional, 12, 13–14, 22
    See also historical injustice

Kant, Immanuel, 6, 70–71, 135
Khmer Rouge regime, 156, 176
Kingsley, Ben, 3
Kiss, Elizabeth, 147
de Kock, Eugene, 175
Korsgaard, Christine, 114

Langer, Lawrence, 60
law, 25, 32
learned helplessness, 64
Levi, Primo, 188
Little School, The (Alicia Partnoy), 4
Luis, Roberto, 163
lustration, 145
Lu Xun, 59, 64

Mamet, David, 72
Margalit, Avishai, 157
mass rape, 11, 35, 65
McCold, Paul, 223
McGeer, Victoria, 82–83, 175
Miller, William Ian, 124
Milosevic, Slobodan, 192–93
Minow, Martha, 145
Misanthrope, Le (Molière), 56
Molière, 43
Moody, Juanita, 42
moral address, 25, 134–35
moral cost, 6, 65, 158, 181–85, 189

moral relations, 6, 23–24, 96, 162,
169, 210
distortions of, 35, 104, 206
social relations and, 26–27, 98–102
moral repair, 6, 12, 23–28, 33, 38, 65,
73–74, 107–8, 109, 153, 164,
188, 191, 192, 204–5, 210, 218,
229
failures of, 205–6
limits of, 36–38
pragmatics of, 198–99
ordinariness of, 197–98, 201, 206
six tasks of, 28
See also communal responsibility;
hope; trust; wrongdoer,
responsibility of
Mukanyonga, Annonciata, 42
Murekatete, Jacqueline, 107
Murphy, Jeffrie, 113, 121

Nanante, Pashtun Afghani, 182
Narayan, Uma, 157
Native Americans. *See* American
Indians
Native Hawaiians, apology to, 225
Nietzsche, Friedrich, 120, 130, 136
Neou, Kassie, 176
New York Times, 42
Nieves Ayress, Luz de las, 55
normative abandonment, 20, 108, 209
normative alienation, 146
normative confirmation, 26, 96
normative expectation, 24–27, 66,
67–69, 79–80, 81, 95–98, 147, 201
asymmetrical, 101, 102–6
See also hope; trust; resentment
normative isolation, 97, 103
normative surrender, 131
norms, diversity of, 98, 114

objective attitude, 104–6
oppression, 12, 87, 88, 132, 156, 209,
215
Ozick, Cynthia, 158

Pachen, Ani, 177
participant attitude, 25, 79, 104

Partnoy, Alicia, 4
discussion of *Death and the Maiden*, 4
Pettit, Philip, 70, 76–77
Pinochet, General Augusto
regime of, in Chile, 2–3, 16, 193–94
torture under, 2–3
victims of, 2, 16
privilege, 88
post-traumatic stress disorder (PTSD),
93, 94
prosecution, 145
punishment, 8–10, 12, 15, 92, 95, 129,
138, 139–40, 156, 157, 189

reactive attitudes, 25–27, 67–68,
86–87, 135
reparation, 8, 11–12, 22, 36, 145,
203–4, 211
resentment (and indignation), 8, 9,
25–27, 67, 85, 96, 97, 110–49,
154–58, 159, 185, 191
answering, 141–46
bitter, 130
dangers of, 127, 147–48
disgusted, 129–30
emotions of rebuke and, 149–50
envious, 130–31
fearful, 132–33
justified, 137–43
as moral address, 134–35
and offense, 124–25, 126–27
shamed, 131
threat and, 123–33
unjustified, 146–48
See also normative expectations;
ressentiment
responsibility
denial of by wrongdoers, 194–95,
201, 202, 205–6, 212
leveraging, 215, 217
See also communal responsibility
ressentiment, 120, 130, 136
*Restorative Justice and Responsive
Regulation* (John Braithwaite),
182
retribution, 9, 207, 210. *See also*
justice, retributive

revenge. *See* vengeance
Rinser, Louise, 168
Roca, Ana, 4
Rosewood Compensation Act of 1994, 184
Rwandan genocide, 21, 42, 107, 108, 193
Ryan, Cheyney, 188

Second World War, 11, 14, 92, 140, 183, 219, 225
sexual slavery, 11, 37, 194, 202
  by Japan in Second World War, 92, 204
shame, 6, 8, 10, 17, 97, 135, 138, 155, 159, 183, 185, 217. *See also* resentment, shamed
Shay, Jonathan, 93, 163
Simmons, Ruth, 224
Smith, Adam, 111–12, 113, 115–16, 117, 118, 120, 133, 134–35, 149
Sorak, Rosa, and Drago Sorak, 41
Sorak, Zoran, 41
South Africa's Truth and Reconciliation Commission, 14, 21, 58, 156, 172, 176, 177, 207–8, 214–15, 224
Southern Honor (Bertram Wyatt Brown), 100
Sparrow, Robert, 174
Stover, Erik, 21
Strawson, Peter, 25, 79, 104–6, 114, 123, 125, 134
Strang, Heather, 91
Sunflower, The (Simon Wiesenthal), 167
surrender. *See* normative surrender

Teitel, Ruti, 145
The Theory of Moral Sentiments (Adam Smith), 111
Thomas, Laurence, 101
"tort model," 225
torture, 4, 11, 12, 37, 41–42, 65, 145, 162, 172, 194, 214
Transcending (Howard Zehr), 17

trauma, 16, 17, 93–94
tribal trap, 148
trust, 27, 73–109
  asymmetrical, 27
  broad conception of, 80
  damage to, 83, 88–97
  default, 83–88, 96, 210
  focus of, 80–81
  hopeful, 24, 27, 67–71, 82–83, 163
  in moral relations, 20, 21, 23–24, 66, 210
  moral repair and, 28, 73, 74, 165, 191, 199
  motive of, 81–82
  normative expectations and, 83
  reliance and, 74–80
  in self, 167, 178
  See also normative expectation
truth commissions, 11, 145, 172, 212
Tutu, Desmond, 156

unforgivable wrongdoing, 152, 158, 175–90
Uruguay, 13, 41, 175

validation, of victim, 5, 16, 18–19, 31–32, 34, 136, 138, 139–40, 212, 217
vengeance, 4, 5, 16
victims
  experience of, 5–6, 19–20, 163, 208
  feelings of, 17–18, 155
  focus on, 6–7
  primary, 163, 164, 221
  secondary, 163, 164, 221
  second wound of, 20–21
  tertiary, 164
  wrongdoer who is also, 7
  See also forgiveness, primary, secondary, and tertiary victims and; validation; vindication; voice
vindication, of victim, 5, 11, 13, 16, 18–19, 212
voice, of victim, 5, 18, 19, 21, 59, 216
VOCAL (Victims of Crime Assistance League), 139

Wachtel, Benjamin, 223
Weaver, Sigourney, 3
Weinstein, Harvey, 21
Weschler, Lawrence, 41–42, 175–76
Wiesenthal, Simon, 167
Williams, Melissa, 221
wrongdoer
    focus on, 8

reproof of, 30–32
responsibility of, 7, 138, 185, 199–201
role in forgiveness, 165. *See also* responsibility, denial of by wrongdoers

Zalaquett, José, 16
Zehr, Howard, 15, 17, 91, 92